D1201519

Language and history
in Cornwall

Language and history in Cornwall

Martyn F. Wakelin

Leicester University Press
1975

First published in 1975 by Leicester University Press
Distributed in North America by Humanities Press Inc., New Jersey

Copyright © Leicester University Press 1975

Designed by Arthur Lockwood

Set in Monotype Times New Roman
Printed and bound in Great Britain by
William Clowes & Sons, Limited, London, Beccles and Colchester

ISBN 0 7185 1124 7

This volume is published with the help
of a grant from the Twenty-Seven Foundation

Contents

Preface

This book was presented in its original form as a thesis for the degree of Doctor of Philosophy in the School of English in the University of Leeds in 1969. It was then, and still is, unsatisfactory insofar as, due to our lack of really adequate historical evidence, it can present only part of a total picture. This problem is discussed further in my first chapter and need not be elaborated here, but it may at least be emphasized again that a much clearer idea of Cornwall's early history and languages may emerge from the whole body of place-names, whenever these can be collected. Indeed, this whole book emphasizes the urgent need for a speedy examination of all the early documents relating to the county.

My decision to work on the dialects of Cornwall dates from 1962, a period when I was employed as Assistant Editor to the Survey of English Dialects at Leeds University, under Professor (now Emeritus Professor) Harold Orton. Like many other workers in this field, I am greatly in debt to him for his enthusiasm and his encouragement of me in this project, and for his friendly interest at all times. A second debt of gratitude is owed to Mr R.L. Thomson, who spent much time reading this book in its thesis form, discussing it with me, writing to me about it, making a multitude of helpful suggestions, and saving me from many pitfalls. To Professor A.C. Thomas, now so deservedly appointed as the Director of the Institute of Cornish Studies, I am similarly indebted – for giving me his time and kindly advice, as well as for his most generous loans and gifts of various publications and other material, and reading the whole book through in manuscript.

I must sincerely thank Professor H.C. Darby, of the University of Cambridge, for his kind loan of the proofs of his book *The Domesday Geography of South-West England*, prior to publication, and Mr J.E.B. Gover for the loan of his unpublished work 'The Place-Names of Cornwall', as well as for his helpful correspondence over many matters relating to the same subject. Mr L.R. Moir, of the Federation of Old Cornwall Societies, similarly earns my thanks for his ready loans and gifts of books to me and help in other ways.

Among those who have been consulted and have given their advice and practical help in many different ways, I must thank in particular the following: Professor A. McIntosh, of the University of Edinburgh; the late Mr J.R.F. Piette, of the University College of Wales, Aberystwyth, for his kindness in

7

answering numerous questions on Cornish phonology; Mr P.M. Tilling, who generously checked numerous points for me, and Mr M.V. Barry, both formerly of the Survey of English Dialects; Mr H.L. Douch, Curator of the County Museum and Art Gallery, Truro; Miss Christine Hawkridge, Deputy County Archivist of Cornwall; Mr R.D. Hale, County Librarian of Cornwall; Mr Oliver Padel of the Institute of Cornish Studies, who has read the whole book through in manuscript; Mr C.E. Wright of the British Museum; Dr Peter Lucas of University College, Dublin; Mr Stewart Sanderson, Director of the Institute of Dialect and Folk Life Studies at Leeds University, and Professor A.C. Cawley of the University of Leeds; Professor M.L. Samuels of the University of Glasgow; Dr J. Widdowson of the University of Sheffield; Dr R. Alston; Miss D.F. Drake. I owe a special debt to the late Mr R.R. Blewett and all those many other people who have answered questions or who have been of help during my researches in Cornwall itself, especially the informants for the Survey of English Dialects, who spent so much time answering our questions, and also those informants whom we interviewed separately in 1963. Of these last, Mr and Mrs R. Knowles of St Day deserve special mention.

I am grateful to the University of Leeds for their grants of money to enable me to pursue my research in Cornwall, and to Mr Stewart Sanderson for permission to use the base map of *SED* localities and material in the archives of the Survey of English Dialects. I owe a debt of gratitude to all those libraries which have willingly helped me in my work, and especially to Miss N. Hyde, of Royal Holloway College, who has gone to great trouble on my behalf over many things. My grateful thanks are also due to Mrs Kathleen King, who has drawn the maps, and to my wife, Diane, who has helped with the proof-reading.

I must thank the Board of Management of the Athlone Press for permission to use material in Chapters 1 and 4 conflated from my book *English Dialects* (1972). Maps 5 and 6 are reproduced from *The Domesday Geography of South-West England* (1967), by kind permission of Professor H.C. Darby and the Syndics of Cambridge University Press, and map 7 from fig. 32 of *South-West England* (1969), by kind permission of the late Mr A.H. Shorter, Professor W.L.D. Ravenhill, Mr K.J. Gregory and Messrs Nelson, London.

This book will, I fear, prove disappointing to those who urge with such enthusiasm the theory that a Cornish substratum underlies and has materially influenced western Cornish dialect. The onus is on such patriots to prove – convincingly – such a Cornish connexion, if they can. My conclusions point, with few exceptions, in a contrary direction.

Royal Holloway College,   M.F.W.
Feast of the Assumption, 1972

Maps

Tables

Abbreviations

adj.	adjective
AN	Anglo-Norman
BM	British Museum
Bodleian	Bodleian Library, Oxford
Bret.	Breton
coll.	collective
Corn.	Cornish (language)
CP	Civil Parish
CRO	County Record Office (of Cornwall)
f.	feminine
f.n.	field-name
Fr	French
i.m.	incidental material
incl.	including
IPA	(alphabet of the) International Phonetic Association
m.	masculine
ME	Middle English
MnE	Modern English
n.	noun
OE	Old English
OF	Old French
ON	Old Norse
pl.	plural
p.p.	past participle
prep.	preposition
PRO	Public Record Office
p.t.	past tense
sb.	substantive
sg.	singular
UD	Urban District
v.	verb

Books and journals

CIIC	R.S. Macalister, *Corpus Inscriptionum Insularum Celticarum*, 2 vols (1945–9)
DEPN	E. Ekwall, *The Concise Oxford Dictionary of English Place-Names* (4th edn, 1960)
DNB	L. Stephen and S. Lee, *Dictionary of National Biography* (1885–)
EDD	J. Wright, *The English Dialect Dictionary*, 6 vols (1898–1905)
EDG	J. Wright, *The English Dialect Grammar* (1905)
EDS	Publications of the English Dialect Society
EEP	A.J. Ellis, *On Early English Pronunciation, Part V: The Existing Phonology of English Dialects* (1889)
EETS (ES)	Publications of the Early English Text Society (Extra Series; the volumes in the Ordinary Series are not specially identified)
EPNS	Publications of the English Place-Name Society
JBAA	*Journal of the British Archaeological Association*
JEGP	*Journal of English and Germanic Philology*
JRIC	*Journal of the Royal Institution of Cornwall*
LHEB	K.H. Jackson, *Language and History in Early Britain* (1953)
MED	H. Kurath and S.M. Kuhn (eds), *Middle English Dictionary* (Ann Arbor, Mich., 1952–)
OC	*Old Cornwall* (issued by the Federation of Old Cornwall Societies, St Ives, 1924–)
OED	J.A.H. Murray, H. Bradley, W.A. Craigie and C.T. Onions, *The Oxford English Dictionary*, 13 vols (1933–)
PMLA	*Publications of the Modern Language Association of America*
PND	J.E.B. Gover, A. Mawer and F.M. Stenton, *The Place-Names of Devon*, EPNS, VIII, IX (1931–2)
RIB	R.G. Collingwood and R.P. Wright, *The Roman Inscriptions of Britain, I: Inscriptions on Stone* (1965)
SED	H. Orton and E. Dieth, *Survey of English Dialects* (1962–71)
TDA	*Transactions of the Devonshire Association for the Advancement of Science, Literature and Art*
Trans. *Phil.Soc.*	*Transactions of the Philological Society*
VC	*Vocabularium Cornicum*

List of phonetic and other symbols

The phonetic symbols are those of the International Phonetic Association:
a, b, d, f, g, h, k, l, m, n, p, s, t, v, w, z have approximately the values represented by English spelling. The values of the remainder are approximately as follows:

æ   mid-way between ɛ and a
ɑ   as in c*a*rt, but short; Fr p*a*s
ɖ   retroflex d
ʤ   as in *j*eer
ð   as in *th*en
e   as in Fr th*é*
ə   as in chin*a*
ɛ   as in b*e*t
i   as in b*ea*t, but short; Fr s*i*
ɩ   as in b*i*t
j   as in *y*ear
ł   as in i*ll* (velarized l)
ņ   syllabic n
ɳ   retroflex n
ŋ   as in si*ng*
o   as in Fr *eau*
ø   as in Fr p*eu*
œ   as in Fr f*eu*illeton
ɒ   as in b*o*x
ɔ   as in p*au*se, but short; Fr c*o*ter
ɹ   as in *r*un (superior denotes r-colouring)
ʈ   retroflex r (superior denotes r-colouring)
ʃ   as in *sh*ort
t   retroflex t
ʧ   as in *ch*air
θ   as in *th*in

13

u   as in b*oo*t, but short; Fr t*ou*t

ʉ   mid-way between i and u

ɷ   as in b*u*sh

ʌ   as in b*u*t

x   as in Scottish lo*ch*

y   as in Fr t*u*

Y   lowered variety of y

ɤ   unrounded equivalent of o

ʐ   retroflex z

ʒ   as in mea*s*ure

:   indicates that the preceding sound is long, e.g. ɛ:

··   over a vowel indicates centralization, e.g. ë

−   underneath a vowel indicates retraction, e.g. ɛ̠

.   underneath a vowel indicates closer quality, e.g. ɛ̣

ι   underneath a vowel indicates more open quality, e.g. ɛ̦

ˈ   indicates main stress, e.g. ˈmɛnι

[ ]   enclose phonetic symbols

/ /   enclose phonemic symbols

~   'alternates with'

<   'descends from'

>   'becomes'

*   indicates a hypothetical form

To my parents

1 Dialect geography and Cornwall

Dialect or linguistic geography is that branch of linguistics which aims to interpret features of regional dialect as plotted on maps. The origins of such studies go back to the end of the nineteenth century when philologists of the Neo-Grammarian school sought to test their theories about sound-laws on the living, rural dialects of Germany and France. In such surroundings, it was felt, speech could be studied in its natural setting, free from the influences of the written language and other factors.[1]

These early dialect studies yielded some significant results, but of even more lasting significance was the fact that the foundations of traditional dialectology had now been laid down for other scholars to build upon. The basic procedure consisted of the collecting of items of local speech by means of some sort of questionnaire in a network of localities, the results being thereafter plotted on maps. From the beginning of dialect studies, there has been much disagreement about the type of questionnaire which should be used to obtain the best results (as to whether it should be posted to informants for their written responses, for example, or put to them personally question by question by a field-worker, how the questions should be framed, etc., etc.). There has been disagreement as to what items should be collected and about the sort of localities to be investigated. But upon one thing there has been up to recently agreement among dialectologists, namely the *type* of dialect to be examined. It is what Professor Harold Orton has referred to as "traditional vernacular, genuine and old",[2] i.e. the type of dialect representative of a direct development from the language of an earlier period which was unlikely to have been disturbed by outside influences (a standard form of speech, for example). There were various reasons why this type of dialect appeared to be important to dialectologists. One is that it is the oldest type of speech and often embodies features of a stratum of language more archaic

1. For treatments of linguistic geography, see the bibliographies in M.F. Wakelin, *English Dialects: An Introduction* (1972).
2. 'An English Dialect Survey: Linguistic Atlas of England', *Orbis*, ix (1960), 332.

17

than that of the standard language. It is thus of inestimable value in re-constructing and elucidating the earlier stages of the language. Another is that the recording of the most ancient type of dialect has been felt to be a rescue operation by which older linguistic forms might be collected before being finally obliterated by modern communications and the standardization of speech.

Traditional local dialect, it is usually believed, is heard in its purest form in rural localities from elderly people of a working-class status, who were locally born and of a continuous residence (i.e. genuine natives of the locality under investigation), and of minimal education (they would thus not be greatly affected by standard speech).[3]

Dialect items obtained from such informants are plotted on maps and the areas over which they are distributed may be delimited by imaginary lines known as isoglosses. When two or three such isoglosses coincide, there occurs what is known as the bundling of isoglosses. This usually takes place along important geographical or political boundaries, which are thus shown to have been dominant factors in the separation of one dialect from another. Without necessarily implying that speech inside an area defined by the bundling of isoglosses is uniform in every characteristic, it may be said that such territory can be regarded in some respects as a 'dialect area'. Isoglosses and the areas they define are the study of the linguistic geographer, who is also concerned to determine whether or not the boundaries of known dialectal areas coincide with 'culture areas' in a broader sense – whether an area characterized by certain dialectal features is also characterized, for example, by the use of certain types of scythe or shepherds' smocks, or the observance of certain local customs and festivals. Dialect maps also show how a dialect of prestige value (e.g. Standard English) may encroach upon traditional local speech, and how local dialects encroach upon one another.

In England, interest in dialect and in historical linguistics generally first becomes clearly manifest in the sixteenth century, together with the rise of interest in antiquities.[4] A long line of scholars and writers from that time on testifies to continued interest in the subject up to the present date, as does also the compilation of glossaries of local speech and dialect verse, mono-logues and so forth. It was, however, only when the systematic study of dialect started on the Continent that English dialectology was seriously

3. The investigation of urban dialects has recently posed different problems for the dialecto-logist in that here the linguistic variation results not only from geographical but also from socio-economic causes. New methodologies have been and are being evolved to cope with this sort of investigation. See Wakelin, *op. cit.*, 59ff., 155–7, and p. 99 n. 90, below.
4. The Society of Antiquaries had been founded in 1572, and the works of men like Leland, Camden, Carew and Norden testify to antiquarian interests as early as the sixteenth century in "the new spirit of creative inquiry and of crescent nationalism" – F.E. Halliday (ed.), *Richard Carew of Antony: The Survey of Cornwall* (1953), 49.

taken up. The English Dialect Society was founded in 1873, with the special intention of producing an English Dialect Dictionary, and the Editor of this work – ultimately commenced in 1896 – was Joseph Wright, a Yorkshire miner's son who later became Professor of Comparative Philology at Oxford, and who had been trained in the Neo-Grammarian school in Germany.

The compilation of glossaries of local English dialect had been going on almost since the beginnings of interest in dialect in this country. The English Dialect Society performed the most useful work of reprinting some of these earlier glossaries – as also some of the earlier dialect monologues and similar items which had been written – and of printing some new ones. For his *English Dialect Dictionary* (*EDD*), Wright used all these sources, plus dialect words from county histories, accounts of industries (e.g. mining), agricultural surveys, natural histories and other works. *EDD* aimed at a comprehensive inclusion of all dialect words current in Britain or known to have been in use during the previous 200 years (see *EDD*, v). Wright intended to achieve this aim by using material from all the existing glossaries, plus the results of a postal questionnaire sent to 12,000 people. The usefulness of this vast collection is unhappily vitiated by the fact that the material is extracted from glossaries whose dates range over too large a period of time and that the designations of locality are too vague: we need to know precisely where a word was recorded, and not merely that it was recorded in a county or area. The etymologies too are often suspect. But in spite of these and other failings, *EDD*, used carefully, is an indispensable source of earlier forms for the lexicologist.

Besides editing the enormous six-volume *EDD*, Wright also produced an *English Dialect Grammar*, which aimed to provide a general description of all the dialects, exhibiting their main characteristic features, and a monograph on his own dialect of Windhill in Yorkshire.

Most of the early investigators of English dialect were concerned chiefly with vocabulary. The first person to attempt an overall description of the phonology of all the English dialects was A.J. Ellis (1814–90), who in 1889 supplemented his four volumes *On Early English Pronunciation* (1869–74) by a fifth subtitled *The Existing Phonology of English Dialects compared with that of West Saxon Speech* (*EEP*). His aim was:

> to determine with considerable accuracy the different forms *now*, or *within the last hundred years*, assumed by the descendants of the same original word in passing through the mouths of uneducated people, speaking an inherited language, in all parts of Great Britain where English is the ordinary medium of communication between peasant and peasant.[5]

5. *EEP*, 1.

It may be seen from this that Ellis was well within the traditions of his time in attempting to obtain only 'pure dialect' and exclude anything but older forms. His information was obtained by various methods – none of them, unfortunately, very reliable, for example the lists of words whose local pronunciations he tried to obtain via the medium of educated people who did not speak the dialect naturally. However, on the basis of the information he obtained, Ellis was able to define six Divisions, namely Southern, Western, Eastern, Midland, Northern, and Lowland (Scottish). These six major divisions were further divided into 42 Districts "in each of which a sensible similarity of pronunciation prevails",[6] themselves often broken down into Varieties and even Sub-varieties.[7]

Ellis's work can alone lay claim to comprise anything approaching an English dialect survey such as the Dieth-Orton *Survey of English Dialects* (*SED*), which was planned in 1946 and whose Introduction and four volumes of Basic Material were published between 1962 and 1971.

Like earlier, Continental dialect works, *SED* has been from the outset specifically interested in one kind of English – the traditional vernacular described above which would be most likely to be obtained in rural communities. Its basic tool is a questionnaire of some 1,300 questions, aimed at eliciting lexical (chiefly), phonological, morphological and syntactical items from informants most of whom were engaged in farming. The field-work for *SED* was carried out by nine trained field-workers between 1948 and 1961. As to the localities investigated, preference was given to agricultural communities that had had a fairly stable population of about 500 inhabitants for a century or so, and newly built-up localities were avoided. Very few towns were included. Ultimately the network extended to 313 localities distributed the length and breadth of England (but excluding Scotland and Wales).

The informants chosen were almost always over 60, and were mostly men, since men in this country are thought to speak dialect more consistently than women. They had to be genuine natives of the locality under investigation without any significant period of time away, and professional raconteurs and reciters were scrupulously avoided. Two or three informants were generally interviewed in each locality, their responses to the questions being transcribed by the field-workers in the International Phonetic Alphabet on specially prepared sheets divided down the middle, the left-hand side being reserved for the responses, and the right-hand side for any expressions and words from the informants' conversations which the field-worker thought especially noteworthy. This 'incidental material' has proved invaluable as supplementary matter, especially since it is unscripted and was elicited

6. *Ibid.*, 3*.
7. For an appreciation of Ellis's work, see Wakelin, *op. cit.*, 48–51.

completely spontaneously (i.e. not within the framework of the formal question and answer).

The information obtained from the informants formed the basis of the *SED* four volumes of Basic Material. Soon after field-work started, however, it was also decided to make tape-recordings of the unscripted speech of suitable informants in every locality an essential part of the survey, and there is thus now in existence a valuable collection of such tapes from all 313 localities.

It is on the material relating to the county of Cornwall contained in volume IV (Southern) of *SED*, edited by Professor Orton and myself between 1967 and 1968, that the present book is chiefly based. It should be especially noted that new dialect material additional to that collected by *SED* (apart from what is mentioned on pp. 33–4, below) has not found a place in this book for the obvious reason that such material would not be strictly comparable with that of *SED* in its date of collection, *SED*'s having been obtained in 1958, some 17 years ago. This is not to say, however, that a completely new survey in Cornwall would not be very welcome indeed, especially if it were able to operate within a close network of, say, 50 localities instead of the present seven. It is greatly to be hoped that a close-meshed survey of this type will in fact be initiated within the foreseeable future. Moreover, this in itself should be regarded only as a component part of a Linguistic Survey of Cornwall which would include analyses of urban speech (e.g. at Bodmin, Truro, Camborne-Redruth) comparable to those already carried out in some other English towns (see n. 3, above), a thorough examination and analysis of all the early vernacular documents from Cornwall and a new investigation of the place-names. What firm conclusions it may be possible to arrive at about the linguistic history and geography of the county will only be reached when all this work has been carried out. Meanwhile, the present book, based on what is available at the time of writing, offers at least an introduction to the material, and – one hopes – an incentive for these larger projects.

The dialects of Cornwall instantly claim the attention when one notices some of the major differences in pronunciation between east, central and west Cornwall. Immediately striking, for example, are the consonantal and vocalic contrasts between [vɤt], [vɒt] and [fɒt] (*foot*), in which dialectal forms – with initial [v], and vowel nucleus [ɤ] – current in east Cornwall give way to pronunciations approaching those of Standard English as one goes further west. The interest in these features is added to by the existence of a number of Cornish words still in use in west Cornwall, and also by the statement of A.J. Ellis – supported by phonetic data – that the western boundary of his District 11 (which bisects Cornwall by a line running north

21

to south almost through Truro) "is properly the w. limit of dialect in England."[8] All these considerations make Cornwall a tempting prospect for the dialectologist, and it also has the advantage of being an area virtually untouched by scholarly research in this field.

Unlike some other work in dialectology, however, my aim in this book is not to give a description of the speech forms of one county, but rather to correlate *selected* features of local dialect which are apparently significant with historical and historico-linguistic facts, and to draw such conclusions about the linguistic history of the county and the influence of Cornish and English upon each other as may be possible. At the same time, the information gained may enable us to define the border between speakers of English and of Cornish during and subsequent to the Middle Ages. This is a matter about which little is known, and text-book statements still often place the boundary at this period on the Devon-Cornwall border. So, for example, Professor Strang, in her recent (1970) book *A History of English*, states that in the period 1370–1570 "the English-speaking population extended from north of Aberdeen to the Devon-Cornwall border" (p. 156), while the *Encyclopaedia Britannica* (14th edn, s.v. Celtic Languages: Cornish), no doubt following Henry Jenner,[9] states that the boundary between Cornish and English was the Tamar even as late as the fifteenth century. I hope to show that such statements need modification. It will thus be clear that the investigation proposed here is historically orientated, and indeed I venture to hope that it will be of interest to historians as well as philologists.

For the two purposes outlined above, it has been necessary to give a fairly detailed historical and historico-linguistic background. Such a background is not easy to sketch, since little appears to be known about Cornish history (especially that of the Anglo-Saxon period) in any detail, in addition to which the Cornish language is poorly documented and the texts inadequately edited for the most part. The source material, in other words, is scanty, and what there is is often unpublished.

Previous research

Earlier investigations of linguistic matters relating to Cornwall took the two divergent directions of work on the Cornish language, and work on English dialect. Since we are not primarily concerned with Cornish, it is not necessary to discuss the language itself in any detail, and a general statement will suffice. The language of the medieval and later Cornish peoples was a development of the Brittonic tongue which was also the parent of Welsh and Breton, and which was a parallel sister branch to Goidelic, the ancestor of Irish,

8. *EEP*, 156.
9. *A Handbook of the Cornish Language* (1904), 11.

Scottish Gaelic and Manx, both Brittonic and Goidelic ultimately springing from an ancestor which we may call Common Celtic. The Cornish language is preserved in a small number of medieval and post-medieval texts (mostly listed in Chapter 4, below), the earliest records being some late ninth- or early tenth-century glosses on Smaragdus's commentary on Donatus.[10] The language lasted, spoken by a decreasing number of people – mostly the lower classes – until for various reasons it finally petered out altogether in the eighteenth century. The most complete outline of its history is to be found in Henry Jenner's *A Handbook of the Cornish Language* (1904).

The revival of interest in Cornish should be seen as part of the widespread rise of antiquarian and historico-linguistic interests of the sixteenth and seventeenth centuries, in which men like Sir Thomas Browne (1605–1682), John Ray (1627–1705) and George Hickes (1642–1715) played notable roles. One of the earliest of the Cornish antiquarians was William Scawen, Vice-Warden of the Stannaries after the Restoration, whose *Antiquities Cornu-Britannick* was written in about 1680. In this work, Scawen gives a long description of the state of the language in his time, and accounts for its decline by 16 elaborate reasons. Special mention should also be made of Nicholas Boson of Newlyn,[11] a man of some education, who was brought up to speak English, but acquired a thorough knowledge of contemporary spoken Cornish, and in about 1700 produced a short work, *Nebbaz Gerriau dro tho Carnoack* ("A few words about Cornish"). The interest in Cornish gathered momentum with a group of antiquarians of Penzance and its neighbourhood, just when it was dying, at the end of the seventeenth century and the beginning of the eighteenth. The oldest member of this local group was John Keigwin (1641–1710) of Mousehole, who transcribed and translated many of the existing Cornish texts, although not very expertly. He seems to have been the only member of the party with linguistic pretensions, the others being chiefly historians and antiquarians. Among these should be mentioned William Gwavas, barrister, compiler of a collection of Cornish songs, verses, proverbs, letters, and so on, found in the 'Gwavas MS' (BM Additional MS. 28554), and ranging in date from 1709 to 1736; John and Thomas Boson; Thomas Tonkin; Oliver Pender; and Dr William Borlase, author of *Observations on the Antiquities . . . of the County of Cornwall* (1754, 1769), and of a *Natural History of Cornwall* (1758). These men collected words, proverbs, etc., in late Cornish, into which they also translated various passages of Scripture, songs and the like.

10. See K.H. Jackson, *Language and History in Early Britain* (1953), 59–62, for an account of the earliest written records of Cornish.
11. Jenner, *op. cit.*, 32–3 (probably following *JRIC* [1879], see below, p. 92), names him as John Boson, but see C. Henderson, 'Nicholas Boson and Richard Angwyn', *OC*, II.2 (1931), 29–32.

Of a much more scholarly nature is Edward Lhuyd's *Archaeologia Britannica* (1707), a prime source for knowledge of Cornish in its last years. Lhuyd, a Welshman, received considerable assistance from Keigwin, Gwavas and Tonkin in the Cornish sections of his work (the book treats of the other Celtic languages as well), and it is a unique source of information for scholars of Cornish.

The interest in Cornish was passed on to the nineteenth century via Dr William Pryce's *Archaeologia Cornu-Britannica* (1790), an edition (under his own name) of Lhuyd's work, together with a vocabulary and collection of Cornish fragments compiled by Gwavas and Tonkin. The most notable work of this century was that of Edwin Norris and Dr Whitley Stokes. The former transcribed, translated and published the *Ordinalia* (Cornish mystery plays), together with a grammar of Cornish and an edition of the *Vocabularium Cornicum* (1859), while the latter published other Cornish texts – *The Passion* (1861), Jordan's *Creation* (1864), *The Life of St Meriasek* (1872) – and also wrote a good number of learned articles on matters relating to Cornish and other Celtic languages. In 1865, The Rev. R. Williams, a Welshman, published his *Lexicon Cornu-Britannicum*, a substantial glossary of Cornish words taken from various earlier glossaries and from the surviving texts which had then been published. This is a reasonably scholarly work, giving numerous citations of the words *in context*, and is thus, like Lhuyd's work, of invaluable assistance for the study of late Cornish.

Up to this time, interest in Cornish had been of a scholarly, semi-scholarly, or antiquarian nature. It had not yet been suggested that Cornish should be revived as a 'living' language. Henry Jenner (1848–1934) was the first man to learn Cornish with the aim of reviving it as a spoken medium, and in 1904 published his *A Handbook of the Cornish Language*, a book which apparently encouraged many people to learn Cornish. Jenner's *Handbook*, in two parts, 'The History of the Cornish Language and Literature', and 'The Grammar of the Cornish Language', is, like the works of Lhuyd, Norris, Stokes, and Williams, invaluable for the study of Cornish.

Henceforth, interest in Cornish seems to have had two related motives (the first no doubt partly inspired by the second), one scholarly or semi-scholarly, aiming to study Cornish texts and produce dictionaries, learned articles on Cornish, and the like, and another, partly patriotic, the intention here being to facilitate and encourage the learning of Cornish and to develop a new literature for Cornwall. This latter movement, the 'Cornish Revival', with the foundation of the Federation of Old Cornwall Societies (beginning in 1920), the Gorsedd of the Bards (1928), Cornish classes, Cornish Church services, manuals of instruction for would-be learners of Cornish, Cornish by radio (1935), a Cornish Correspondence Circle (1937-9), the *English-Cornish Dictionary* and *Cornish-English Dictionary* (1934, 1938), and numerous Cornish publications, may be read about in J.J. Parry, 'The Revival of Cornish: an Dasserghyans Kernewek', *PMLA*, LXI (1946), 258–68; in A.S.D. Smith's pamphlet, *The Story of the Cornish Language: Its Extinction and Revival* (1947, 1969), and in the pages of the periodical *Kernow* (1934–6), and is not our concern here except for the fact that it has been responsible for the study of Cornish in a semi-scholarly way. The late R. Morton Nance was one of the great figures of the movement, producing an enormous stream of books and articles on Cornish and Cornwall, and he is not without his disciples and successors. The Federation of Old Cornwall Societies still enjoys a fairly vigorous existence, and there are a great many Cornish enthusiasts and patriots of one sort and another. Meanwhile, new, scholarly editions of all the Cornish texts together with a Cornish dictionary compiled on the lines of the *Oxford English Dictionary*, an historical phonology of Cornish, and all the other necessary linguistic apparatus, are still awaited.

Early works on the English dialect of Cornwall are concerned almost exclusively with vocabulary, except in so far as they attempt imitated pronunciations of words or give lists of phonetic features. None of these works distinguishes between words of Cornish and English origins, those dealing exclusively with Cornish having been already mentioned above.

Mention should first, however, be made of the works of Andrew Borde and Richard Carew. Borde, in the appendix to Chapter I of his *The Fyrst Boke of the Introduction of Knowledge* (written by 1542, published 1547), treats of Cornwall, giving 26 lines of English dialect from the county, which is clearly of an east Cornwall variety. As the first specimen of early MnE dialect from Cornwall, the passage is reproduced in an appendix to the present book, and no further comment is required here. Carew, in his *Survey of Cornwall* (1602), besides listing a few dialectal items such as *pridy* 'handsome', *shune* 'strange', *hoase* 'forbear',[12] uses dialect words himself, and also comments on the language of the county (see below, pp. 89–90). His work abounds in such dialect words as *dornes* 'door-jambs', *moldwarps* 'moles', *angle-touches* 'earth-worms', *polled* 'beheaded', *quurt up* 'fill up' (of chinks), and it is clear that Carew, with his interest in language, deliberately introduced these dialect words into his works (see, for example, besides the *Survey*, his poem *A Herring's Tail*).[13]

Apart from Pryce's work, cited below, no glossaries or works of any kind as such on the English dialect of Cornwall, however, appear to have been written before the early nineteenth century. Apart from Borde and Carew, therefore, we are totally without this type of evidence for the history of the dialect. But from the nineteenth century on, as is the case with regard to most counties, dialect glossaries, tales, monologues and similar works

12. See Halliday's edition, 128. Subsequent references are always to this edition.
13. Ed. Halliday, *op. cit.*, 279–99.

proliferated, and a large number are cited in the bibliography to *EDD*. The following, all of which were used in the compilation of *EDD*, is a selection of those deemed to be most important.

1. W. Pryce, *Mineralogia Cornubiensis* (1778). [Pp. 315–31 contain a glossary of items used in the tin-mines.]

2. R. Polwhele, *A Cornish-English Vocabulary; a Vocabulary of Local Names, chiefly Saxon; and a Provincial Glossary* (1808, 1816, 1836).

3. W. Sandys (Uncle Jan Treenoodle), *Specimens of Cornish Provincial Dialect* (1846).

4. T.Q. Couch, 'A List of Obsolete Words, still in use among the Folk of East Cornwall', *JRIC* (March 1864), 6–26.

5. T. Garland, 'A List of Words in Common Use in West Cornwall', *JRIC* (April 1865), 45–54.

6. T.Q. Couch, 'Appendix to a List of Obsolescent Words and Local Phrases in use among the Folk of East Cornwall', *JRIC* (April 1870), 173–9.

7. M.A. Courtney and T.Q. Couch, *Glossary of Words in Use in Cornwall:* West Cornwall by Miss M.A. Courtney; East Cornwall by T.Q. Couch (English Dialect Society, No. 27, 1880). [This is the most ambitious glossary to deal exclusively with Cornwall. Both sections are also provided with phonetic notes on the dialects (these do not, however, add materially to the points under consideration in the present book). A frontispiece map is given, showing an approximate line of division between the dialects of west and east Cornwall. This starts at Crantock Bay, and passes, north-east of Truro, to Veryan Bay. (This isogloss is discussed in my Conclusion, below.)]

8. F.W.P. Jago, *The Ancient Language, and the Dialect of Cornwall, with an enlarged Glossary of Cornish provincial Words* (1882).

9. J. Thomas, *Randigal Rhymes and a Glossary of Cornish Words* (1895).

Many other nineteenth-century works relating to the English dialect of Cornwall are listed in *A Bibliographical List of Works that have been Published, or are known to exist in MS., Illustrative of the Various Dialects of English* (English Dialect Society, No. 2, 1877, pp. 19–28). In addition, numerous notes and letters on lexical matters are to be found in the volumes of *The Journal of the Royal Institution of Cornwall, Old Cornwall* and other local journals. Finally, *A Glossary of Cornish Sea-Words*, compiled by the late R.M. Nance, has been edited by P.A.S. Pool (1963), and Nance also left a manuscript collection of dialect words.

All the investigators named above were concerned chiefly with vocabulary, and their imitated pronunciations and phonetic notes are usually very inadequate. The only work before *SED* to attempt a serious phonological description of English dialect in Cornwall was Ellis's *EEP* (see above, pp. 19–20), and any investigation of the present-day dialects of Cornwall must therefore take into account the data collected by him, even though it is recognized

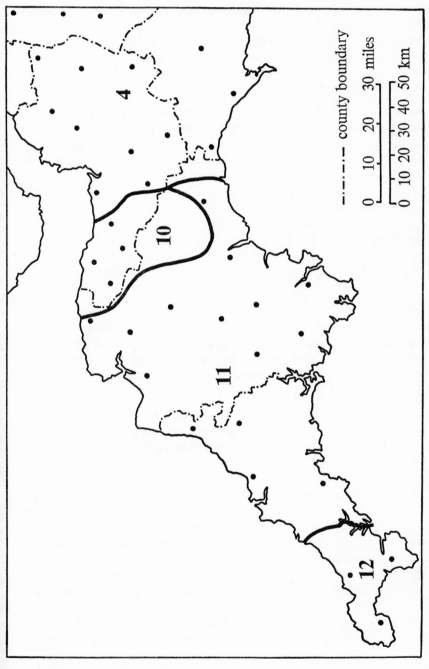

Map 1. Ellis's Districts 10, 11 and 12, with dots representing SED localities.

that Ellis's methods are open to criticisms of a serious nature and that his information is somewhat haphazard.

For present purposes, the relevant Districts distinguished in *EEP* are 10 (pp. 145ff.), 11 (pp. 156ff.) and 12 (pp. 171ff.). These Districts (shown on map 1) together form Ellis's 'west Southern Group', comprising the following area and having the following 'character' (p. 145):

> *Boundaries.* The e.b. is the w.b. of MS. [Mid Southern] and the other boundaries are formed by the Bristol and English Channels.
>
> *Area.* The w. portion of Sm. [Somerset], all but the extreme sw. of Dv., all Co. and the Scilly Isles. This represents comparatively recent, and in w.Co. very recent, overrunning of a Celtic language (Cornish or West Welsh) by English. In D 12, w.Co. and Scilly, a true dialect has apparently never been formed.
>
> *Character.* Besides the general S. character with the (R) very strongly developed in the e. but gradually weakening on going w. (till in D 12 the received *r* is perhaps quite established),[14] there is also the striking change of O′ [= ME $\bar{o}$] into (yy₁), closely resembling Fr. (y), which sharply limits this group towards the e.

District 10 ('northern West Southern') comprises west Somerset and a small portion of north-east Devon. District 11 ('southern West Southern') comprises all of Devon except for the area north of Exeter and east of Tiverton (in District 10), and east Cornwall. District 12 ('western West Southern') consists of west Cornwall, and Ellis's definition of the boundary between Districts 11 and 12 is worth quoting (p. 156):

> There was much difficulty in determining the w.b. [west boundary], concerning which I collected several opinions, and finally follow the information of Rev. W.H. Hodge, which I believe to be most accurate. Begin at the Black Rock in the middle of the entrance to Falmouth Harbour, and go through the centre of the water-way to Truro. Then proceed by land e. of Kenwyn (1 nnw. Truro) and w. of St. Erme (4 nne. Truro), e. of St. Allen (4 n. Truro) and w. of Newlyn (8 n. Truro), and also west of Cubert (9 nnw. Truro), but e. of Perran Zabulo (8 nnw. Truro) to the sea in Ligger or Perran Bay. This border was determined by noting the change of speech. Mr. Rawlings, speaking only from general impressions, said the b. was probably a straight line from St. Anthony, on the e. horn of Falmouth Harbour to St. Agnes Head (9 nnw. Truro). This line, beginning practically at the same point as the other, and ending only 5 m. to the sw., must be considered as practically identical with it. Mr. Sowell, who wrote the Cornish-English version of the *Song of Solomon*

14. This feature was unremarked by *SED*, which recorded [ɾ] throughout Cornwall.

for Prince L.-L. Bonaparte, inclines to a line from St. Austell to Padstow. According to Mr. Hodge, Mr. Herman Merivale in his "Historical Studies" lays down the border between Celt and Saxon, no doubt at a much earlier date, from Down Derry (8 sse. Liskeard) to St. Germans (7 se. Liskeard), thence to St. Ive (4 ne. Liskeard), South Hill (7 nne. Liskeard), North Hill (7 n. Liskeard), Altarnun (7 wsw. Launceston), Minster (13 wnw. Launceston), and to the sea by Forrabury (14 nnw. Launceston). This line is just a few miles w. of the e.b. of Co. itself.

Ellis further remarks that "the w.b. of D 11 is properly the w. limit of dialect in England."

Ellis divides District 11 into three Variants, Var. i north Devon, Var. ii south Devon and Var. iii east Cornwall. The localities under Var. iii from which he gives dialect samples are Camelford, Cardinham and St Columb Major, while Millbrook (Cornwall, 2 miles south-west of Plymouth) is included under Var. ii. Under the heading 'Alphabetical County List' pp. 32*–67*, however, Ellis gives the names of *all* the localities from which he received information, county by county, although this information is published for only some of them in *EEP* itself. He received information from 19 localities in Cornwall (see p. 35*), distributed between Districts 11 and 12. In addition to the four mentioned above, these comprise for District 11: Landrake, Lanivet, Lanreath, Padstow, Poundstock, St Blazey, St Goran, St Ive, St Stephen's and Tintagel.

Ellis comments in general terms on the character of the pronunciation of each District in his work. In District 11, this is, he says, "essentially the same as that of D 10, with a few distinguishing particulars." Under District 10 (see pp. 146–7), he singles out for detailed comment the reflexes of ME $\bar{\imath}$, $\bar{u}$, $\bar{\rho}$ and i, and retroflex consonants after [ɽ], as well as giving the equivalents of most of the other ME vowels and diphthongs. The 'distinguishing particulars' of District 11 are the reflexes of ME *æg* and *eg*, ME $\bar{\imath}$ and $\bar{u}$. These are commented upon in some detail, while other points are dealt with in the Notes appended to the dialect samples. Reference will be made to Ellis's comments in the appropriate sections of Chapter 5, below.

Ellis's District 12 'western West Southern' comprises Cornwall west of Truro, together with the Scilly Isles. Its eastern boundary is as described above. There are apparently no Variants, but a dialect sample is given from Marazion, and also a conjecturally palaeotyped[15] list of words from the Introduction to Miss Courtney's *West Cornwall Glossary*, to which are added some from the Marazion specimen mentioned above, supplied by Mr Rawlings of Hayle (Henry Jenner's father-in-law). The other localities in

---

15. See *EEP*, pp. 76*–88*, for an explanation of Ellis's Palaeotype.

District 12 from which Ellis received information were (p. 35*): Gwennap, Penzance, St Just in Penwith and Stithians.

Ellis says (p. 171) that no 'character' (of the pronunciation) can be given. He notes, however, that "most of the WS. [West Saxon] characters seem to have disappeared", and that "we find scarcely a vestige of Dv. phraseology or pronunciation ... Many words of Cornish origin remain." Ellis seems to think that "a haphazard speech ... appears to prevail", and he has been told that the 'mode of speech' varies very much from place to place. Finally, Ellis reproduces from T.Q. Couch's *East Cornwall Glossary* (he refers to it as *East Cornwall Words*) some comments by 'Tregellas'[16] on the distinctively west Cornwall intonation, together with some from the same source on the western limit of the voicing of initial fricative consonants, which appear to agree precisely with the boundary between east and west Cornwall adopted by him.

Ellis's work was the natural precursor of the Dieth-Orton *Survey of English Dialects*. The *SED* localities in Cornwall all conform to the 'small village' type chosen for investigation throughout the country. All of them appear to be of some antiquity, although now often disturbed by housing estates on their fringes and main roads running through them. In all of them, agriculture is a staple occupation (but note that St Day, below, is a mining village). Their situations are shown on map 2. Further elaboration seems unnecessary, but fuller portraits of the village can, of course, be found in some of the books dealing with the counties of England (e.g. those by John Betjeman and Arthur Mee – see the Bibliography, below). The *SED* localities investigated and informants interviewed in Cornwall (all in the autumn and winter of 1958) are set out below, the details slightly modified from those given in *SED*, volume IV, pp. 46–51. The National Grid reference follows the name of the locality, and this itself is followed by the populations of the civil (c) and ecclesiastical (e) parishes as determined in the 1951 Census. A superior *r* after the informant's initials indicates that a tape-recording was made of him (her).

1. Kilkhampton (SS/2511; 907°, 880ᵉ)

1. W.J.T.   77; native; father and mother from district, father farmer; local school till 11; farmer; lifelong resident; wife native, wife's father farm-labourer.
2. R.H.ʳ   82; native; father and mother natives, father farm-worker; local school till 10; farm-worker; lifelong resident; wife born Bradworthy (4¾ east-north-east), Devon, of Bradworthy parentage, wife's father farm-labourer.

16. This is J.T. Tregellas, *Peeps into the Haunts and Homes of the Rural Population of Cornwall* (1868), 2.

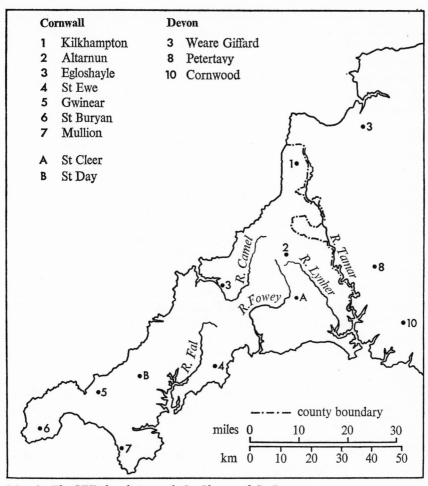

Cornwall		Devon	
1	Kilkhampton	3	Weare Giffard
2	Altarnun	8	Petertavy
3	Egloshayle	10	Cornwood
4	St Ewe		
5	Gwinear		
6	St Buryan		
7	Mullion		
A	St Cleer		
B	St Day		

Map 2. The SED *localities with St Cleer and St Day.*

3. F.J.G.ʳ 77; native; father and mother from district, family carriers here "several generations"; local school till 10; carter and carrier; except for First World War, lifelong resident; wife from district, wife's father sawyer.

4. R.P. 78; native; father and mother natives, father farmer; local school till 12; farmer; lifelong resident; wife born Hartland (8 north-north-east), Devon.

2. Altarnun (SX/2281; 700ᶜ, 601ᵉ)

1. W.C. 77; native; father and mother from district, father farmer; local

school till 12; farm-labourer; except for three years with the Duke of Cornwall's Light Infantry in First World War, lifelong resident; bachelor.

2. T.W.B. 70; native; father and mother from district, father tin-miner; local school till 12; farm-worker; except for service with the Devonshire Yeomanry in First World War, lifelong resident; wife born Alton, Hants, but resident of the locality since 12, wife's mother from district, wife's father railwayman.

3. T.W.S.[r] 74; native; father and mother born next parish, father farmer; local school till 12; farm-worker and shepherd; except for three years farming in next village during First World War, lifelong resident; wife from district, wife's father farmer.

3. Egloshayle (SX/0072; 413[c], 1425[e])

1. W.T.L.R.[r] 70; native; father and mother from district, father miller; Wadebridge (¾ north-west) school till 13; miller and small-holder; except for service with the Duke of Cornwall's Light Infantry in First World War, lifelong resident; wife from district.

2. H.E.P. (female) 77; born St Mabyn (2¾ east-north-east); father and mother natives, father wagoner; Wadebridge (¾ north-west) school till 12; housewife; lifelong resident; husband from district, dead 24 years, railwayman, lifelong resident.

4. St Ewe (SW/9846; 668[c], 720[e])

1. J.J.[r] 76; native; father born Mevagissey (2½ east-south-east), mother native, father shepherd; local school till 13; farm-worker and small-holder; lifelong resident; wife born Mevagissey.

2. F.J.L.[r] 64; native; father and mother natives, father farmer; local school till 13; farmer; lifelong resident; wife born Lostwithiel (11¾ north-east), wife's father farm-worker.

3. G.S. 68; native; father and mother born Newquay (14 north-west), father farm-labourer; local school till 11; farm-labourer; except for ten months farming in Hants, and one year with Duke of Cornwall's Light Infantry in First World War, lifelong resident; bachelor.

5. Gwinear (SW/6037; 1155[e])

1. G.H.E. 73; native; father and mother from district, farmed same farm as son; local school till 13; farmer; lifelong resident, has "always lived on same farm"; wife born Gulval (7¾ west-south-west), wife's father farmer.

2. E.H.W. 63; native; father and mother from district, father traction-engine driver; local school till 13; farm-worker; except for service with

the Royal Engineers and the Northumberland Fusiliers in First World War, lifelong resident; wife native, wife's father farm-worker.
3. J.G.ʳ   77; native; father and mother from district, father farm-worker and tin-miner; local school till 12; farm-worker, tin-miner and local quarryman, munition worker in First World War; lifelong resident; wife native, wife's father and mother from district.
4. R.A.P.   54; native; father and mother born Camborne (4 east-north-east), father tin-miner; local school till 14; blacksmith, builder and carpenter; lifelong resident; wife from district, wife's father farmer and tin-miner.

6. St Buryan (SW/4125; 1072ᶜᵉ)

1. J.A.   72; native; grandfather, father and mother natives, father stone-dresser, grandfather local blacksmith; local school till 13; quarryman, general labourer; lifelong resident; wife native, farm-worker.
2. W.T.S.ʳ   70; born St Levan (2¾ south-west); father and mother from district, father farm-labourer; local school till 12; farm-labourer; except for 18 months with the Duke of Cornwall's Light Infantry in First World War, lifelong resident; wife native, wife's father and mother from district, father farmer.
3. A.G.   75; native; father and mother natives, father farm-labourer; local school till 12; farm-labourer and nursery foreman; except for two years with the Royal Navy in First World War, lifelong resident; wife and wife's father and mother natives.

7. Mullion (SW/6819; 1154ᶜᵉ)

1. C.E.T.ʳ   83; native; father and mother natives, father farm-labourer; local school till 12; farm-worker, later watchman at Lizard (4½ south-south-east) Wireless Station 30 years; lifelong resident; wife native, wife's father shoemaker.
2. W.H.W.ʳ   73; native; father and mother natives, father farm-labourer; local school till 12; farm-labourer; except for five years with the Duke of Cornwall's Light Infantry in the First World War, lifelong resident; wife native, wife's father gardener.

The present author has long felt that the number of localities investigated in Cornwall might have been larger,[17] and in July 1963 he and Mr P.M.

17. It has indeed been suggested more than once that the *SED* network of localities as a whole is not close enough, and, although the criticism was answered by Dieth (see H. Orton and E. Dieth, 'The New Survey of Dialectal English', in *English Studies Today*, ed. C.L. Wrenn and G. Bullough [1951], 68–9), it must, of course, be admitted that a closer mesh would have been in every way desirable. But time and money were not available

Tilling (then Editorial Assistant to *SED*) visited two further localities in Cornwall, with the hope of augmenting the *SED* network. These localities were St Cleer and St Day. Attempts were made at recordings at these places, but without actually completing a full questionnaire at either of them. Tape-recordings were, however, also made, and I have decided in the present book to make limited use (generally in note form) of both the transcriptions and the tape-recordings from these two places to supplement when helpful the information given from the *SED* localities. This is particularly desirable in the case of St Cleer, since it is the centre of a large area in south-east Cornwall where there is a considerable gap in the *SED* network. Details of the two additional localities and their informants are as follows:

St Cleer (SX/2468; 1616°, 1657°)

1. N.C.[r] 89; native; farmer, retired; lifelong resident.
2. W.H.L.[r] *c.* 75; native; road-worker, retired; lifelong resident.

St Day (SW/7342; 3758 – with Lanner, now a ward of Camborne-Redruth U.D. and C.P., 1695°)

1. R.J.K.[r] 70; native; father from Kea (5 east), mother from Truro (6 east-north-east); local school till 14; brickworker, miner, retired; lifelong resident; wife and wife's father and mother natives.

---

for this, and accordingly our conclusions must be based on what has been done. To extend the network at this late date would mean that parts of the material were not truly comparable. In any case, I hope my conclusions will show that even seven localities in Cornwall are sufficient to allow significant boundaries to be established, although more localities would have inevitably given them a more precise location.

2 Present-day Cornwall

Since Sir Cyril Fox's classic exposition,[1] the notion of the division of Britain into two parts, based on the country's natural composition, has become a commonplace. The northern and western Highland Zone and the eastern Lowland Zone are each characterized by special features which are of primary importance for British history, and thus for the history of language in Britain. The Highland Zone has, generally speaking, a more rugged, mountainous character, poorer soil and higher rainfall than the Lowland Zone. This means that, as R.G. Collingwood rather sombrely put it:

> In the highland zone communication by land is everywhere difficult, and water-transport, except by sea, impossible; the character of the soil makes agriculture and stock-farming alike a precarious matter, with small profits and great liability to loss; and the cold, wet climate is a hindrance to every kind of activity and a handicap to every form of civilized life.[2]

This, in turn, means that throughout history there has always been a difference between the richer, more comfortable and more prosperous life of the Lowland Zone and the harsher, poorer life of the Highland Zone.

Roughly speaking, the Lowland Zone consists of eastern England as far west as the base of the Devon-Cornwall peninsula, the beginning of the Welsh hills, the Pennine chain and the uplands of County Durham and Northumberland. The Highland Zone is in three parts of unequal size – Scotland, with the Border Counties and the Pennine chain; Wales; and the south-western peninsula. It is the third of these areas in which we are specially interested for the purposes of this book – a long peninsula of land, somewhat remote from the rest of England by virtue of the surrounding sea on three of its sides and the Somerset levels, a large area of fen and marsh, at the neck of the peninsula. Such remoteness might well foster the tendency, as Lady

1. *The Personality of Britain* (1932; 4th, rev. edn, 1943).
2. R.G. Collingwood and J.N.L. Myres, *Roman Britain and the English Settlements* (2nd edn, 1937), 3.

Aileen Fox points out,[3] for individual cultures to develop in the region differing from the southern 'norm'. On the other hand, within the area itself there are few hills of any magnitude and the relief features – ranging mainly from 200 to 600ft, only Exmoor, Dartmoor and Bodmin Moor presenting extensive areas of over 1,000ft – present no obstacles to penetration and communication.

At the western end of the south-western peninsula is the present-day county of Cornwall, separated from its neighbours by the River Tamar, and thus even more set apart than they. We must now turn to a consideration of the county's characteristics in greater detail.

Natural features

Seventy-five miles long, and 45 miles broad at its widest point, Cornwall has a coastline of some 200 miles and an area of 1,357 square miles (including the Scilly Isles). The county is formed from a mass of Carboniferous and Devonian slates, shales and grits, with several intrusions of granite and other igneous rocks.[4] The granite masses, which are the visible parts of a deep-seated granite ridge running from Dartmoor to the Scilly Isles, form the higher relief features, comprising: Bodmin Moor (highest point, and the highest point in the county, Brown Willy, 1,375ft); Hensbarrow Down or the St Austell granite (highest point, Hensbarrow Beacon, 1,026ft); the Wendron Moors area (highest point, Carnmenellis, 819ft); and the West Penwith area, rising sharply only in the north-west of the area. Flanking these four main bosses are a number of smaller outcrops of more irregular shape.

Sometimes the granite has undergone certain modifications, the most familiar of these being the process of kaolinization. This has occurred on a large scale in the central and western portion of the St Austell granite mass, but all the granite outcrops are affected to some extent, and kaolin or china clay has been worked outside the St Austell area at various times, notably on the south and west sides of Bodmin Moor.

Nothing need be said of the volcanic and minor intrusive rocks, except to refer to the greenstones, which occur throughout the county, while the best known of the rocks of the complex Lizard series is serpentine. The principal minerals in Cornwall are tin and copper, but lead, zinc, antimony and silver are also found sporadically, the chief metalliferous regions being the areas around Wendron Moors, St Ives and St Just, lying on margins of two of the granite masses.

3. A. Fox, *South West England* (1964), 15.
4. On geology, see R.M. Barton, *An Introduction to the Geology of Cornwall* (1964).

The greater part of present-day Cornwall is taken up with arable and grassland. There is very little woodland, and that mostly in central Cornwall. It may be confidently surmised, however, that much forest has disappeared since medieval times.[5] Today, apart from woodland planted mainly around country houses in the eighteenth and nineteenth centuries and plantations established during the present century, the steep slopes of the valley sides of the Fal, Fowey and Camel contain the only important areas of woodland in the county, and some of the smaller rivers have similar fringes. A small percentage of the county consists of grass and heather moorlands, chiefly on the granite areas, of which Bodmin Moor is the most extensive. There is also a small area on Goonhilly Down, on the serpentine rock of the Lizard. Note should be made, too, of the St Breock Downs between Newquay and Wadebridge.

There are no very large rivers in Cornwall. The Tamar, rising in the far north-east, and almost making the county an island, was, according to William of Malmesbury,[6] fixed as the eastern shire boundary in the tenth century, and it has always served as an isolating factor to Cornishmen, though ever since Brunel's bridge was built in 1859, with the consequent increase in visitors, their sense of isolation must have been considerably diminished. Of the Tamar's tributaries, the Lynher (the largest one) and the Ottery are the most important, and were probably political boundaries for some time during the Anglo-Saxon period. The Camel and the Fowey both rise in or near Bodmin Moor and flow southwards, but the former eventually turns north and emerges in the Padstow estuary. The coincidence of these two rivers with the hundred boundaries Trigg/West in the east and Pydar/ Powder in the west makes this a very important boundary indeed, as the sequel will show. In the west, the Fal, rising on Hensbarrow Down, and emerging in the south at Falmouth, is the only river worthy of mention.

In general, the landscape of Cornwall, predetermined by its physical composition, has probably changed very little since early times. The coastal areas have apparently been affected most. Since before historic times a silting process has been going on in the river estuaries, although at a somewhat slower rate in modern times. Tregoney on the River Fal was, for example, an active port until 1600, and within the last 200 years the estuaries at Hayle, Pentewan, Porthluney and Par have been silted up, while similar minor

5. See C. Henderson, 'An Historical Survey of Cornish Woodlands', in *Essays in Cornish History* (1935), 135–51. The woodland recorded in Domesday Book is charted on a map (fig. 74) in H.C. Darby and R.W. Finn, *The Domesday Geography of South-West England* (1967), from which it can be seen that woodland was more frequent on the southern side than elsewhere, presumably, as today, in the incised river valleys. For the distribution of present-day woodland, see A.H. Shorter, W.L.D. Ravenhill and K.J. Gregory, *Southwest England* (1969), fig. 16.
6. *De Gestis Regum Anglorum*, ed. W. Stubbs (Rolls Series, 90 [1887]), 148.

changes proceed along the coast even now. Areas of blown sand occur chiefly on the exposed north-west coast, and there are extensive dunes at Padstow, Bude, Perranporth and Hayle, those at Perranporth having reached a height of 270ft. Along the cliffs the opposite process of erosion is going on, however. These changes need not detain us here, but we may note that the rivers of the south coast, which formed the most favoured landing ground for early visitors to Cornwall, could carry vessels further inland, toward the moorland hills, than they can today.

Divisions within Cornwall [7]

The most important non-physical division within the county is the hundred. The hundred first becomes clearly recognizable as a unit of local government in England in the tenth century, but it was probably an institution with a long history behind it even at this date.[8] Although it now has nine, Cornwall apparently had six hundreds originally, namely Trigg, Wivel, Pydar, Powder, Penwith and Kerrier. Trigg was later divided into three, Trigg, Lesnewth and Stratton, this trisection being unrecorded at the time of Domesday Book, and Wivel was divided into two, (modern) East and West, its bisection being already known at the time of Domesday Book. It is probable that the median boundary was based on a customary ridgeway from the neighbourhood of Launceston to that of St Michael's Mount, while the lateral boundaries appear to have been based on natural features: in the east these are the River Camel between Trigg and Pydar and the River Fowey between Wivel and Powder; in the west, originally the Portreath valley and stream between Pydar and Penwith and the Restronguet stream and creek between Powder and Kerrier. The later divisions, however, are not demonstrably so arranged, and must have been based only in part on natural boundaries, in part probably on the bounds of co-extant land-holdings.

There are evidently good reasons for regarding the six ancient hundreds of Cornwall as pre-English in origin, preserving to some extent the internal divisions of the peninsula in the post-Roman era.[9] The bisection of Wivel may represent part of a reorganization by Athelstan, as Professor W.G. Hoskins suggests,[10] "to arrange an area of overwhelmingly English character on lines closer to those of the other southern shires."[11] There is evidence,

7. This section owes much to the paper by Professor A.C. Thomas, 'Settlement-History in Early Cornwall, I: The Antiquity of the Hundreds', *Cornish Archaeology*, III (1964), 70–9.
8. See P.H. Blair, *An Introduction to Anglo-Saxon England* (1956), 232, 235–6.
9. This was not the opinion of Henderson (see *Essays*, 108), who believed that the fact that the four western hundreds all met together at one point excluded the possibility of their development from Celtic tribal divisions.
10. *The Westward Expansion of Wessex* (1960), 22.
11. Thomas, *op. cit.*, 72.

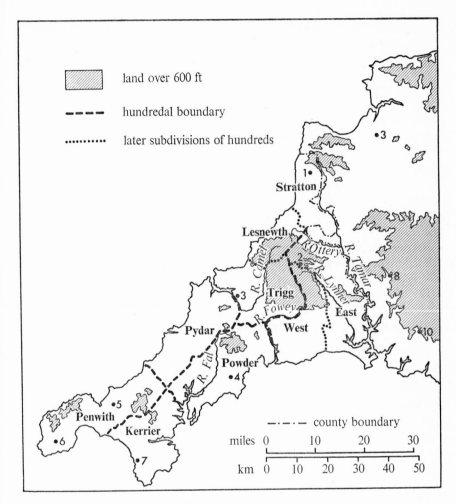

Map 3. Hundreds and physical features.

on the other hand, that the trisection of Trigg took place before Domesday Book, but the early forms of the name Trigg (cf. Gaulish *Tricorii*, a tribal name meaning 'those with three armies' – *corio*-'army')[12] suggest a tripartite division prior to Athelstan, even if only ratified later.

Of the other administrative divisions, the primary subdivision of the hundred was, until at least the sixteenth century, the tithing, adopted from the Anglo-Saxons and extended in Norman times, but replaced by the parish

12. See *DEPN*, s.v. Trigg, and, further, *LHEB*, 587.

from the fourteenth century onwards. The manor, a unit of property, was independent of the parish in origin, and probably earlier. Still impossible to define adequately, the manor seems to have consisted of a community, embracing one village or more (or perhaps one village sometimes being part of two or more manors), and comprising various grades of free and servile tenants, with certain officers – steward, bailiff, reeve and so on – the whole being held by a lord. Although the manorial system seems to have been inaugurated by the Normans, it may have replaced a similar Anglo-Saxon system, and a connexion may therefore exist between the manor and the late Saxon vill and the pre-Saxon tref. The parish is in origin an area allotted for purposes of support to a religious foundation selected to serve as an *ecclesia*. In Cornwall, where between a third and a half of the pre-medieval Celtic chapelries were thus selected, the parochial system seems no older than the twelfth century.[13] There are now 254 parishes in Cornwall. None of the smaller administrative units mentioned in this paragraph – past or present – appears to have had any bearing on dialectal differences in the county.

Population trends and settlement [14]

Various changes in the distribution of the county's population took place in the seventeenth and eighteenth centuries, mostly due to shifts in the emphasis on mining. Until the 1951 census, however, the population figures for Cornwall as a whole had shown a steady increase, as the following table demonstrates:

1086	19,033[15]
1377	51,411[16]
1700	105,800[17]
1801	192,281[18]
1861	369,390

In 1951, however, the figures were 345,442, a drop of some 24,000 over the previous 90 years, and in 1961 they were 341,746. At least part of this decline can be accounted for by the depression and poor harvests of the 1840s, by the failure in the mining industry from the 1860s onwards, and in the fishing

13. Henderson, *Essays*, 109, suggests "possibly not before 1100".
14. See B.S. Roberson, *Cornwall* (1941), chap. III.D.
15. J.C. Russell, *British Medieval Population* (Albuquerque, 1948), 53.
16. *Ibid.*, 132.
17. L.E. Elliott-Binns, *Medieval Cornwall* (1955), 68–9.
18. *Ibid.*

industry between the two world wars. Many Cornishmen went to America: it has been estimated, for example, that in the hundred years preceding the First World War almost 100,000 men left Cornwall to find a living there.[19] Others went to Australia (for gold) and South Africa (for gold or diamonds).[20]

At the present day the most thinly populated area of the county extends from the north-east across the high land of Bodmin Moor, plus other infertile downs and moors. Even the other rural areas, however, have only a moderate density of population, generally speaking, in contrast with the principal holiday resorts, the industrial areas of west Cornwall, the china clay area, the Truro-Falmouth district, the inland centres of Bodmin, Launceston and Liskeard, the Tamar valley area and the south-eastern district associated with Plymouth.[21]

Cornwall is essentially a rural county, its population distributed between small towns, villages and isolated settlements. There are no large urban agglomerations, and the only places approaching industrial towns are the former mining centres of Camborne and Redruth, and also St Austell. The first two do not show much tendency to expand now, due to the decline in mining, but there is a considerable area of scattered settlement linked with Camborne-Redruth, extending north and east almost to Truro. The only other towns of any size are Penzance, Falmouth, Newquay, Bodmin, Truro, Saltash and Launceston. The first three have old harbour nuclei and modern expansion associated with their development as seaside resorts. Bodmin and Truro share the honours of county town, although the latter is more flourishing.

There is also a group of smaller towns, local market centres, e.g. Helston, Wadebridge, Lostwithiel, Liskeard, Camelford, and fishing ports which are also resorts, e.g. Looe, Polperro, St Ives, Padstow. There are few genuine village settlements in Cornwall – the most typical are fishing villages, closely packed round a small harbour, e.g. Mevagissey, Port Isaac, Mousehole, Boscastle, some of which are expanding due to the tourist trade.

The rest of the county is either un-nucleated or hamletted, a settlement-type exemplified by small clusters at cross-roads, and half-a-dozen houses round the parish church, but nothing approaching the agricultural villages of south-east England. These scattered settlements mostly consist of a farmhouse, a labourer's cottage, or three or four houses together. Of these settlements, some eight to 12 usually occur in any one square mile fairly consistently throughout the county.

19. See J. Rowe, 'Cornish Emigrants in America', *Folk Life*, iii (1965), 25–38.
20. C. Berry, *Portrait of Cornwall* (2nd edn, 1971), 109.
21. See Shorter, Ravenhill and Gregory, *op. cit.*, 195–8.

Occupations [22]

Apart from relatively small manufacturing industries such as tanning and leathermaking, textiles and papermaking, the chief traditional industries of Cornwall are farming, fishing and mining.

Mixed farming has always been one of the chief occupations in Cornwall, although interest in it has fluctuated very severely from time to time, and it has suffered from difficult climatic and geological conditions. From Carew's account,[23] we gather that Cornish agriculture saw an improvement in the sixteenth century, before which, he tells us, it had been very much neglected. And agriculture has continued to be one of Cornwall's main industries. Oats and mixed grain are the main cereal crops at present, but there are also root crops, and cattle, sheep, pigs and poultry are kept. Dairying is especially important in west Cornwall and in the Lizard and Land's End peninsulas. The total area under crops and grass is about three-quarters of the total area. The farms are mostly small: in 1967, out of almost 12,000 holdings, one in five was of five acres or under.[24] Fruit, flower and vegetable growing is carried on largely in Mount's Bay and the Fal and Tamar valleys.[25]

Fishing claims to be Cornwall's oldest industry, although Cornish ships and ports are first mentioned in official records only at the beginning of the thirteenth century. The industry, although (especially the pilchard fishery) once extremely flourishing, and engaging in a brisk export trade over centuries, has, for various reasons, suffered a grievous decline this century, and fishermen have often had to turn elsewhere for employment, either abroad or, for example, to the seasonal tourist trade in the county itself. However, although the Cornish pilchard industry is nearly defunct, pilchards are still caught all the year round, mackerel and herring fishing are done – although not with the same success as hitherto – and crab and lobster fishing still remain fairly prosperous. The principal fishing places are Newlyn, Mevagissey and Looe, although only Newlyn can now claim to be a thriving fishing port.[26] In recent times, fishing has become quite popular among holidaymakers, and Looe is now the centre of the shark-fishing sport.

The search for tin in Cornwall, which started in the Bronze Age, went on throughout Roman and medieval times, going through successive periods of

22. See Berry, op. cit., chap. V; Encyclopaedia Britannica, 14th edn, s.v. Cornwall; A.K. Hamilton Jenkin, The Story of Cornwall (1934, reprinted 1962), chap. VIII; F.E. Halliday, A History of Cornwall (1959); Shorter, Ravenhill and Gregory, op. cit., chaps. VII, VIII.
23. pp. 101ff. On Cornish medieval farming, see J. Hatcher, Rural Economy and Society in the Duchy of Cornwall 1300–1500 (1970).
24. Berry, op. cit., 112.
25. For further details of land utilization, see Roberson, op. cit., chap. III; Shorter, Ravenhill and Gregory, op. cit., 148–56.
26. For the varied fortunes of the Cornish pilchard industry, see J. Rowe, Cornwall in the Age of the Industrial Revolution (1953), chap. VII.

decline and prosperity. Up to the end of the Middle Ages, tin 'mining' had meant that the tinners worked in the open air, uncovering the alluvial ore which lay beneath layers of sand and gravel in the moors and stream beds. It was not until the fifteenth century, when the richer stream grounds were becoming exhausted, that the tinners started searching for the actual veins of mineral in the hillsides and cliffs. This sort of mining started in earnest after the dissolution of the monasteries, when the gentry were eager to exploit the mineral resources of their newly acquired lands. The primitive equipment used, however, made depth mining uneconomical, and Elizabeth's reign was a period of depression in the industry. Carew's *Survey* describes the mining of the time,[27] and notes that when the industry began to fail, the Cornish people returned to agriculture, which they had previously neglected.[28] Mining with poor, but gradually improved, apparatus, and in terrible conditions, continued right up to the present century, mining at really deep levels becoming practicable during the eighteenth century. From the sixteenth century onwards the balance of tin-mining activity moved more markedly to the western parts of Cornwall. Tin-mining in Cornwall reached its peak in 1871, but declined very shortly afterwards, mainly due to an increase in output overseas. After the slump of the 1890s, there was a slight revival in the First World War, but mining had all but ceased again by 1922. The rise in the price of tin in 1926–8 caused some new activity, especially in the Redruth-Camborne area, but ten years later the output was still lower than in 1919. Mining was, however, carried on in several places during the Second World War, but none of the smaller wartime workings is now in operation. In recent years, however, the prospect of a world shortage of base metals has resulted in renewed attention being given to several of the old mining areas of south-west England.

Copper was discovered in large quantities in Cornwall about the beginning of the eighteenth century. This made an enormous difference to the mining industry, and thousands more men were taken into employment. West Cornwall was earlier the most important area for copper mining, especially Camborne-Redruth-Gwennap, but declined in importance and the shift of emphasis moved mainly to east Cornwall and west Devon. By the mid-nineteenth century the mines of Cornwall were producing three-quarters of all the copper in the world, and nearly half of the tin. Then came the decline, and by 1900 copper mining had virtually ceased. Exhaustion of the copper lodes and competition from mines – both tin and copper – in other areas of the world account for the drastic decline of the Cornish mining industry.

The mining of china clay began in about 1755: St Austell became the most important centre of the industry in Cornwall, and indeed throughout

27. pp. 88ff.
28. p. 101.

the world. A large amount of the clay is exported: in 1961, over a million tons were shipped abroad, and the industry still creates new records every year.

In addition to the mining of tin, copper and china clay, iron has been worked near Lostwithiel and elsewhere; the area south of Liskeard and the Chiverton mines and East Wheal Rose were most productive of lead and zinc; granite is quarried in the Penryn district; road stone is also quarried, the largest group of quarries being at Penlee (Penzance), St Keverne (Lizard), Clicker Tor, and Hingston Down; slate is quarried and largely exported, for example from the Delabole quarries near Tintagel. Serpentine is produced from the Lizard district.

The holiday industry [29]

As something of a compensation for the decline in the Cornish mines and fisheries, the tourist trade, promoted by the introduction of railways, started seriously in the middle of the last century, Cornwall being particularly popular because of its romantic aspect, its appeal to antiquity and its wild, rugged scenery. From this time onwards, hotels and bungalows have proliferated, and what was started in the nineteenth century by the railways was continued in the 1920s and 1930s on the roads. The county is deservedly popular on account of its coastline, its cliffs and coves, and its picturesque fishing ports, and seaside resorts such as Bude, Newquay, St Ives, Penzance, Falmouth and Looe are immensely popular, as are also the much smaller resorts, such as Port Isaac and Mevagissey. It has been estimated that in 1969 over 2,250,000 holidaymakers came into Cornwall from outside between May and October.[30] Some native Cornishmen are concerned with the holiday trade (although many are still farmers, fishermen and even miners). These have been joined by a large number of people from outside the county, who keep boarding houses, shops and the like, while others are retired people or people who prefer to live in Cornwall rather than elsewhere.[31] Partly on account of all this, it is not easy to find native people who speak a broad dialect, and the county has been well and truly 'sacked' by both holidaymakers and immigrants.

It may be said in conclusion that, although Cornwall's two ancient industries, fishing and mining (for tin and copper, at least) have greatly declined, the county prospers in its china clay industry and in its tourist trade.

29. A specially interesting account of early visitors to St Ives is to be found in chap. XXIII of J.H. Matthews, *A History of the Parishes of Saint Ives, Lelant, Towednack and Zennor* (1892).
30. Berry, *op. cit.*, 116.
31. In a small village I visited, three shops were all kept by non-Cornish people, while in places like Newquay, Yorkshire dialect is a commonplace!

Communications [32]

Thomas Martyn's map of the county (1745), showing several east–west routes, with a number of less important roads from north to south, gives the chief roads at the time it was drawn, and probably represents a network not very different from the one in existence in late medieval times.[33] Down to the end of the eighteenth century, almost all the merchandise of the county was carried on the backs of mules or ponies, including coal, copper ore, merchant goods and farm produce. Many of the ancient tracks which they used can still be traced. The earliest mention of a coach being used in Cornwall is in 1644, when Charles I came down in one to fight the Earl of Essex. The appalling condition of the Cornish roads at that time makes it clear that they were not intended for wheeled traffic, and, in fact, it is doubtful whether, right up to recent times, ordinary people travelled far, unless they were forced to by business or other urgent need. After about 1750, the roads began to improve. In 1745 the first turnpike in Cornwall was constructed from Falmouth to Grampound, via Truro, and in 1759 an Act of Parliament was made for constructing or repairing a road from Launceston to Camelford, and on to Truro via Wadebridge and St Columb. In 1820 the mail-coach service was extended to Penzance. The improvement in the main roads heralded the introduction of the stage-wagon, travelling regularly from Falmouth to London, and from now onwards both transport and roads began to improve, no doubt with improved facilities (accommodation and so on) along the roads. This was the coaching era, and it reached its height about the middle of the last century. By this time, the main roads had been improved out of all recognition.

Coaching lasted longer in Cornwall than elsewhere, but the first railway line was laid down in 1814, and from then on the days of coaching were numbered. After Brunel's famous bridge over the Tamar was completed in 1859, traffic began to leave the roads, and the coaches disappeared, with the consequent desertion of inns along the routes. In 1865 the main line reached Penzance, and branches were flung out to the north and south, the spread of the railways to the coast being a great stimulus to the holiday industry, heralding the modern development of numerous resorts such as Falmouth, Newquay and St Ives. In more recent years, however, the railways have declined, and many of the smaller branch lines have been closed, while the roads are again enjoying increased usage. The county is served by a good network of A-class roads, of which the A30 from London traverses the county from the Tamar to Land's End. Although many of the smaller

32. See Hamilton Jenkin, *op. cit.*, chap. VI; W.G.V. Balchin, *Cornwall* (1954), chap. VII; Shorter, Ravenhill and Gregory, *op. cit.*, chap. IX.
33. Elliott-Binns, *op. cit.*, 38, n. 1.

roads are still very narrow, they are in constant use by holidaymakers during the summer. Bus services linking the smaller villages are not very good, even in the season.

Cornwall today

Dr A.L. Rowse makes the following observation in his book *Tudor Cornwall* (1941): "Up till this very century, Cornish life remained very much *enfoncé* in its old grooves: you can trace in the parish registers how long and how continuously a given family remains attached to its own village, its old places. All this had scarcely changed up to the last war."[34] It is certainly true that in some respects the Middle Ages in the remote west can be said to have extended itself up to the beginning of the present century: Dr Rowse notes, for example, that ploughing with oxen was still the practice at Bodrugan near St Austell "within living memory".[35]

But for a very long time now, Cornwall has been subjected to a process of modification in her ways of life: a partial failure of some of the ancient industries, combined with the advent of a new industry – that of tourism – has meant the virtual breakdown of the old life, although efforts continue to be made by Cornish patriots to capture its customs, speech and other features. The process of disintegration has naturally been greatly assisted by the presence of the numerous settlers from other parts of England and by the media of mass communication.

In these circumstances, although from the point of view of its generally pre-urbanized nature Cornwall would seem to be an ideal region in which to record local dialect, good dialect informants are now in fact difficult to find, and the traditional speech of the county is much modified. To give but one example, *EDD* lists a great many Cornish loan-words, while *SED* found a mere handful. Neither have any subsequently come to light on tape-recordings made since the *SED* 'impressionistic' recordings were completed. The fishing dialects urgently need to be investigated, and these may well yield material of the greatest interest, especially that of a lexical nature.

34. p. 21.
35. p. 41.

3 The historical background

Early settlements [1]

To early visitors, who mostly, no doubt, proceeded by sea, the narrow Cornish peninsula offered a sheltered southern coast, with numerous estuaries inviting access inland via the wooded rivers. The more exposed northern coast had only St Ives and the Camel estuary, but from here it was perfectly easy and possible to cross to the south coast. From either coast, the granite masses, with their expanses of moorland, would spring to the eye, offering an inviting prospect for settlement.

Evidence of settlers of various prehistoric cultures may be seen in Cornwall. The Neolithic peoples established settlements (e.g. Carn Brea, near Camborne), chiefly in the Land's End peninsula. These were joined, at the beginning of the second millennium B.C., by a small group of 'Beaker' peoples, whose sanctuaries – stone circles mostly 70 to 80ft in diameter, and usually on open moorland – are well known in the county, e.g. the Hurlers, the Stripple Stones and others on Bodmin Moor. The Beaker peoples were also responsible for the free-standing stones or menhirs which are numerous in Cornwall, e.g. Maen Pearn, Constantine (broken up in the eighteenth century), although their known settlements are coastal, and concentrated in the Land's End peninsula.

1800–1500 B.C. was the formative period of a Bronze Age culture and society in the south-west, but in this area the early Bronze Age civilization was poor as compared with that in Wessex further east. 1500–500 B.C. was a period of stability, showing little change (apart from increase) in the population or its way of life. Some Bronze Age peoples were pastoralists, living in enclosed and/or nucleated settlements surviving, in Cornwall, chiefly on Bodmin Moor, and in Devon on Dartmoor. Others were agriculturalists, whose settlements have been found at Gwithian and on Bodmin Moor, on

1. For this and the following sections, see A. Fox, *South West England* (1964); and H.O'N. Hencken, *The Archaeology of Cornwall and Scilly* (1932).

the eastern side of Dartmoor, and to some extent in the valleys of the East Dart and the Plym. Peoples of the early and middle Bronze Ages buried their dead in barrows, of which several thousand survive.

The Celtic peoples

The first Celtic peoples came to Britain in the declining years of the Bronze Age culture, and are usually credited with inaugurating the Iron Age in Britain. There were, however, probably Celtic-speaking peoples here in the earlier Bronze Age – before 1000 B.C. These were then reinforced by the three waves of invasion definitely recognized on archaeological evidence as Celtic (there is documentary evidence only for the last wave), which took place in, respectively, the fifth and fourth centuries B.C., the third and second centuries B.C., and the late second to the mid-first century B.C.

The archaeological record of the Iron Age in Cornwall consists of cliff castles, hill forts and earthworks, and the remains of numerous villages. In addition to these settlement sites, the Iron Age peoples modified the landscape agriculturally, and also continued tin-streaming for the benefit of a tin trade which had begun in the late Bronze Age. At the end of the Iron Age, members of these Celtic tribes in the south-west, together with Bronze Age peoples who lived on the high moorlands, were known as the Dumnonii.

The Roman Conquest

The conquest of the south-west under the Emperor Claudius was virtually complete by A.D. 47–8. We need not deal here with the various stages of the occupation: the Dumnonii as a whole remained unaffected by the military campaigns. Exeter was founded in A.D. 50–5 as a social and administrative centre, and was known as Isca Dumnoniorum. The town is important in that for the first time the whole of the Dumnonian people were under one centre of administration. The territory governed from Isca Dumnoniorum extended from Land's End to the Blackdown Hills-River Parrett boundary of the territory of the neighbouring Durotriges, although prior to the Roman Conquest the Dumnonian territory may have extended somewhat further to the east.

During the Roman occupation, the inhabitants of the south-west remained much as they had been since prehistoric times. Native settlements were concentrated in the Land's End area, where, on present archaeological evidence, four types of native settlement have been distinguished, namely the single isolated irregular hut; the courtyard-house village type, the classic example of which is Chysauster; a mixture of courtyard-houses and circular huts; and finally the courtyard-house within a 'round'. Archaeological finds do not suggest much change in the native way of life. There were no towns west of Isca Dumnoniorum, and only one Roman villa has been found; this is at Magor, near Camborne. Mixed farming remained the basis of the Dumnonian economy. The canton was backward and conservative – an area of poor, isolated native settlements, mainly in the Land's End area, and influenced little by imperial power.

In the south-west, the main roads of Roman Britain ended at Isca Dumnoniorum, but smaller roads linked the canton with the rest of the province. In the south, west of the River Exe, one road crossed the River Teign at Teignbridge. To the north of Dartmoor a length of road at North Tawton made for the Tamar, while a third road, to the north-west, may also have existed.[2] In Cornwall, although no constructed roads have been identified with certainty, the presence of five milestones of the mid-third and early fourth centuries,[3] together with several forts, leaves no room for doubt that even remote Cornwall was included in the system. A special reason for this was probably metal-prospecting.

The sub- and post-Roman eras

The end of Roman Britain, from a combination of causes, was quite complete by the middle of the fifth century, although there are signs of the decline of Roman civilization in the south-west long before this. The immediate result of the passing of Roman rule was that the Roman military organization and defences became native British organization and defences. The whole of Britain from the mid-fifth century to the foundation of the Saxon kingdoms in the sixth and seventh centuries was now governed by native Celtic princes.[4] Overall political cohesion was lost, and an era of petty kings and independent local dynasties, warring with each other, came into being. Because of this, the country as a whole could offer no effective resistance to the Saxons.

Archaeology has revealed, however, continuity of a sort in civil organization, in religion (both Christian and pagan), and in art, all bearing the indisputable traces of Roman influence. The use of Latin, for example on funerary stones, continued, and indeed these inscriptions on stone afford a valuable idea of the standard of culture of the western Celtic peoples,

2. See I.D. Margary, *Roman Roads in Britain* (3rd, rev. edn, 1973), 84–5 (map) and 117–22.
3. *RIB*, nos. 2230–4. See also W. Page (ed.), *A History of the County of Cornwall*, Part 5: *Romano-British Remains* (1924), with a note on the milestones and roads of Cornwall by R.G. Collingwood, pp. 26–32.
4. Before the end of Roman Britain came, however, indications of growing independence of Roman rule were shown in the south-west by the election of local rulers or 'protectors', who were later regarded as kings, instead of there being the usual local councils subordinate to Roman power.

who, after the departure of the Romans, probably maintained a conservative and relatively high grade of civilization as compared with eastern Britain: in the Lowland Zone, Roman culture very largely broke down owing to the collapse of Roman government and the general unrest of the times.[5]

The structure of Dumnonian society during the 'Dark Ages' is bound to remain, at best, only partly known, and any reconstruction of it must be necessarily a tentative one. No records comparable with the Welsh laws of later times (though even these were modified to some extent by English influence) have survived to tell us how Dumnonian society lived. Certain deductions may, however, be made. A number of institutions were common to Celtic societies from a very early period, and it may be confidently assumed that at least the framework of the traditional society, as revealed in the early epic literature of Ireland and Wales, continued to exist throughout the Roman period and into the Dark Ages, although necessarily modified, first of all to at least some extent by Roman government, and secondly – after the departure of the Romans – by the poverty and backward nature of a Dumnonian society which was (ultimately) constantly under threat of invasion from outside.

The most important of the Celtic institutions was hereditary kingship. At the time of the Roman Conquest, Britain had been divided into a large number of independent Celtic kingdoms, each ruled by its own royal house. These had adopted a republican type of government under the Roman Empire, centred in the tribal centre or *civitas* of each state: this was Isca Dumnoniorum in the kingdom of Dumnonia. When the Romans left, these republics probably became hereditary monarchies, and we must note the continued existence of Celtic kings in the south-west (although recorded only disconnectedly) into late Anglo-Saxon times as revealed by the *Anglo-Saxon Chronicle*, by one or two epigraphic inscriptions, and by the testimony of place-names (the place-name element *lis*, *les* (Welsh *llys*), meaning 'chieftain's hall' or the like, has frequently survived in Cornish place-names, perhaps suggesting the existence of a number of petty 'kings' within the county).[6]

There were no towns in dark-age Cornwall. There had only ever been one in the entire kingdom of Dumnonia, namely Isca Dumnoniorum, where

5. *LHEB*, 112–20.
6. The supreme overlordship of Dumnonia can presumably be placed in Devon during the sub-Roman period, but by the mid-seventh century this area was in Saxon hands, and the British had in general been pushed further west. It is even possible that the kingship is to be located in Cornwall as early as the sixth century: this depends upon an equation of the *Kynvawr* of the Royal Dumnonian genealogies with the *Cvnomori* of the Castle Dore inscribed pillar of *c*. 500. See p. 52 of H.M. Chadwick, 'The Foundation of the Early British Kingdoms', in *Studies in Early British History* (1959), 47–60, and (on the pillar), *LHEB*, 291, *CIIC*, vol. I, no. 487.

corporate town life seems to have continued into the fifth century.[7] As the occupation of the kingdom proceeded further west, the kings and their subjects were pushed further and further west too, the kings apparently continuing to govern the subjects under their rule who lived at Isca Dumnoniorum and in other places scattered throughout the old kingdom for some hundreds of years.

Our knowledge of settlement in dark-age Cornwall is derived from archaeological evidence as well as from place-names. The oft-cited Castle Dore excavations on the south coast revealed that a former defensive site – an Iron Age hill-fort, deserted in the early first century – had been re-occupied, the spaciousness of the excavated buildings being consistent with re-use as the enclosure for the palace of a Cornish king. Evidence for similar re-occupation is forthcoming from Chun, in Penwith.

For evidence of humbler settlements, the archaeological finds at Gwithian (west Cornwall) indicate an economy based on shellfish-gathering, fishing, pastoralism and a little agriculture. The distinctive 'grass-marked' pottery found here, and from some 20 sites in the county, replacing the earlier 'Gwithian style' pottery, is parallelled only from north-east Ireland, and is evidence for an immigration from that area to west Cornwall perhaps about 600. The presence of parish dedications to a group of saints traditionally considered Irish – Phillack, St Ives, St Erth, Gwithian, Gwinear – the distribution of which corresponds well with the grass-marked pottery, would seem to support this theory.[8]

Religion

Virtually all our knowledge of Christianity in Cornwall at this period is derived from a few inscribed memorial stones of the fifth and early sixth centuries.[9] It is, however, fairly clear that the Christian religion had made some headway in the peninsula. Christianity was almost certainly well established in Britain by the second century,[10] and in the south-west there were probably British monasteries at Sherborne, Shaftesbury and Glastonbury from early times. The Church in Cornwall would have been of a monastic character, as elsewhere in the Celtic world: according to Charles Henderson, 98 of the 254 existing parishes were originally monastic foundations – probably in their beginnings merely a number of small huts clustered

---

7. As revealed by current excavation. I owe this information to Professor Charles Thomas.
8. See A.C. Thomas, 'Cornwall in the Dark Ages', *Proceedings of the West Cornwall Field Club*, II (1957–8), 59–72.
9. *Ibid.*, 61.
10. R.G. Collingwood and J.N.L. Myres, *Roman Britain and the English Settlements* (2nd edn, 1937), 270.

round a church.[11] Medieval tradition apparently holds that the Cornish Church was closely dependent on the Church in Wales from the earliest times.[12] In the sub-Roman period, Christianity continued, perhaps occasionally reinforced by contact with Roman Gaul, and rekindled somewhat later by missionaries from south Wales, Ireland and Brittany. The British Church in Cornwall kept its own usages, at least to some extent, even after the British bishop Kenstec submitted to Archbishop Ceolnoth of Canterbury in the ninth century.[13]

The Irish in Cornwall

Irish expansion had affected south Wales by the end of the fourth century, when the Déisi from south-east Ireland settled in Pembrokeshire. The presence of Irish settlers in Cornwall too is attested by memorial stones inscribed in ogam (the late-Roman Irish alphabet based on incised linear strokes) as well as by stones inscribed in Roman lettering but containing Irish names. These are all mainly distributed in north-east Cornwall, spreading across the border into Devon. Supported by independent archaeological evidence, there thus appears to be evidence of Irish immigration into north Cornwall in the late fifth and early sixth centuries, perhaps not from Ireland direct but from the Irish settlements in south Wales. This is again supported by the presence of a group of parish dedications common both to an area of south Wales and to an area in Cornwall more or less coincidental with that of the ogam inscriptions, in which all the saints belong to a group known as the Children of Brychan, the semi-legendary king of Brecon, whose name appears to be Irish Brocan or Brocagnus.[14] In addition to this movement into north-east Cornwall, as mentioned above, a second Irish 'invasion' took place into the west of the county, perhaps in about 600, emanating this time from (north-east) Ireland direct.

Professor Thomas gives us a picture of Cornwall in about 800 which may be accepted for a period somewhat earlier than this, and which we may term 'Cornwall on the eve of the Anglo-Saxon invasion'. In the west, he says, numerous little domestic sites shared a culture part Cornish, part Irish; in the east, similar conditions obtained, with slightly different ceramic styles. Numerous oratories and field churches could be seen, the pattern being enlivened by the occasional large monastery.

11. *The Cornish Church Guide and Parochial History of Cornwall* (1925, reprinted 1964), 18.
12. Chadwick, *op. cit.*, 144.
13. See Bede, *Historia Ecclesiastica*, V.18; A.W. Haddan and W. Stubbs, *Councils and Ecclesiastical Documents relating to Great Britain and Ireland* (1869–78; reprinted 1964), vol. I, 674–5, 676 (A.D. 909).
14. See Thomas, *op. cit.*, 63–4.

Into this backwater slowly intruded the pressure of a not dissimilar agricultural people with a different language and ancestry, though with much the same material equipment and nominally the same religion. As events moved towards the inevitable supremacy of Alfred's Wessex, and the united England of the bretwaldas, the existence of a potentially hostile Celtic flank, tainted with archaic and heretical Christian practices, had to be taken into account. Cornwall had to be incorporated, politically and religiously, into England.[15]

The Anglo-Saxon advance and settlement

There is evidence that Germanic pirates had been a menace to Britain since the third century A.D.[16] The first stage of serious invasion did not begin, however, until c. 450, and consisted of widespread, marauding raids, penetrating even to the far west, but without extensive permanent settlement. The colonization of Wessex presents numerous problems, which it is unnecessary to discuss here. It is enough to say that by the middle of the seventh century the Saxons had advanced to within a few miles of the Dumnonian boundary, which was probably formed naturally by the River Parrett, the Blackdown Hills and the River Axe.[17]

There has been much speculation about the occupation of Devon, and again there is no need to enter into the various arguments that have been advanced, especially since it is the territory of present-day Cornwall that is our objective and not that of Devon. However, since it appears that east Cornwall was occupied by the beginning of the eighth century, the occupation of Devon must have taken place during the seventh century. Indeed, we know from the Life of St Boniface, who is traditionally believed to have been born of English parents at or near Crediton in 675–80, that a Saxon abbey of Exeter supervised Boniface's early education,[18] and this must make the foundation of the abbey not later than 685–90, if not earlier (there is, in fact, reason to believe that it was founded by Cenwealh in the year 670, although this depends on ancient tradition embodied in late land-charters, reconstructions of lost originals).[19] This, in turn, puts the occupation of east Devon at a date earlier in the seventh century.

15. *Ibid.*, 68.
16. P.H. Blair, *An Introduction to Anglo-Saxon England* (1956), 6. Civil settlements had, however, probably begun as early as the second century, under Roman auspices. See M. Dillon and N.K. Chadwick, *The Celtic Realms* (1967), 47–8.
17. See F.M. Stenton, *Anglo-Saxon England* (3rd, rev. edn, 1971), 63; *PND*, xv–xvi; *LHEB*, 205.
18. Vita S. Bonifacii, *Monumenta Germaniae Historica*, Scriptores II, ed. G.H. Pertz (Hanover, 1829; reprinted Stuttgart, 1963), 335.
19. W.G. Hoskins, *The Westward Expansion of Wessex* (1960), 16–17.

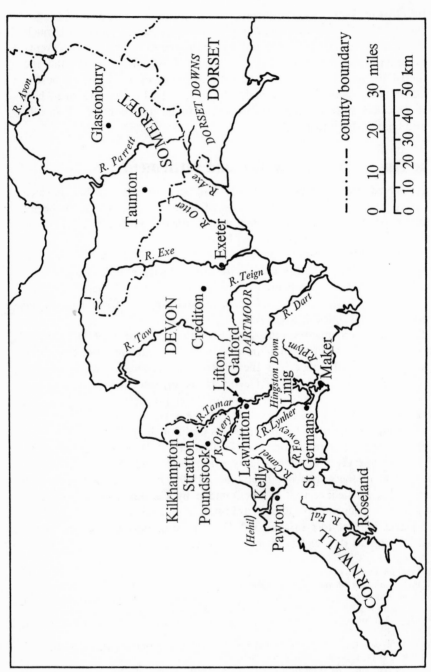

Map 4. The Anglo-Saxon advance and settlement.

Assuming, then, that most of Devon was occupied during the seventh century, we may turn to Cornwall. In 710, King Ine of the West Saxons was able to give 20 hides of land at *Linig* (? = 'fertile land near the Lynher'; *Lin-* + OE *eg, ig*), by the Tamar, to Glastonbury Abbey, and if the supposition is correct which places this territory between the Tamar and the Lynher, south-east Cornwall must have been in English hands by this time, probably as a result of the battle fought in the same year (see further below). Now, the English place-names in this area are quite numerous, but nowhere as numerous as in north-east Cornwall: here, the place-name nomenclature contains an overwhelmingly English element, suggesting early and substantial settlement, perhaps earlier and more substantial than the territory further south just described. The lack of Cornish place-names from Poundstock down the River Ottery to the River Tamar, and the presence of a very large number of English ones in the same area, strongly suggests that the Ottery formed a racial boundary for a period long enough for the Anglo-Saxons to settle down in this north-east area, and give names to their settlements – names very similar to those of north Devon. The West Saxon boundary here was not the Tamar but the Ottery.

On place-name evidence it may therefore be inferred that north-east Cornwall was in English hands even before the land further south, i.e. before 710, and this necessarily pushes us back to a date at the end of the seventh century or the beginning of the eighth, not too far removed in time from the date 682, in which year, according to the *Anglo-Saxon Chronicle*, "Centwine drove the Britons as far as the sea": Hoskins suggests that this battle (the site of which is unspecified by the *Chronicle*) took place somewhere west of the River Taw and north of Dartmoor, and that by it the British were pushed westward to the Atlantic coast into what is now north-east Cornwall.[20] It need hardly be observed that, in any case, north Devon and north-east Cornwall were easier places to cross (or to avoid) the Tamar than at its wider lower reaches – a consideration which presumably did not escape the Anglo-Saxon invaders.

The further penetration of the present-day county of Cornwall is evidently referred to in a number of entries in the *Anglo-Saxon Chronicle*. These form a skeleton which, amplified by other evidence, gives a reasonably clear picture. The *Chronicle* references are quoted from the Laud version, but with corrected dates.[21]

710: Ine and Nun his mæi gefuhton wið Gerente Weala cininge. "Ine and Nun his kinsman fought with Gereint, king of the 'Welsh' [i.e. Cornish]." [The site of this battle is unknown, but if the Dumnonian kingdom had

---

20. *Ibid.*, 17–18.
21. The quotations are taken from C. Plummer, *Two of the Saxon Chronicles Parallel* (1892–9).

been pushed back as far as or beyond the Tamar, it was presumably just west of the river, possibly, on other evidence, between the Tamar and the Lynher (see p. 58, below). Nunna was king of Sussex.]

753: Her Cuðred Wæst Seaxna cyning gefeaht wið Wealas. "In this year, Cuðred, king of the West Saxons, fought with the 'Welsh'."

756: Her Cuðred Wæst Seaxna cining forðferde ... Sigbriht ... feng to Wæst Seaxna rice and heold .i. gear. "In this year, Cuðred, king of the West Saxons, died ... Sigeberht ... succeeded to the West Saxon kingdom and ruled for one year."

757: Her Cynewulf benam Sigebriht his mæge his rice ... and se Cynewulf oft feaht mycclum gefeahtum wið Britwealas. "In this year, Cynewulf deprived Sigeberht, his kinsman, of his kingdom ... and this Cynewulf often fought great battles with the 'Welsh'."

815: ... þy geare gehergode Ecgberht cining on West Walas fram east-weardum oð westewearde. "... In this year, King Egbert harried among the West Welsh from east to west."

825: Her wæs Weala gefeoht and Defena æt Gafol forda. "In this year, there was a battle between the 'Welsh' and the men of Devon at Galford [in Devon]."

838: Her com micel sciphere on Wæst Wealas and hi to anum gecyrdon and wið Ecgbriht Wæst Seaxna cining winnende wæron. Þa fyrdode him togeanes and wið him feaht æt Hengestesdune and þær ægðer aflymde ge þa Wealas ge þa Deniscan. "In this year, there came a great [Danish] fleet to the West Welsh, and they joined forces and fought with Egbert, king of the West Saxons. Then he made an expedition against them, and fought with them at Hingston Down, and put to flight there both the 'Welsh' and the Danes."

Added to the references in the *Anglo-Saxon Chronicle*, the tenth-century *Annales Cambriae* [22] record (in their curious assortment of Latin and Old Welsh) for the year 722:

> an'. Beli filius elfin moritur. et bellum hehil apud cornuenses. gueith gart mailauc. Cat pencon. apud dexterales brittones. et brittones uictores fuerunt. in istis tribus bellis. "Anno [722]. Beli the son of Elfin dies, and there took place the battle of Hehil in the land of the Cornish, the battle of Gart Mailauc, the battle of Pencon in the land of the southern Britons. And the Britons were the victors in these three battles."

The entry records, that is, three British victories against the English, one of them being at *hehil* in Cornwall. Stenton regards *hehil* as modern Hayle

22. Ed. E. Phillimore, 'The *Annales Cambriæ* and Old-Welsh Genealogies from *Harleian MS.* 3859', *Y Cymmrodor*, IX (1888), 141–83; see p. 160.

in west Cornwall,[23] but an identification with a locality somewhere on the River Camel estuary would seem to be more appropriate, as Hoskins suggests.[24] The old name for the Camel estuary was apparently *Hehil* or *Hægel*, and the word is preserved in Egloshayle 'church on the River Hayle', and in Hell (or Hayle) Bay.[25]

The references in the *Anglo-Saxon Chronicle* and the *Annales Cambriae* show the West Saxon kings fighting sporadic battles against the *W(e)alas* (i.e. the inhabitants of the now shrunken kingdom of Dumnonia), and making inroads into what is now Cornwall from the early eighth century onwards. Egbert (ruled 802–39) seems to have been the first to penetrate to the far west. In 825 the *W(e)alas* advanced eastward into Devon and fought against the West Saxons at Galford, several miles to the east of the Tamar, and in 838 they joined forces against the Saxons with a Danish fleet, but were again defeated by Egbert, this time at Hingston Down, near Callington, and just to the west of the Tamar. Although the whole of Cornwall had now presumably passed under the domination of Wessex, possible archaeological evidence for the survival of native kings down to the early tenth century (see pp. 59–60, below) suggests that Egbert's conquest, at least as far as the inhabitants were concerned, was nominal only.

With this outline before us, we may now attempt to fill in the picture of the invasion in greater detail. The English conquest of Devon had begun in the seventh century, or so we have suggested, and was no doubt virtually completed by Centwine. By the time of the battle of 710, the British of Dumnonia had probably already been driven back west of the Tamar. The earliest surviving record of the division of the peninsula into two halves is from some Latin verses written at the end of the seventh century.[26] By the middle of the eighth century, Devon was fully organized as one of the shires of Wessex, along with Berkshire, Hampshire, Wiltshire, Dorset, Somerset and perhaps the Isle of Wight.

A certain amount of supplementary evidence is available from ecclesiastical sources. In 705 an episcopal see was founded at Sherborne by Ine (ruled 689–726), who appointed his kinsman Aldhelm as its first bishop, giving him jurisdiction over the whole English Church west of Selwood. Aldhelm had previously been abbot of Malmesbury, and while there had written his celebrated letter to Gereint, king of Dumnonia, and the clergy of his realm,[27] solemnly urging them to come into line with Roman practice with regard

23. *Op. cit.*, 73.
24. *Op. cit.*, 19.
25. See E. Ekwall, *DEPN*, s.v. Egloshayle, Hayle, and *English River-Names* (1928), s.v. Hayle. Ekwall agrees with the identification proposed here.
26. See *TDA*, LXIV (1932), 108–9.
27. Bede, V.18. See Haddan and Stubbs, *op. cit.*, vol. III, 268–73.

to the date of Easter and the tonsure, and then inveighing at some length against the Britons on the other side of the Bristol Channel. About 705 an entry in the surviving register of Sherborne makes it clear that king Gereint endowed the new see of Sherborne with "five hides of land at Macuir [modern Maker] by the Tamar". Finberg sees in this gift "a gesture of appeasement by the weaker party" in response to "an undertone of implication [in Aldhelm's letter] that if misfortune should ensue, the Cornishmen would have only their schismatic selves to thank for it."[28]

In 710, however, war broke out again, and Ine's victory over the British was followed by his gift to the third English abbot of Glastonbury of 20 hides of land at *Linig* by the Tamar, territory, as already suggested, almost certainly somewhere between the Tamar and the Lynher.[29] This seems to confirm the suggestion that the battle of 710 was fought between the two rivers, and that the racial boundary was now the Lynher in the south and the Ottery in the north-east.

We have already referred to the solid area of English place-names in north-east Cornwall between the Ottery and the Tamar. In this area, 90 per cent of the place-names have been computed to be of English origin,[30] as are by far the greater proportion of those in Devon.[31] The Anglo-Saxons had crossed Devon, probably entering Cornwall north of where the Tamar rises, and settling in fairly substantial numbers in the north-east corner of the county. We may further postulate that at the beginning of the eighth century the West Saxon kings had extended their borders as far as the Ottery-Lynher boundary. This does not, of course, mean that all the Britons in the area were exterminated: on the contrary, there is very good evidence that settlements of Britons remained for several centuries in all parts of the Dumnonian peninsula, as also in other parts of Britain. This evidence we shall discuss further. In east Cornwall we now have the situation of two different peoples living side by side. The Anglo-Saxon colonists were governed by the laws of Wessex, but the British, under their native dynasty, continued to be ruled by the kings of Cornwall. The old kingdom of Dumnonia, now pushed beyond the Ottery and the Lynher, continued to exist in shrunken form, and enclaves of its subjects continued to live scattered throughout the whole peninsula, subject to its kings.

There now seems to be a more or less complete blank for just over a hundred years, during which time we know (from the *Anglo-Saxon Chronicle*) that fighting between the British and English continued, but we know very

28. 'Sherborne, Glastonbury, and the Expansion of Wessex', *Transactions of the Royal Historical Society*, 5th series, III (1953), 101–24; see pp. 106–7.
29. *Ibid.*, 108.
30. *Ibid.*, 113, quoting J.J. Alexander in *TDA*, LXV, LXVI.
31. *PND*, xix.

little else. The next evidence available from charters relates to Egbert's reign (802–39). Egbert's victories over the British allowed him to be a generous benefactor to the Church. He gave her a tenth of the lands he had won beyond the Tamar. Two charters now lost, Finberg 74 and 76,[32] tell of his further generosity: sometime between 815 and 839 he endowed the see of Sherborne with three estates, *Polltun* (Pawton in St Breock), a manor which included six or seven parishes and parts of four more,[33] *Cællwic* (probably Kelly in Egloshayle),[34] and *Landwithan* (Lawhitton), comprising Launceston and four neighbouring parishes. Further, the Sherborne list of founders records gifts from Egbert of 12 hides of land at *Kelk* (Kilkhampton), and 18 at *Ros* (? Roseland) and *Macor* (Maker). Kenstec, the Cornish bishop, was now compelled to acknowledge the Archbishop of Canterbury as his canonical superior,[35] but it seems that the Cornish Church continued with its own usage in spite of canonical and royal pressure.[36]

Native kings, however, continued to reign in Cornwall, and the Celtic inhabitants of the county still adhered to their own tribal code. For the English colonists, the king of Wessex appointed two high-reeves: the headquarters of one was at Stratton, and he administered from there all the English settlements in the district of Trigg (i.e. the modern hundreds of Trigg, Lesnewth and Stratton). The sparser southern settlements (the proportion of English to Cornish place-names in the southern part of the area between the Tamar and the Lynher has been computed to be 40 per cent)[37] were administered from Lifton, a royal manor just across the Tamar on the Devonshire side.

King Athelstan presumably completed Egbert's work, not only asserting his supremacy over the remaining local native kings in Britain,[38] but, according to William of Malmesbury, compelling the Britons who lived in Exeter to withdraw.[39] The native Cornish dynasty probably came to an end at

32. Charters thus cited are as listed in H.P.R. Finberg's calendar, *The Early Charters of Devon and Cornwall* (1963).
33. Cf. C. Henderson, in *Essays in Cornish History* (1935), 121.
34. Henderson, *Cornish Church Guide*, 57; Hencken, *op. cit.*, 249.
35. Haddan and Stubbs, *op. cit.*, vol. I, 674–5.
36. *Ibid.*, 676 (A.D. 909).
37. Finberg, 'Sherborne', 113, quoting J.J. Alexander, *op. cit.*
38. See the *Anglo-Saxon Chronicle*, MS. D, 926. The "Huwal West Wala cyning" of this annal is regarded here not as a king of Cornwall but of the west Welsh, probably the famous Hywel Dda, king of Dyfed (south-west Wales), by whom a number of Athelstan's charters are attested (see Blair, *op. cit.*, 220). *West Wala* is thus, in this later entry, to be interpreted literally as 'west Welsh', whereas in the earlier entries for 815 and 838, *West Walas, Wæst Wealas* mean 'Cornish' (cf. the semantic shift in OE *Scottas* from 'Irish' to 'Scots', which probably took place in the period after the death of King Alfred).
39. *Willelmi Malmesbiriensis Monachi, De Gestis Regum Anglorum*, ed. W. Stubbs (Rolls Series, 90 [1887]), 148.

about this time.[40] It was Athelstan who, according to William of Malmesbury,[41] fixed the Tamar as the shire boundary, and possibly he who reorganized the six ancient divisions of Cornwall into hundreds on the English model, thus bringing the county more fully and more genuinely into the kingdom of Wessex.

In 909 the large Sherborne diocese had been divided into three: Dorset remained to Sherborne; Somerset was made into a new bishopric, with its see at Wells; Devon and Cornwall were made into yet another, under a diocesan bishop with a see at Crediton. In 926 Athelstan attached a large endowment to St Germans, and made it the seat of a bishop – a *chorepiscopus* acting for the bishop of Crediton – at the same time appointing a bishop with a British name, Conan, to officiate west of the Tamar.[42] Athelstan was also a benefactor to various churches in the county, especially St Buryan.[43] The further fortunes of the see do not concern us. A line of Anglo-Cornish bishops followed Conan, until finally in 994 King Athelred the Second gave Bishop Ealdred a charter authorizing him to rule over the diocese with full episcopal authority.

Looking back on the Anglo-Saxon settlement in Cornwall from the tenth century, two points should be made. First, the settlement was probably not always a military or an official one: some early colonists doubtless moved into the county in a peaceful fashion, simply intending to make a home there. Finberg, indeed, suggests that at least some of the early campaigns into Dumnonia may merely have been "defensive actions undertaken to protect the colonists against attack by hostile neighbours. Political annexation would follow, as the aftermath of victory."[44] The same may be equally true of the occupation of what is now Cornwall.

Secondly, the question of to what extent the British remained in the Dumnonian peninsula should be briefly considered.[45] Evidence has now been

---

40. The latest king of whom we have record is 'Ricatus' (*CIIC*, vol. II, no. 1051), whose name appears to be embodied in the inscription *Regis Ricati crux* on a cross at Penzance dated probably not earlier than the beginning of the tenth century, according to Hencken, *op. cit.*, 248.

41. *Loc. cit.*

42. Finberg, 'Sherborne', 119, regards this appointment as a "substantial concession to native sentiment", which would suggest that at this time the British element in Cornwall was still strong enough to make itself felt. This is supported by the fact that Athelstan fixed the shire boundary on the Tamar, and not on the Ottery-Lynher. All of this suggests that at this time the English were still at the settler or colonist stage.

43. See Finberg (charter) 78; Henderson, *Essays*, 96–7.

44. 'Sherborne', 109.

45. On the whole question of British survival in general, see Collingwood and Myres, *op. cit.*, 444ff.; *LHEB*, chap. VI; P.H. Reaney, *The Origin of English Place-Names* (1960), 83ff.; M.V. Barry, 'Traditional Enumeration in the North Country', *Folk Life*, VII (1969), 75–91 (who gives numerous references).

produced for widespread British survival throughout England,[46] and there is good evidence for British enclaves throughout the whole of what was the old kingdom of Dumnonia, together with a British quarter in Exeter at least until the tenth century, when, according to William of Malmesbury, the British in the city were expelled by King Athelstan, and driven into Cornwall.[47] Their existence in Exeter up to this time is perhaps recorded in the medieval name for present-day Bartholomew Street, namely *Britayne*, the British quarter probably being roughly marked off by this very street, and coinciding with the original area of ancient British settlement.[48] It is also perhaps attested in the Celtic dedications of two Exeter parishes, one to St Petroc and one to St Kerrian.[49]

Celtic place-names, though infrequent, are to be found throughout Devon, probably indicating groups of British, e.g. Walreddon (perhaps < OE *weala-ræden* 'community of Britons').[50] The implications are clearly that, not only in Exeter, but throughout old Dumnonia, groups of British were allowed to live in accordance with their own ancient laws and custom. Although most of them probably belonged to the poorer classes, an occasional Celtic name is found among the names of those licensed to make money at the Exeter mint in Saxon times.[51]

The Norman Conquest

The Norman Conquest gives us, for the first time in English history, some sort of a systematic account of certain affairs of the country. The Domesday Book, although not in any sense a complete survey or census, is nevertheless an invaluable record of tenure and population, and provides much incidental information. It is useful to us here for two special reasons.

Firstly, Domesday Book provides us with our first real knowledge of settlement and population distribution, and maps 5 and 6 give details of these as recorded there. It should be noted that for several reasons the figure of 330 settlements recorded in Domesday Book for the present-day county of

46. Sites can be found that have had a continuous existence from Roman into Saxon times. See H.P.R. Finberg, *Roman and Saxon Withington: A Study in Continuity* (1955); and also 'Continuity or Cataclysm', in *Lucerna* (1964), 1–20.
47. *Op. cit.*, 148.
48. W.G. Hoskins, *Two Thousand Years in Exeter* (1960), 12. But *PND*, 21, suggests that this street, like Little Britain in London, may owe its name to a settlement of Bretons.
49. See T. Kerslake, 'The Celt and the Teuton in Exeter', *Archaeological Journal*, xxx (1873), 211–25.
50. *PND*, xx–xxiii.
51. See further Hoskins, *Two Thousand Years in Exeter*, 13, and Finberg, *The Early Charters of Devon and Cornwall*, 26–7. For the survival of British-speaking peoples in Dorset, see Hoskins, *The Westward Expansion of Wessex*, 20–1 (but the evidence is doubted by Jackson, *LHEB*, 239).

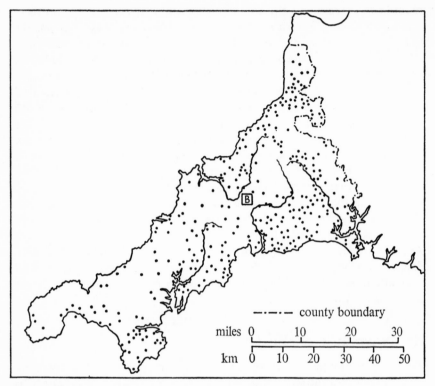

Map 5. Domesday settlements. (B indicates the borough of Bodmin. The dot in the bay, off the south-west coast, represents St Michael's Mount.)

Cornwall[52] cannot be accurate, however (cf. below). The large manors mentioned in Domesday Book (e.g. Pawton, Connerton, Bennerton) probably included a number of small unnamed places, and consisted of a centre with outlying farms and hamlets rather than of single large villages. Moreover, there are several entries in which no place-name appears, and finally, where two or more adjoining places bear the same basic name today, it is not always clear whether one or more than one existed in 1086.

The main feature to be noticed with regard to settlement distribution is the almost complete absence of settlement from the granite areas, presumably on account of their unattractiveness due to infertile soils and exposure to the winds. The small streams of the county were apparently favoured places for settlement. Generally speaking, settlements become less numerous as one

52. References are always to the present-day county, which is not quite the same as Domesday Book Cornwall, since it has gained some territory from Devon and lost some to it.

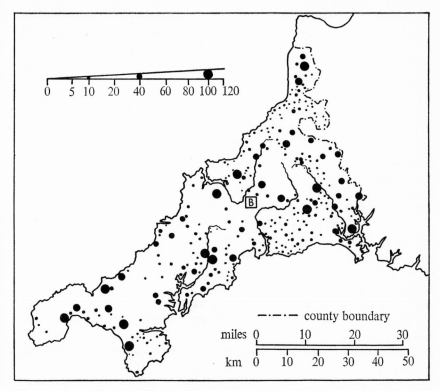

Map 6. Domesday population. The area of each circle is proportional to the population of each settlement. (B indicates the borough of Bodmin.)

proceeds towards the west. There were a surprising number in the Lizard peninsula, although the majority were without recorded plough-teams, and some were also without recorded population.

The total recorded population in Domesday Book for Cornwall amounts to 5,439, but this total needs to be multiplied perhaps four or five times to obtain the actual population. Allowing three and a half persons to the average household, J.C. Russell computes the total population of the whole county in 1086 as 19,033.[53]

The Domesday Book figures show the paucity of working plough-teams and of population as compared with, for example, Devon and Somerset, not to mention the rest of southern England. The density of teams never

53. *British Medieval Population* (1948), see pp. 34ff., 53. It should be noted that the total population of the county can be estimated from the Domesday survey with a limited degree of accuracy, for (a) we cannot be sure that everyone was counted, and (b) serfs were probably counted as individuals, while the rest may represent heads of households.

rises above 1·4 per square mile, and that of the population never more than 5 except along the eastern border where the county adjoins Devon, and where an influx of English population had taken place. Here, the recorded population was 5·2 persons per square mile in the north (roughly down to the Ottery) and 5·8 in the south.[54]

The second reason for the importance of Domesday Book for our purposes is that the three basic types of place-names it records tell us at least something of the Anglo-Saxon occupation. English place-names represent the Anglo-Saxon settlements made since the beginning of the eighth century, Cornish place-names obviously represent Celtic settlements (although some of these presumably included Englishmen by the time of the Norman Conquest), while Cornish place-names with an English suffix, e.g. *tūn*, suggest Celtic settlements taken over by the English.

As observed above (pp. 55, 58), present-day English place-names are especially numerous in two eastern areas, and this situation is reflected in Domesday Book. In the north-east, between the Ottery and the Tamar, the names are 90 per cent English, cf. the following examples from Domesday Book (DB): Milton, DB *Middeltona*; Lee, DB *Lega*; Norton, DB *Nortone*, Woolston, DB *Ulnodestone*; Widemouth, DB *Witemot*, *Widemot*; Bennacott, DB *Betnecote*; Boyton, DB *Boietone*. In the south-east, between the Lynher and the Tamar, they are 40 per cent English, cf. Climson (in Stoke Climsland), DB *Clismestone*; Bicton, DB *Bichetone*; Halton, DB *Haltone*; Pillaton, DB *Piletone*. Between these two areas, however, Cornish names predominate, almost reaching right up to the Tamar. This is the area covered by the estate of Lawhitton (see p. 59, above), and it has been suggested that the Celtic inhabitants may have been left undisturbed in this district.[55] North and south of this middle area, however, Cornish names are very much less in evidence, except right in the south-east corner of the county, where a number of Cornish names are found, e.g. Sheviock, DB *Savioch*; Maker, DB *Macretone* (comprising a British borrowing from Latin *maceries* 'enclosure'+ OE *tūn*). Perhaps the wide lower reaches of the Tamar formed something of a barrier to the Anglo-Saxons of south-west Devon (cf. p. 55, above).

The English place-names in east Cornwall are mostly of a very similar type to those of west Devon, as one would expect. The great majority of these, containing elements such as *bearu* 'grove', *lacu* 'stream', *pytt* 'pit', *ēa* 'water', *gehæg* 'enclosure', do not, however, occur in Domesday Book English names, which consist almost entirely of names with elements *ton* and *cot*, *cote*, though *Taccabear* (Tackbear)[56] and *Tirlebere* (Thurlibeer) in

54. See Darby and Finn, *op. cit.*, figs. 70, 72 respectively, and cf. figs. 86, 84, 85 in the same work.
55. *PND*, xxi.
56. Now in Devon; see *PND*, 135–6.

the north-east may contain *bearu*. The OE *tūn* 'enclosure, farmstead, estate, village' is very common in the east, and is in use with Cornish first elements, as shown below, sporadically throughout the county. OE *cot*, *cote* 'cottage, hut, shelter, den' is much rarer, and is chiefly confined to the north-east: here it is indeed quite common, as in DB *Wescote* (Westcott), *Alueuacote* (Alvacot), *Horniecote* (Hornacot), and *Betnecote* (Bennacott). It does not occur in the south-east in Domesday Book. This agrees with the distribution of the element in Devon.

The English place-names recorded in Domesday Book for central and west Cornwall are almost negligible, except for the occasional OE *tūn* added to a Cornish name. Such hybrids do, in fact, occur throughout the county, for example: DB *Chilchetone* (Kilkhampton), recorded in 1194 as *Kilkamton*, perhaps from an Old Cornish name comprising Cornish *kyl* 'recess', and (e.g.) *loch* 'pool' + OE *tūn* (the last part of the name was early associated with the common English termination *-hampton*), DB *Glustone* (Blisland; the *G* is probably an error, since it occurs in no other documents, but the first element is in any case obscure), DB *Pautone* (Pawton), < Corn. *pol* (or OE *pōl*) 'pool' + OE *tūn*, DB *Rieltone* (Rialton), < a Corn. personal name + OE *tūn*, DB *Tedintone* (Tehidy), perhaps < a Corn. personal name + OE *tūn*, DB *Conarditone* (Connerton), ? < *Connar* (personal name) + OE *tūn*, DB *Bennartone* (Bennerton), < an obscure first element + OE *tūn*, DB *Henlistone* (Helston), < Corn. *hen* + *lis* 'old court' + OE *tūn*, DB *Winetone* (Winnianton), < a personal (? saint's) name (cf. Irish Finnian)[57] + OE *tūn*. DB *Alwaretone* (Alverton) seems to be the only completely English compound name in the west: Domesday Book states that this manor was held by one Aluuard, i.e. OE Ælfweard, and there seems no reason to doubt that his name forms the first element of this place-name.[58] The names above, then, comprising Cornish and OE elements, represent Celtic settlements taken over by the Anglo-Saxons.[59]

To sum up. The place-names recorded in Domesday Book can give us some idea of the extent of the Anglo-Saxon settlement of Cornwall by 1086. In the extreme north-east of the county, a small triangular area bounded on the west by the River Ottery, shows evidence of extensive Anglo-Saxon occupation, its nomenclature being chiefly English, and consisting both of totally English names (some elements in them being comparable with those in Devon place-names) and Celtic names given an OE termination. To the south and west of this small area, Celtic settlements are greatly in the majority,

57. The Domesday Book form may be defective: the name appears as *Winienton* 1195, *Wynienton* 1296, etc. The simple name appears once as *Gwynyon next Nampyan* 1439, and there is a nearby promontory Pedngwinian Point.
58. But Ekwall, *DEPN*, s.v., suggests 'Ælfwaru's tūn' in spite of this.
59. Cf. Henderson, *Essays*, 23.

65

but in the south-east, except for a small area in the extreme south, the names are again shared with English or partially English ones. In the rest of the county, the nomenclature is overwhelmingly Cornish, apart from some hybrid names consisting of a Cornish word compounded with OE *tūn*, these being indicative of large or important manors developed by the Anglo-Saxons from original Celtic settlements. From the picture as we have it in Domesday Book, the north-east and south-east stand out as being Anglo-Saxon territory, the rest still mainly Cornish.

It must not be forgotten, however, that Domesday Book does not record all the names of places then in existence (cf. pp. 61–2, above), and there are some which, although not recorded until long afterwards, are undoubtedly of an early type, and were in existence at the end of the Anglo-Saxon period. With the help of these, we are able to show that the Anglo-Saxon settlement had, in fact, almost certainly proceeded somewhat further to the west than the Domesday Book nomenclature implies. In the north, the Ottery may nevertheless still have been the main boundary between the Anglo-Saxons and the Cornish, although scattered English settlements no doubt existed all the way down the peninsula. In the south, in the present-day hundred of West, although, taking the place-names as a whole, Cornish names are in the majority, English place-names are to be found in every parish, being specially numerous in those north of the River Fowey, i.e. Cardinham, St Cleer, Warleggan, St Neot and Liskeard. Some of these may be of later medieval origin, but a large number are of an early type, and we may thus assume that the English occupation was fairly complete all over south-east Cornwall.

In central and west Cornwall the later names reflect the same situation as those of Domesday Book in being mostly Celtic. An interesting type, however, occurs in this predominantly Celtic area, illustrated by such names as Coyssawsen (first recorded 1338), Nansawsan (1311), Tresawson (1278), Trenithon (*Treveythin Sauson* 1293), Porth Sawsen (no early examples), Carsawsen (1556), Bejowsa (1397), Coswinsawson (1345), all of which contain as second element the word *Sawson* 'Saxons'.[60] These, although late, may date from a period when there were sufficiently few English settlers in the district for such designations to be meaningful.

The overall situation thus seems to be that the Anglo-Saxons had colonized the north-east and the south-east fairly completely, and had settled sporadically in places right down to the west. The completeness of the Anglo-Saxon conquest is suggested by the fact that in Domesday Book only three manors were held at the time of Edward the Confessor by men having Cornish names. These were all in the west of Cornwall.

60. Cf. Tresawsen (first recorded 1327) in Lanreath, east Cornwall, which, however, occurs in a parish in which the farm-names are nearly all Cornish.

The foregoing, although not necessarily implying that the Anglo-Saxons were very important numerically, suggests that by the time of the Norman Conquest they had a good deal of influence. Domesday Book shows them as overwhelmingly the chief landowners in the county, and their importance is also shown by sources other than Domesday Book, for example the famous Bodmin Gospels (BM Additional MS. 9381), written in the early tenth century at Bodmin. Forty-seven entries of manumissions are recorded in the fly-leaves and margins, either in Latin (chiefly) or in OE – but not, it should be noted, in Cornish – covering the period 940–1040, 122 slaves thus being recorded as having secured freedom. Of these, 98 have Cornish names, 12 Anglo-Saxon, and 12 Latin or biblical. Of the 33 liberators named, 24 have Anglo-Saxon names and only 5 Cornish. This would seem to suggest that a large proportion of the slave-class was Cornish (without, however, implying that they had been made slaves by the Anglo-Saxons: more likely, perhaps, they had inherited their serfdom from some hundreds of years before the Anglo-Saxon conquest).[61] The Bodmin manumissions also show Anglo-Saxon influence in another way: generally, the system of spelling used in Old Welsh, Old Cornish and Old Breton sources is in all important respects identical, and does not change in any radical way between the earliest documents of the eighth century and those at the end of the eleventh, but even at this early period, the scribes of the manumissions used Anglo-Saxon letters such as ð, þ and þ, which are very rare in Old Welsh and lacking altogether in Old Breton.[62] In addition to the evidence of the manumissions, it is to be noted, too, that all 27 witnesses to Cnut's charter (1018; Finberg 54, p. 19) to Bishop Burhwold of St Germans bear Anglo-Saxon names.[63] All this evidence points in the same direction as that of Domesday Book, and shows a county ruled by an Anglo-Saxon minority, who lived chiefly at the eastern end of the county, but had settlements and extended their authority throughout.

This virtually closes an examination of the evidence for the Anglo-Saxon settlement of Cornwall. Archaeological evidence is so disappointing as to be hardly worth considering. There are no remains of any specifically Anglo-Saxon churches in Cornwall, although place-names such as Stowe Barton, Rhude (< OE rōd) Cross, Minster and Warbstow (St Werburga's stow), all

61. Serfs amounted to about 21 per cent of the total of the population of Cornwall in Domesday Book, Cornwall being, next to Gloucestershire, the county in which they were relatively most numerous. See Darby and Finn, op. cit., 320. Hoskins tentatively suggests that the present-day distribution of ethnic groups in the south-west may have interesting historical implications. See The Human Geography of the South West (1968).
62. See LHEB, 67–8. Jackson remarks that "The Bodmin Gospels is an instructive MS. in respect of AS. influences in Cornwall." See also pp. 59–60. The Bodmin Manumissions are edited by M. Förster, 'Die Freilassungsurkunden des Bodmin-Evangeliars', in A Grammatical Miscellany offered to Otto Jespersen (1930), 77–99.
63. Haddan and Stubbs, op. cit., vol. I, 686–8.

in east Cornwall, are probably indicative of former Anglo-Saxon churches or chapels.[64] A (? tenth- or eleventh-century) pillar stone in the churchyard at Lanteglos by Camelford apparently read in the nineteenth century (the text has now deteriorated) *Ælselð ⁊ Genereð wohte* [*i.e. worhte*] *ðysne sybstel for Ælwyneys soul ⁊ for heysel* "Æ. and G. raised this pillar for Æ.'s soul and for themselves" (or "for Heysel"),[65] while zoömorphic designs on three Cornish crosses – at Lanherne, Sancreed and Waterpit Down – consisting of a dragon whose body forms a series of undulations, each filled in with a Stafford knot made by the tail, have parallels at Bexhill and Aycliffe (Co. Durham), and are clearly in an Anglo-Saxon tradition.[66] Only two Anglo-Saxon hoards have so far been discovered, namely the famous chalice, silver scourge and associated objects at Trewhiddle,[67] deposited *c.* 875, and the Tywardreath hoard of silver coins,[68] probably deposited *c.* 928–30. The full implications of these finds are not at present very clear, but neither of them seems to add materially to what we know of the Anglo-Saxon settlement from other evidence.

The period under review in the preceding pages is one of the first importance in the history of Cornwall. Since the time that Athelstan had asserted his supremacy, Cornwall had been properly a part of England. The Cornish people, although ethnologically, culturally and (to some extent) linguistically apart, were now for the purposes of administration part of the English nation. This state of affairs continued and developed under a strong Norman rule. Henceforth our interest in the two peoples will be mainly confined to a study of the ways in which their languages mingled and affected each other, and to the historical background of these linguistic developments. It merely remains for us to sketch, before turning to this, a bird's-eye view of the Cornish scene as it would have appeared just after the Norman Conquest.

In the later medieval period – just after the Conquest – three settlement forms seem to have co-existed in the south-west: the single farm, the hamlet, the village. Single farmsteads were probably quite common, those excavated suggesting that the building was rectangular in form – a 'long house', in

64. Marhamchurch and Cubert are often quoted as being Anglo-Saxon dedications, but the former is possibly St Marwen's (or Morwenna's) church, and the latter St Cubertus's church, both local (Celtic) saints. See Henderson, *Cornish Church Guide*, 130–2 and 51 respectively.

65. A.G. Langdon, 'Early Christian Monuments', in *The Victoria History of the County of Cornwall*, ed. W. Page (1906), 407–49 (see p. 416); Hencken, *op. cit.*, 265; E. Okasha, *Hand-list of Anglo-Saxon Non-Runic Inscriptions* (1971), 90–1.

66. Langdon, *op. cit.*, 443; J. Romilly Allen, *Old Cornish Crosses* (1896), 352.

67. See D.M. Wilson and C.E. Blunt, 'The Trewhiddle Hoard', *Archaeologia*, xcviii (1961), 75–122.

68. See R.H.M. Dolley, 'The Tywardreath (Fowey) Treasure Trove', *Numismatic Chronicle*, 6th Series, xv (1955), 5–9.

fact, divided into three parts, living-room, sleeping-room and byre. (This type was probably the characteristic house-form in the south-west throughout the Middle Ages from the fourth century onwards and in early modern times.) Single farms of this type would be surrounded by their enclosed-field system. The hamlet, a cluster of farm-houses and associated buildings, usually grouped without any formal plan, sometimes with enclosed fields, sometimes with miniature open-field systems, appears to have been widely distributed throughout the county during the Middle Ages. Although some doubt exists as to how we may distinguish between the hamlet and the village, the latter may perhaps be regarded as a nucleation of a large number of houses in a setting of streets, crofts and lanes, surrounded by common arable fields and meadow, the lay-out of these villages, moreover, often surviving in more or less original form up to recent times.[69] These were the ingredients of the medieval Cornish landscape. It is, furthermore, now considered that these various forms of settlement filled the landscape to a remarkably larger degree than has been previously thought, both on the low-lying ground and the more elevated parts, and that most of the farms found on the modern map would have been in existence by 1350 at the latest.[70]

The origin and growth of towns [71]

If we accept the presence of a market or fair as an indication of some form of town life (i.e. a community of larger numbers than usual in which some inhabitants are not concerned exclusively with farming), small, early towns were already in existence, according to Domesday Book, at Liskeard, Trematon, St Stephens (Launceston), Methleigh and Bodmin (which is mentioned as having 68 houses). We further know from other evidence that a market or fair or both existed at St Michael's Mount or on the mainland near it round about the same time. From the Domesday Book mention of 40 *cervisarii* at Helston (probably tenants who paid their dues in ale) and the record of ten salt-pans at Stratton, we are perhaps justified in assuming that these settlements too were on the way to becoming small towns.

Towns originated, however, in Cornwall – as elsewhere in England – not just from the natural growth of small settlements but by the founding of 'boroughs' by kings and powerful barons, who recognized the potential value of urban centres as sources of considerable revenue. By the middle

69. See A.H. Shorter, W.L.D. Ravenhill and K.J. Gregory, *Southwest England* (1969), 106.
70. *Ibid.*, 110, where it is suggested that for 1086 "we should think of a total in the order of 1,800 farms".
71. *Ibid.*, chap. 6. See also Henderson, *Essays*, 19–25; A.L. Rowse, *Tudor Cornwall* (1941), 95; M.W. Beresford, *New Towns of the Middle Ages* (1967), 401.

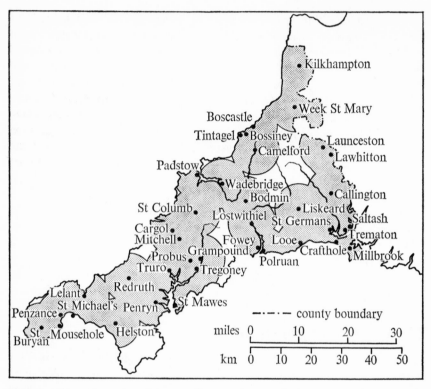

Map 7. The early towns of Cornwall. Dots denote places which had been styled boroughs or had markets by the middle of the fourteenth century; the shaded areas are within five miles of a borough or market.

of the fourteenth century, the number of places which were either boroughs or market towns had grown from the half-dozen or so of the eleventh century to between 30 and 40 (see map 7). The map clearly shows that the two parts of the county still relatively free of urban settlement were the Bodmin Moor area and the Lizard.

Mining also led to the growth of towns, especially after the introduction of shaft mining soon after the middle of the fifteenth century, which gave a permanence of location not offered by the searching of tin in streams, and therefore had a significant effect on settlement growth. This was true not only of the coinage towns – at first Bodmin and Lostwithiel, and (to a lesser extent) Truro and Helston, then later Liskeard and Penzance (first made a coinage town in 1663) – but also of places actually associated with the mining process: Callington, St Austell, Camborne, Redruth, St Day and St Just.

There was also growth of the seaports which exported the tin and imported the requirements of the mines, and these, like the choice of coinage towns, show how mining in Cornwall moved ever in a westerly direction. In the first half of the seventeenth century, the most important ports were in the east – Fowey, Looe, Millbrook, Saltash – but by the end of the century they had been surpassed by those in the centre and west: Truro, Penryn, Falmouth, Penzance, St Ives and Padstow.

4 Cornish and English

The use of English in Cornwall had presumably been spreading ever since the Anglo-Saxon occupation of the county had begun in the early years of the eighth century. Chapter 3 traced that occupation up to the Norman Conquest, by which time Cornwall can be said to have been absorbed into the English nation as a political and administrative unit. From this time onwards, we cannot trace the development of the Anglo-Saxon 'occupation', for there is no material evidence for what had become merely a mingling of races. What we are specifically interested in is the adoption of the English language in Cornwall, and the present chapter will consider the evidence for this. For these purposes, it is not necessary to outline the history of Cornwall from the Middle Ages onwards: the details of the Anglo-Saxon conquest and occupation are of the greatest importance for our purposes, for obvious reasons, but this is not the case with the later history of Cornwall where, during the later and post-medieval periods, social affairs were probably very much the same as elsewhere,[1] except that the county was poorer and more sparsely populated than some others, and more remote from the central government. A detailed history of social affairs in Cornwall might throw some light on the subject in hand, but the compilation of such a history would probably not be justified by the *linguistic* conclusions that could be drawn from it, and it is therefore preferable to concentrate on linguistic history and evidence rather than on social history and evidence. I have, however, thought it relevant to discuss briefly reasons why Cornish was given up in favour of English, and here social affairs are considered as far as is helpful.

First, however, it is relevant to summarize the situation with regard to the English language as it existed in the Middle Ages.

The OE period is generally accepted as having lasted until *c.* 1150. Four dialects can be distinguished from the extant MSS., namely Northumbrian

---

1. Cf. L.E. Elliott-Binns, *Medieval Cornwall* (1955), 70.

(north of the River Humber), Mercian (in the large stretch of territory between the Thames and the Humber), Kentish (present-day Kent and parts of the neighbouring counties), and West Saxon (the rest of southern England). Of these, West Saxon assumed the status of a written standard form towards the end of the period.

The Norman Conquest had a profound effect on the writing of English literature, as on English culture in general. The literature produced in the transitional period (1050–1150) is meagre, and the West Saxon standard form ultimately disappears (the ME descendant of West Saxon was south-western). When English literature fully re-emerges, it is written in a variety of different dialects, of which none has the precedence. The ME dialects were classified by Moore, Meech and Whitehall, in 1935,[2] on the basis of an examination of 266 texts, into ten dialect areas, of which Cornwall comprises part of the southern area, but for various reasons this ME dialect survey was not completely satisfactory, and much research is at present in progress on the ME dialects, of which the survey being conducted by Professor Angus McIntosh and Professor M.L. Samuels deserves special mention.[3] However, in any new classification of ME dialects, we may take it that the dialect of west Somerset, Devon and Cornwall is likely to emerge not only as 'southern' but more precisely as 'south-western'.[4] In our consideration of ME dialect material (as also of OE), it must, of course, be remembered that the evidence is primarily that of written, not spoken, dialects, of traditions and practices of local scriptoria, not necessarily that of local speech. Nevertheless, reasonable inferences about medieval speech-habits may be drawn from the written evidence.

In the fourteenth century we can again begin to see the rise of a standard written dialect – this time the dialect of the capital, London, which, for various reasons, chiefly commercial, had begun to emerge as the national centre after the Norman Conquest. This incipient standard underwent changes in its linguistic character during the late Middle Ages, ultimately becoming a Central Midland type of dialect, brought about, so it is now believed, by the immigration of considerable numbers of Midlanders into the capital.[5] From this time on, it was only a matter of time before dialectal features disappeared from the written page, as late ME texts show.

In spoken English, however, the regional dialects continued to flourish,

2. S. Moore, S.B. Meech and H. Whitehall, *Middle English Dialect Characteristics and Dialect Boundaries* (1935).
3. See A. McIntosh, 'A New Approach to Middle English Dialectology', *English Studies*, XLIV (1963), 1–11; M.L. Samuels, 'Some Applications of Middle English Dialectology', *ibid.*, 81–94.
4. So far, however, there has been no systematic analysis of ME texts from Cornwall, or of the *Ordinalia*, which contain a certain amount of ME.
5. See Samuels, *op. cit.*, and E. Ekwall, *Studies on the Population of Medieval London* (1956).

although we may be able to see, even as early as the fourteenth century, the rise of a *spoken* standard, parallel with the written one. The evidence for this, consisting mainly of inferences,[6] is not very good at first, but from the sixteenth century onwards there are definite statements by writers that one particular type of English is regarded as 'the best', namely that of educated London speech, the Court, and the universities. In the early days of this standard, it contained numerous social varieties, and often adopted regional and vulgar forms. It was, in fact, much more 'permissive' in its usages than is its present-day descendant. However, in the eighteenth century there was a drive towards 'fixing the pronunciation', the chief guiding principle being contemporary orthographical conventions, and since this time, most of the variants in Standard English pronunciation have, in fact, gradually disappeared.

At the same time, regional dialects had also started gradually to disappear under the influence of education, especially since the time of universal and obligatory education, which teaches and advocates the use of the 'prestige' dialect, Standard English, as distinct from the regional forms of the English language, which had started to become 'non-prestigious' forms ever since the rise of the standard dialect. It has also been assisted by the movement from the countryside into towns which had been taking place since the end of the Middle Ages, at first into London, but later into other centres, until, with the Industrial Revolution, the severance of the population from the land began to be complete.[7] This perhaps applies only to a limited extent in Cornwall, where no towns of any size have developed, and where farming has continued to be the chief occupation.

Having discussed the types of English in use in the country as a whole, we may now turn to the evidence for the adoption of English (which may comprise any or all of these varieties – we shall return to this later) in Cornwall. This consists of place-names, Cornish and English medieval documents, and the statements of writers.

Place-names [8]

The theory at the basis of the present use of place-name material is as follows. Numerous phonological changes took place in the Cornish language between,

6. See M.F. Wakelin, *English Dialects* (1972), 27–8.
7. The majority of English people have lived in towns since soon after 1850, 77 per cent of them since 1901 and 81 per cent since 1951. See E. Jones, *Towns and Cities* (1966), 30.
8. My access to place-name material has been via Mr J.E.B. Gover's unpublished work 'The Place-Names of Cornwall' (1948), and I am grateful to Mr Gover and to the English Place-Name Society (in whose archives one copy is now deposited) for allowing me to use this material. It must unfortunately be conceded, however, that even this corpus of place-names represents only a part of all the available material, which is as yet uncollected *in toto*.

say, *c.* 1100 and the time of its extinction in the eighteenth century, some of which can be approximately dated. Some of the Cornish (i.e. as distinct from English) place-names show evidence of these changes, the geographical location of the name showing the change being related to the time at which the change took place, i.e. the early forms (without change) occur in east Cornwall, but the later forms (with change) occur further west, since here the Cornish language was still alive and changing. To quote an excerpt from a paper by the late C.L. Wrenn:

> The decline of the Cornish language is well indicated by the forms and distribution of the word *BOD* "dwelling." In areas early anglicised, such as much of the Bodmin neighbourhood, names in *BOD-* persist because, there, Cornish early ceased to exist so that the name-form remained unchanged and failed to share the proper Cornish development of *bod* into *bos* which took place in the twelfth and thirteenth centuries. Thus west Cornish names occur frequently with *bos* as first element, since there the native Celtic continued to develop as a living changing language, as contrasted with the fossilized *bod*-type common in east Cornwall. Still further west, in remote areas where Cornish lingered on till the early modern period, we find names in *Boj* (*Bodʒ*) which was the later development of *Bos* (*Boz*). We find *BODMIN*, for example, as contrasted with *BOSWYN*, from *BOS GWYN* "white dwelling," in Camborne parish; and still further west there is *BOJEWYAN* in St Just-in-Penwith, which seems to stand for *Boj* plus the personal name *YWAIN*, and is recorded in the *Feet of Fines* for 1302 as *BOSYWEYN.*[9]

Mr Gover has applied the same theory to Cornish place-name elements containing *-nt*.[10] It is known that Old Corn. *-nt*, which still remains at the time of Domesday Book, e.g. in *Trenant* (modern Trenance in St Austell and in Mullion), had become *-ns* by the time of the *Vocabularium Cornicum* (for which, see p. 78, below). It seems, therefore, that in those parts of the county where *-nt* remains in place-names, the Cornish language is likely to have become extinct by a date not later than the time of the *Vocabularium*, whose date of composition is estimated by Jackson as *c.* 1100.[11] According to Mr Gover's calculations, this would confine the Cornish-speaking area at that time to the west of a line drawn from Padstow up the Camel to the south of Bodmin and from there to the sea at Par, passing just to the east of Lostwithiel and Tywardreath.

9. 'Saxons and Celts in South-West Britain', *Transactions of the Honourable Society of Cymmrodorion*, Session 1959, 38–75.
10. *Op. cit.*, xxi.
11. *LHEB*, 61. Jackson, *op. cit.*, §110, dates the change *-nt* > *-ns* as the second half of the eleventh century.

Using Mr Gover's place-name material as a basis, it is possible to apply this test to two further Cornish phonological features[12] which can be dated with some precision:

1. *-d>-s* ([z]). There is a little early evidence for supposing that this change was already beginning *c.* 1100.[13]

2. *-n(n)->-dn-, -n>-dn*. This change probably began *c.* 1500, and the evidence for it is as follows: Middle Corn. *-n(n)-* and *-n>-dn-* and *-dn* in Modern Corn. There is no trace of this change in the *Ordinalia*, the MS. of which dates from the fifteenth century (see below, p. 79). The first examples of it, in fact, are to be found in the word *bennath* (<Latin *benedictio*), which occurs twice spelled *bedneth* in *Meriasek* (ll. 198, 225), 1504 (for which, see below, p. 79). On the evidence of place-names, however, this feature was probably not general until later in the sixteenth century, since the earliest examples are *c.* 1570 (Carnwidden in Stithians), 1584 (Towednack, parish name), and 1591 (Nanquidno in St Just-in-Penwith).

In the first of these tests the element *bod* alone was used. The first indisputable easterly signs of *bos* appear to be in Bosmaugan (just to the north-east of Lostwithiel) and in Boscarne and Boskear (both in Bodmin parish, which name, however, never has *-s* spellings).[14] West of these points, *bod* and *bos* continue westwards together, appearing in a few cases as *boj*[15] (or with comparable spellings), the most westerly example of *bod* occurring in the parish of St Clement. After this, *bos* and *boj* alone occur. The deduction here, roughly speaking, seems to be that in the places whose names contain the element *bos* Cornish was still being spoken after *c.* 1100, i.e. in a good many places west of Bodmin, but that in some places in this area (represented by *bod*-names) the speaking of Cornish had ceased by this time. It may be plausibly suggested that the lack of *-s* spellings in the name Bodmin itself is due to Bodmin's early assumption of urban (? county town) status in which Cornish was relegated to use by lower-class speakers, while English

---

12. Other phonological features might perhaps have been chosen, and some were, in fact, examined, e.g. *ty* ('house')>*chy*, final *-m>-bm*, and also the prefixing of ME adjectives to place-names, such as *michel, litel, overe, nithere*. But none of these characteristics is of sufficiently consistent occurrence to allow isoglosses to be drawn.

13. This evidence is set out in *LHEB*, §52.

14. Boscastle (north-east coast) is eliminated from consideration because its origin is *Boterelscastel* (1302, 1370), and the first element is therefore not *bod*. Boslymon (between Bodmin and Lostwithiel), Bossiney (near Tintagel) and Bosent are doubtful because in each case the second element begins with *s* or *c*, and the final *s* of the first element may represent an assimilation to this.

15. Not many conclusions can be drawn from these occurrences of *boj*, since they are very few, and there are no really early spellings. But their distribution is as follows: Bejowan in St Columb Minor, Bogee in St Ervan, Bejowans in Cubert, Bojea in St Austell, Bojorrow in Mawgan-in-Meneage, Bejowsa in Camborne, Bojewyan in St Just-in-Penwith, Bojawens and Bojuthno in Sancreed.

was spoken here earlier than in the surrounding countryside. We thus have a situation in which, about 1100, English was vastly predominant as far west as Bodmin. West of Bodmin, as one might expect, there was no uniformity: in some places Cornish was still spoken (*bos*-names), in some places English (*bod*-names). The line that can be drawn here is roughly the same as that of Mr Gover for -*nt*~-*ns*, as might be expected (since the dates of the sound-changes are similar).[16]

From an examination of the Cornish place-names containing -*n(n)*- and -*n*, there emerges a body of names in west Cornwall in which -*n(n)*- has become -*dn*- and -*n* has become -*dn*. The easternmost parishes in which names containing these late forms occur are (south to north): Veryan (Carn Pednethan), Gerrans (Pednvadan), Feock (Chywine [*Chegwidden* 1841], Pill Point [*Pednapill Point* 1597], Porthgwidden), Perranarworthal (Trewedna), Gwennap (Mennergwidden) and Illogan (Tolvadden). The deduction here, roughly speaking, is that in the places whose names contain -*dn*- or -*dn* Cornish was still being spoken after about 1500, i.e. in some places west of the group of parishes listed above, but that in places whose names contain -*n(n)*- or -*n* preserved, Cornish had ceased to be spoken. We thus have a situation in which, about 1500, English was vastly predominant as far west as the above parishes. West of this line, Cornish was still being spoken in quite a number of places.

The two lines distinguished above are very roughly equatable with the lateral hundred boundaries.

It would not, of course, be wise to assume that, from the above, a deduction can be made about every place in Cornwall whose name contains these elements. The theory, it is hoped, is generally valid, but place-names, because of their frequent paucity of early spellings, and because of their habitual conservatism in spelling, are not always a reliable guide in linguistic matters. What are needed now are a thorough and complete examination of all the place-names of the county, with special attention to their early forms, and a similar investigation of the history of every parish individually and the documents relating to it. Only when both of these have been done will it be really possible to form a definite conclusion as to the relative uses of Cornish and English in any one place at any one time.

We may now turn to a consideration of the second class of evidence mentioned above.

16. Cf. C. Henderson, in *Essays in Cornish History* (1935), 144n., discussing place-name evidence: "It is convenient for philological purposes, to divide Cornwall by a line from Padstow through Bodmin to Fowey." This remark was presumably generally based on Henderson's knowledge of place-name forms.

Documents

1. Documents in the Cornish language

The Cornish documents are mostly listed and described by Jenner, in Chapter II of his *Handbook*. Excluding the Bodmin Manumissions, whose implications are dealt with above (p. 67), the only documents relevant to the present enquiry are as follows:

(a) The *Vocabularium Cornicum*. This is a Cornish version of Ælfric's Latin-OE glossary (*c.* 1000), Cornish glosses being substituted for the OE ones. Extant only in BM MS. Cotton Vespasian A XIV (ff. 7a–10a), it is the largest known Old Cornish document, but the presence of a few Welsh forms in the gloss makes it probable that the scribe was a Welshman, who occasionally added or substituted his own forms.[17] Its composition is dated *c.* 1100.[18]

(b) The 'Charter Fragment'. BM Additional Charter 19491 contains on the back a fragment of 41 lines of Cornish verse. The charter relates to St Stephen-in-Brannel, and its date is 1340. The verse, however, is in a hand dated by Jenner as *c.* 1400.[19] The subject of the verse, although obscure, is obviously popular in intention, and includes some advice to a lady as to her behaviour to her future husband. It may be a part in a (? secular) play or an interlude.[20]

(c) *Poem of Mount Calvary* or *The Passion*. This is a versified narrative of the Passion in 259 stanzas of eight heptasyllabic lines (but written as four lines) each. It is extant in BM MS. Harley 1782, in a fifteenth-century hand, but was composed in the fourteenth century. There are four later copies.[21]

(d) The *Ordinalia*. This is a dramatic trilogy consisting of *Origo Mundi*, *Passio Domini*, and *Resurrectio Domini*. The plays were probably written

---

17. *LHEB*, 61. Brecon and Monmouth have both been suggested as the place of compilation of this MS., which contains, beside *VC*, Lives of Celtic saints, extracts from monastic cartularies, a 'Kalendar', a short tract *De Situ Brecheniauc*, and a list of contents. See K. Hughes, 'British Museum MS. Cotton Vespasian A. XIV ("Vitae Sanctorum Wallensium"): its Purpose and Provenance', in *Studies in the Early British Church*, ed. N.K. Chadwick (1958), 183–200.
18. *LHEB*, 61. Ed. J.C. Zeuss in *Grammatica Celtica* (2nd edn, by H. Ebel, 1871), 1065–81; E. Norris, *The Ancient Cornish Drama* (1859), 311–435; E. Van T. Graves, *The Old Cornish Vocabulary* (University Microfilms Incorporated, Ann Arbor, 1962).
19. *A Handbook of the Cornish Language* (1904), 26.
20. Ed. W. Stokes, 'Cornica', *Revue Celtique*, IV (1879–80), 258–62; H. Jenner, 'Descriptions of Cornish Manuscripts – II', *JRIC*, XX (1915), 41–8; R.M. Nance, 'The Charter Endorsement in Cornish', *OC*, II.4 (1932), 34–6, 'New Light on Cornish', *OC*, IV.6 (1947), 214–16; E. Campanile, 'Un Frammento scenico medio-cornico', *Studi e Saggi Linguistici* (Supplement to *L'Italia Dialettale*, XXVI), III (1963), 60–80.
21. Ed. W. Stokes, *The Passion, A Middle-Cornish Poem*, Appendix to *Trans. Phil. Soc.* (1860–1), 1–100.

at Glasney College, near Penryn, since there are some local references. The plays are extant in Bodleian Library MS. 791, dating from the fifteenth century, the date of composition, however, being perhaps late fourteenth century.[22] There are three later copies.

(e) *The Life of Saint Meriasek.* This is a dramatized Life of the patron saint of Camborne, and was perhaps written for performance there. It is extant in a single manuscript, Peniarth 105 (National Library of Wales), the colophon of which states that it was finished in 1504 by 'Dominum Rad[ulphum] Ton',[23] perhaps a canon of Glasney College.[24]

(f) The Tregear Homilies. The homilies are extant only in BM Additional MS. 46397, and are translations into Cornish by one John Tregear of 12 of the 13 homilies in Edmund Bonner's *A Profitable and Necessary Doctrine, with Certain Homilies Adjoined thereto,* plus a thirteenth homily in a different hand, and not in Bonner's original. Bonner's work was published in 1555, during Mary's reign. No date appears in the Cornish version, but if translated, as it would appear, for congregational use, it must have been written between 1555 and 1558, when Mary died. The thirteenth homily, on palaeographical grounds, is probably later. Tregear himself has not been identified, though he may have belonged to the Tregear(e) family of Crowan, and neither is it known for what parish the homilies were translated.[25]

(g) *The Creation of the World.* This play is partly based on the earlier *Origo Mundi,* and was composed, or transcribed,[26] by William Jordan of Helston, in 1611. Five copies of the play are known, and there is also a fragment.[27]

(h) *The Story of John of Chy-an-Hur.* This is a folk-tale of some length, of a labouring man who lived at Chy-an-Hur ('the Ram's House') in St Levan,

22. Ed. Norris, *op. cit.* D.C. Fowler discusses date and provenance in 'The Date of the Cornish "Ordinalia"', *Mediaeval Studies,* xxiii (1961), 91–125, and suggests 1350–75 as the date of composition on the evidence of the place-name forms (he also discusses [p. 104] the date of *The Passion*). See also R. Longsworth, *The Cornish Ordinalia: Religion and Dramaturgy* (1967), 5–8.
23. This decipherment was made by R.M. Nance, according to F.E. Halliday, *The Legend of the Rood* (1955), 15, n. 2. Mr Halliday also notes that *Richard* Ton was curate of Crowan, near Camborne, in 1537. The older reading of the name in the colophon was 'Hadton', i.e. Hatton.
24. Ed. W. Stokes, *The Life of Saint Meriasek, Bishop and Confessor: A Cornish Drama* (1872).
25. Part of one homily is printed by R.M. Nance, 'The Tregear Manuscript', *OC,* iv.11 (1950), 429–34. For a description of and report on the MS., see Nance, 'More about the Tregear Manuscript', *OC,* v.1 (1951), 21–7.
26. W. Stokes (ed.), *Gwreans an Bys, the Creation of the World: A Cornish Mystery, Trans. Phil. Soc.* (1864), Part IV, 4, suggests that Jordan was perhaps merely the transcriber; he thinks the English of the stage directions is earlier, and that the references in the play to Limbo suggest a pre-Reformation date of composition. As against this, one must remember that traditional beliefs and practices died slowly and late in Cornwall. See n. 88, below, on the late use of the Roman mass in Cornwall.
27. Ed. Stokes, *op. cit.*

and went east seeking work, and of what befell him. It first appears in Lhuyd's *Archaeologia Britannica* (1707), but Lhuyd says it "was written about forty years since", i.e. *c.* 1667. There are several other copies, listed by Jenner (pp. 33–4). The work seems to be a genuine, popular version in Cornish of a very old folk-tale, first written down in Cornish at the beginning of the Cornish 'revival'.[28]

(i) Songs, verses, proverbs and other fragments. These are to be found in BM Additional MS. 28554 (the 'Gwavas MS'), ranging from 1709 to 1736; in the Borlase MS., *c.* 1750 (now in the County Record Office, Truro, accession no. DD.EN/2000); in Pryce (n. 28, below); in D. Gilbert's editions of *The Passion* (1826) and of Jordan's *Creation* (1827). But most of those in the Borlase MS. and those in Pryce and Gilbert were probably taken from the Gwavas MS. and from Tonkin's MSS. These are all listed in detail by Jenner (pp. 34–46), and need not be itemized individually here, but special care should be taken to distinguish genuinely popular and spontaneous works from those artificially created as part of the learned revival of interest in Cornish.

This is the extent of genuine, popular literature composed in Cornish, although it is certain that more, now lost, once existed, at least several genres being represented – drama, Arthurian romance, saints' Lives, liturgical matter.[29] The literature so far mentioned brings us to the period of learned and semi-learned interest in Cornish, dealt with in Chapter 1. This latter is not important here, since it tells us nothing about the earlier relationship between Cornish and English, which is our concern in the present chapter.

There are several important conclusions to be drawn from the literature mentioned above. First of all, with the exception of the *Vocabularium Cornicum*, whose place of origin is unknown, the literature which remains was almost certainly all composed in west Cornwall (BM Additional Charter 19491, containing the 'Charter Fragment', relates to St Stephen-in-Brannel, *The Passion* evidently has associations with west Cornwall,[30] and the Tregear Homilies may be associated with Crowan). There is nothing in Cornish known to have been composed in east Cornwall (cf. the English manuscripts, below). This in itself suggests that in east Cornwall the Cornish language had been given up fairly early, since the localizable documents of the fifteenth century and later come from the west of the county.

Secondly, all the Cornish literature mentioned above is of a popular

28. Also printed by W. Pryce in his *Archaeologia Cornu-Britannica* (1790), by D. Gilbert at the end of his edition of Jordan's *Creation* (1827); and most recently by R.M. Nance, *John of Chyannor or The Three Points of Wisdom*, Cornish Language Board (1969).
29. See M.F. Wakelin, 'The Lost Literature of Medieval Cornwall' (forthcoming).
30. There is a tradition that the MS. was found in the church at Sancreed. See Jenner, *Handbook*, 26.

nature, catering for widespread religious tastes. There are no official documents written in Cornish of any sort whatsoever, as far as is known, even in the late fifteenth century, when there are, as one would expect, some legal documents from the county at least written not in Latin but in English. It is true that most of the legal documents we possess are, in any case, from east Cornwall, where we naturally expect English rather than Cornish, but the evidence clearly shows that the language of official documents in fifteenth-century Cornwall was either Latin or English, but not Cornish, in both east and west Cornwall. This is in distinct contrast to the language of fifteenth-century popular literature, which appears to have been in Cornish in west Cornwall and in English in east Cornwall.

The language of the fourteenth-century and subsequent Cornish literature is heterogeneous. A number of English, French and Latin words appear even in the *Vocabularium Cornicum*,[31] and the plays contain a great many more, although there do not seem to be so many in the Charter Fragment or *The Passion*, and it has been suggested that there is a significant distribution of the English element in the plays, and that it is used for special dramatic purposes:[32] Fowler notes the fact that the first identifiable English phrase is spoken by the Devil, while God "invariably speaks pure Cornish." Jenner notes[33] that English sentences in Jordan's *Creation* are given to Lucifer or one of his angels, who appear only to speak Cornish when on their good behaviour, and relapse into their own tongue when they become especially excited or vicious. As far as the English loans are concerned, these are not merely words and short phrases and tags, but whole lines and couplets in English, the verse in some places becoming macaronic. This couplet, for example, occurs in the middle of a stanza otherwise completely in Cornish:

> nygh for sorw y am ful woud
> thow harlot for goddys bloud
>   (*Origo Mundi*, 2670–1)

The following is a typical example of a macaronic verse:

> henna me a wra hep let (That I will, without delay)
> an elles the difl yow fet
> ganso the dre yn y wlas (With him, home to his country)
> bot yowr doctours y yov fet
> bys yn iherusalem sket (Even to Jerusalem, straight)
> god yeue yow al yfle gras.
>   (*Passio Domini*, 1635–40)

31. For references to works dealing with foreign elements in *VC*, see *LHEB*, 60.
32. Cf. Fowler, *op. cit.*, 105, n. 34: "The *Ordinalia* contains a larger admixture of English words and phrases ... but this appears to be deliberate stage business, and cannot be regarded as representing a later accommodation of English elements in the Cornish language."   33, *Op. cit.*, 31.

And then there is the refrain sung by the three Marys at the Sepulchre:

> ellas mornyngh y syng mornyngh y cal
> our lord ys deyd that bogthe ovs al
> *(Resurrectio Domini, 733–4)*

The English element[34] is also present in the later plays. It should be stressed again that these are not merely occasional borrowed words, naturalized (though these, too, abound), but also foreign syntactical structures lifted bodily and used as if part of the Cornish language. The implications of these large chunks of English are puzzling, even taking into account possible dramatic distribution and the unlikely fact that in some cases they were taken directly from an original source as yet undiscovered. Does the heterogeneity of the language – even taking these factors into account – indicate that the people of west Cornwall spoke Cornish, but with an enormous admixture of English and French, a sort of pidgin Cornish, reflecting the linguistic heterogeneity of the plays? Or does it simply mean that they spoke Cornish but could understand English when the occasion demanded? For some of the populace the answer seems to be 'probably both', but the situation is obviously one of great complexity.

First of all, although it is impossible to say to what extent the language of the plays is a faithful reflection of the contemporary spoken language, it at least seems evident that a very large infiltration of English had taken place, even only on the evidence of the fully integrated English words in the plays.[35] Furthermore, 'people' is too vague a term for our purposes, and it becomes clear that several classes need to be distinguished in any consideration of the speech of medieval west Cornwall:

1. Some people spoke only Cornish, but with a generous admixture of foreign (French, English) words and phrases, but many, or perhaps most, of these understood English to varying extents. These were probably the lower classes. Incidentally, there is no doubt that some people knew only Cornish at a much later date, as witness the famous Prayer Book rebellion of 1549 (see p. 98, below).

34. Whole lines of French also occur in the *Ordinalia*:

parles vous et synour myn
(parlez, vous êtes seigneur mien)   *(Origo Mundi, 1911)*
vos eet bon se dev ma eyd
(vous êtes bon, si Dieu m'aide)   *(ibid., 2680)*

The latter example is preceded by a line in English, and followed by Cornish. These verses invite comparison with ME macaronic verse.
35. Examples of such words are: *vody* (mutated form of *body*), *Origo Mundi*, 2069; *an lahe* (='the law'), *ibid.*, 2602; *worthye* (<OE *weorþian*; ='worship' v.), *Passio Domini*, 105; *yet* (<OE *geat*; ='gate'), *Resurrectio Domini*, 115; *kestalkye* (<English *talk*), *Meriasek*, 236; *londia* (='land' v.), *ibid.*, 1093. Fowler, *op. cit.*, 113–20, appends a long list of English words from the *Ordinalia*, some of which, however, should be treated with caution.

2. Some people spoke English only, and it is not clear to what extent, if any, this class understood Cornish. These were the upper and middle classes.

3. Some people clearly understood both languages, and acted as intermediaries when necessary. Among these must have been some of the lower clergy, many of whom were of humble birth, and thus native speakers of Cornish, but had also learned English. Such was perhaps the writer of the *Ordinalia*, and an earlier example is Henry Marsely, the rector of St Just-in-Penwith, who acted as an interpreter when Bishop Grandisson visited St Buryan in 1336 (see p. 88, below). Later examples of priests who preached and administered the sacraments in Cornish are discussed below, and it looks as though many parish priests, both before and after the Reformation, were able to act as intermediaries. Finally, it is clear from the substantial English element in the Tregear Homilies that the translator, though familiar with both English and Cornish, was probably more so with English, since he interposes not only less familar English words but also common ones such as *not, indeed, meek, food*, and in more than one place corrects his English to the equivalent Cornish.[36]

The plays and the Tregear Homilies show that there was a public for Cornish drama and pulpit oratory up to the beginning of the seventeenth century (cf. also Carew, pp. 89–90, below), but also that, as time went on, they were more and more for audiences many of whom were familiar with English, and who spoke a version of Cornish more and more influenced by it.

The documents from the fifteenth century and later show that this influence was not restricted to lexical items, but was also phonological in nature. It appears, from the extant Cornish documents, that the Cornish sounds were gradually assimilated to English sounds, and took part in later changes together with them. The following are examples:

1. Cornish *ī* was assimilated to late ME *ī*, and took part to some extent in its further development to MnE [aɪ].[37] Boson of Newlyn, *c.* 1700 (see p. 23, above), writes *oy* in *choy* (Corn. *chy* < earlier *ty* 'house').[38] James Jenkins of Alverton, near Penzance, who died in 1710, composed a Cornish song of five stanzas, of which there is a complete copy in the Gwavas MS.,[39] and wrote *eye* for the pronoun 'they' (*y* in the *Ordinalia*). Lhuyd, in 1707, writes *ẏi* and *ei* in the pronoun *ny* 'we', *ei* in *why* 'you' and *jy* 'they', and *ai* in *hy* 'she',[40] and gives *ey, ei* as pronunciations of the letter *y*, instancing

36. See R.M. Nance, 'More about the Tregear Manuscript', *OC*, v.1 (1951), 23.
37. See Jenner, *Handbook*, 60.
38. Since the reflex of ME *i* found in west Cornwall by *SED* is usually [æɪ] today, [ɒɪ] being mostly confined to east Cornwall, perhaps *oy* simply = [əɪ] or the like.
39. See Jenner, *Handbook*, 35, for other copies and further details.
40. *Archaeologia Britannica* (1707), 244.

83

try 'three' and *kyn* 'back'.[41] There is no doubt that these spellings indicate a diphthongal pronunciation at the beginning of the eighteenth century for what was formerly *ī* (i.e. [i:]), but precisely what the pronunciation was it is not easy to say. According to Dobson,[42] the orthoepists' spelling *ei* indicates [əi] "or some closely related diphthong", the forerunner of present-day English [aɪ], and, in view of the notation *yi* and Lhuyd's statement that *ẏ* is like *i* in *bird* or *o* in *money*,[43] it looks as if Lhuyd's diphthong is something between [əi] and [aɪ], there being good reasons for supposing that the sound [aɪ] was never heard in careful southern English speech before 1700.[44]

2. Corn. *ou* ([u:]) was assimilated to late ME *ou*, and took part to some extent in its further development to MnE [aʊ].[45] Cf. Chapter 7, below, s.v. *Bullies, Croust, Gook, Groushans*.

3. Corn. *wa* > *wo* (see p. 122, below). Jenner instances *gwander* and *wartha*, which, he says, were pronounced *gwonder* and *wortha* (or *worra*).[46]

4. Corn. *u, eu, ue* ([ø:]) > *ē* ([e:]). Jenner states that this change is detected as early as *The Passion* (i.e. the fifteenth century).[47] This sound may have fallen in with late ME [ø:] (<OE *ēo*) in the west and south, which was not unrounded to [e:] until the fourteenth century,[48] and perhaps not until even later in remote Cornwall.[49]

5. Corn. *ū* in words like Middle Corn. *tūs* 'men', *rūth* 'red', *būgel* 'shepherd' was either unrounded, perhaps (on place-name evidence) in the sixteenth century,[50] to [i:], sometimes being spelled *ee*, e.g. *tees*, or became *ew* (i.e. [iu], [ju:]) in certain contexts – before *gh*, in final position, and in some loanwords.[51] The Corn. sound thus seems to have become anglicized in one of two directions: either it was unrounded, or it became a diphthong, perhaps following the path of development of the English diphthong which resulted from ME *iu* (i.e. [íu] > [iú:] > [ju:]). Similarly, Corn. *ü* (short) in words like Middle Corn. *grüglon* 'heather-bush' (see p. 192, below) was unrounded to [i] or [ɪ]. There is, of course, no absolute certainty that these developments were the result of English influence: however, although OE *ẏ* was unrounded to *ĭ* in Devon and Dorset as early as the tenth or eleventh century,[52] this may have been a process that went on over a long period of time (the rounded ME sound remained in some areas until the fifteenth century),[53] and conversely, the Corn. place-name spellings may reflect a

41. *Ibid.*, 230.   42. *English Pronunciation 1500–1700* (2nd edn, 1968), §137.
43. *Op. cit.*, 225.   44. Dobson, *op. cit.*, 662.
45. See Jenner, *Handbook*, 58, §5. (2); 59, n. 2.   46. p. 56.   47. p. 59.
48. K. Brunner, *An Outline of Middle English Grammar*, trans. G. Johnston (1963), §10.
49. [ø:] < OE *ēo* appears as *u* in *buth* (< OE *bēoþ*) in the *Ordinalia* – one of the usual representatives of [ø:] in western ME.
50. 'The Place-Names of Cornwall', 724.
51. Jenner, *Handbook*, 51, 58–9. Jenner observes that "the *u* of the earlier MSS. probably once represented approximately the French *u* or the German *ü*, the *u* of Devon and East Cornwall English".   52. Brunner, §11.5.   53. *Ibid.*

change which took place somewhat earlier than the time it is first evidenced in written form, thus bringing the unrounding processes in Cornish and English closer together in time than appears at first sight.

6. Corn. *oi* (=Welsh *oe*) in words like Middle Corn. *coid, cois* 'wood' (< Old Corn. *cuit*) appears from the sixteenth century onwards with *o, oo, u* spellings (*gos, goose, coose, gus, cus, cuz,* etc.), presumably representing pronunciations [o:], [u:]. The [u:] form is presumably a development from [o:], suggesting that Corn. [o:] fell in with the development of English *ọ̄*.

This English influence on Cornish phonology has been dwelt on at some length, since it is obviously relevant to any consideration of suggested Cornish influence on English, whether from a substratum (see Chapter 5, below) or in any other way. For Cornish influence to be proved, it has first to be shown that English owes something to Cornish. As will be seen from the sequel, except in the case of a small number of loan-words and other items this is not proved. On the other hand, there is evidence that Cornish was influenced to a considerable extent by English, in lexis and phonology (probably more examples could be adduced than those given above), and possibly, therefore, in morphology and syntax too,[54] though these have not been dealt with here. While a thorough examination of all available Cornish material from these points of view is obviously very desirable, it can be stated, even on the present evidence, that, far from being influenced by Cornish, English itself was the influencing agent, dominating Cornish so completely that the latter's sound system became assimilated in some respects at least, and perhaps in a greater number, to that of English. It is thus impossible to accept theories such as those of Mr E.G.R. Hooper, who, in an article[55] in 1931, states that the dialect of west Cornwall "is a key to Cornish in three ways": 1. It gives us "practically all the *sounds of Cornish* as last spoken", as an example of which Mr Hooper instances only the "lightly guttural *gh*" in the exclamation *Aw! Awh!* (Corn. *Ogh!* 'Oh, alas', etc.). Since the precise phonetic quality of the sounds of Cornish, as of any other dead language, are now irrecoverable, this argument – still tenaciously held by enthusiasts – is of doubtful value, but even if [x] could be heard in such exclamations in 1931 (which is open to question), it is surely but feeble evidence on which to base such a broad generalization. 2. The dialect of west Cornwall apparently preserves Corn. word-order, idioms and intonation. There is possibly more truth in this, as a study of the intonation of west Cornwall dialect might show. Mr Hooper's example of *there's a cow to you* 'you have a cow', cited as a syntactical structure modelled on Corn. *yma bugh dheugh-why*, seems reasonably convincing (unless derived by simple

54. Cf. Jenner, *Handbook*, 158: "In later Cornish there was a strong tendency to assimilate the order of words and the construction of sentences to those of English."
55. 'Dialect as a Gateway to Cornish', *OC*, II.2 (1931), 34–5.

omission of the word *belonging*), and although no examples of such structures were found by *SED*, I am told that they can still be heard. But the simple omission of *to* before an infinitive, which he also cites, is widespread in dialect, and no evidence of the influence of Corn. syntax, and likewise the use of *you* in such phrases as *very hot, you*, can hardly be regarded as a relic of Corn. *yu* 'it is', 'is it?', since a) this interjection appears to have been recorded by *SED* outside Cornwall – see VII.5.1, Wilts 2, 6, 8 (and cf. Cornwall 3), VII.5.8, Gloucs 7, VIII.3.3, Wilts 2; and b) it occurs in contexts, even in Cornwall, where it cannot possibly mean 'it is' or 'is it?' – see VII.5.2, Cornwall 4. 3. The existence of Corn. words in west Cornwall dialect cannot, of course, be disputed. Whatever the state of dialect in 1931 regarding the retention of archaic features, it is clear that it is at the present time of no use whatever to the student of Cornish, and it is my opinion that it never was. Nevertheless, the notion of 'Cornish continuity' still exercises a fatal fascination and is dearly cherished among Cornish patriots.

Finally, with regard to the plays, it has been suggested that not merely some of the language but also the drama itself may have been borrowed from English. The plays are, to quote E. Hoblyn Pedler,[56] "exotics transplanted from English soil", although no sources have been recognized in extant ME drama. There is certainly nothing in the drama, or, in fact, in any extant Cornish works (as far as is known), to suggest that the remaining literary monuments are peculiarly Cornish in outlook or ideas: all are in the traditions of ordinary medieval literature. Perhaps, therefore, Jenner's reference to the plays as "just the contemporary drama of Christendom in its local form"[57] is the fairest judgment that can be made at present.

2. Documents in the English language

For the Bodmin Manumissions and their implications, the reader is referred to p. 67, above. The following ME documents are of Cornish provenance:[58]

(a) PRO S.C.8/124/6187, before 1427. Petition of William Moorton, Mount St Michael.

(b) PRO C1/12/202, 1430. Petition of Richard Trewe (or ? Crewe) relating to St Austell.

(c) Bodleian MS. Tanner 196, 1430. Registrum Prioratus de Launceston. Fos. 8aff. comprise various matters in Latin and English relating to the election of William Shyre as prior, 1430, the English being on fos. 40b–41b, 42a–43a and 53b–54b.

56. In an Appendix to Norris, *The Ancient Cornish Drama*, vol. II, 508. For similar points of view, and also another, see Longsworth, *op. cit.*, 1–3.
57. In 'The Cornish Drama' (four unpublished lectures given at Exeter University, c. 1928, and now deposited in the Morton Nance Bequest at the County Museum, Truro), 50.
58. Professor Angus McIntosh kindly acquainted me with the PRO documents and several of the others.

(d) Rotuli Parliamentarum, IV, 403, 1432. Petition of the Commons of Cornwall.

(e) PRO C1/9/195, 1434. Memorandum relating to Thomas Treffrye of Fowey.

(f) PRO C1/9/394, 1434. Memorandum relating to Fowey.

(g) BM Cart. Antiq. Harley 57.A, 35, 1434. Award of John Treffry, Thomas Broun and others, in a dispute over land, between the prior of Bodmin and Richard Flamank. Printed in W. Dugdale, *Monasticum Anglicanum* (1846), II, 462–3.

(h) BM Harley MS. 2399, fos. 47a–61a, *c.* 1450–75.[59] This is a poem in a popular vein on the Child Jesus, written by Canon Johannes Bowyer, of Bodmin. Ed. C. Horstmann, *Sammlung Altenglischer Legenden* (1878), 111–23.

(i) CRO DDA. 6, 1458. Indenture from Saltash.

(j) Bodmin church accounts, 1469–72. Printed by J.J. Wilkinson in *Camden Miscellany*, VII (1875).

(k) CRO DDP. 221/5/1, 1480. Accounts of the keepers and the Guild of All Saints, St Thomas (Launceston), in Latin and English.

(l) CRO DDT. (2). 214, 1489. Deed relating to Burlorne, near Bodmin. Written at Bodmin.

(m) CRO (reference lost), 1491. Indenture from *Treuoruke* (presumably Trevorrick in St Columb Major).

(n) CRO Accession 247,[60] 1492. Contract for making new furniture for Bodmin church.

(o) CRO Accession 247, 1494. Indenture from Bodmin.

(p) CRO DDT. (2). 47, 1495. Deed relating to Burlorne, near Bodmin. Written at Bodmin.

(q) CRO Accession 247, 1498. Indenture from Bodmin.

(r) CRO Accession 247, 1498. Deed relating to Naylor's Chantry at Bodmin.

The above documents, all of a fifteenth-century date, represent all the ME from Cornwall that I am at present aware of.[61] Their distribution, as one would expect, is almost entirely confined to east and central Cornwall, and there are quite a number of documents from Bodmin.

As explained further in Chapters 5 and 7, there is apparently no Cornish element in the English documents, phonological, lexical, or of any other type as far as can be seen.[62] After the fifteenth century, documents in English

---

59. I am grateful to Mr C.E. Wright for this estimate of the date.
60. No individual shelf numbers are available for the Bodmin Borough documents.
61. This is not, of course, counting the scraps of English found in the *Ordinalia* and other Corn. works.
62. A possible phonological exception is the word *plaeth* 'plaice', a pronunciation found, according to Nance (*Glossary*) at Mousehole. In Middle Cornish, words of French origin ending in [s] are sometimes spelled with *th* in the MSS., e.g. *fath* 'face', *grath* 'grace',

from Cornwall naturally become more and more common, but these have not been individually examined for present purposes since, as is well known, later documents gradually lose the distinctively local features present in earlier ones. See further pp. 101–2, 181, below.

Statements

We may now turn to a series of statements on Cornish and the English of Cornwall, recorded in official documents or made by travellers, visitors, antiquaries and men of letters. Their collective evidence serves two purposes – the establishment of a Cornish-English boundary, even if only tentatively, at various periods, and enlightenment about the type of English used in the county. It is obvious that references which make no mention of locality are of little value to us, since we cannot tell to which part of Cornwall they refer, a matter of prime importance. Most of the following are quoted by Jenner (pp. 9ff.):

1. 1328–9.[63] In a letter from John de Grandisson, bishop of Exeter, 1327–69, to certain cardinals, the writer states that "linguam eciam, in extremis Cornubie non Anglicis set Britonibus extat nota". It should be noted that the bishop refers here not to the whole of Cornwall, but to the 'extreme', i.e. the westernmost, part. [F.C. Hingeston-Randolph (ed.), *The Register of John de Grandisson, Bishop of Exeter (A.D. 1327–1369)* (1894–9), I, 97–8.]

2. 1336. On 12 July, the parishioners of St Buryan, after a long and bitter struggle between the Crown and the diocese over the status of the college of secular canons at St Buryan, made a formal submission to Bishop Grandisson.[64] The principal parishioners made their submission in English or French (although their 13 names are mostly Cornish), and the rest made theirs in Cornish, interpreted by Henry Marsely, rector of the neighbouring parish of St Just-in-Penwith. A sermon followed, translated into Cornish by the same priest. [*Grandisson Register*, II, 820–1.]

3. 1339. A licence was granted to J. Polmarke to help the vicar of St Merryn (near Padstow) in the cure of souls, part of his duties being to preach in Cornish. [*Grandisson Register*, II, 910.]

4. 1349. On 26 April, the prior of Minster died from the Black Death, and the death roll among the tenants and labourers of the priory was so high that it became impossible to support the members of the community.

---

plath 'place' (beside *fas, gras, plas*), suggesting an actual pronunciation with [θ]. In this instance, it appears that the [θ] ending of the Corn. word has been preserved in local fishermen's dialect.
63. This reference and numbers 2, 3 and 5 are given by L.C.J. Orchard, 'Some Notes on the Cornish Language in the Fourteenth Century', *OC*, III.2 (1937), 79–80.
64. See *Grandisson Register*, vol. III xliii–xliv.

Nor could a chaplain be provided for the parish, since none of the survivors could speak Cornish. [Quoted in *Grandisson Register*, III, lxix, and by L.E. Elliott-Binns, *Medieval Cornwall* (1955), 89–90, from Patent Rolls, 29 Edward III, pt II, m. 19.]

5. 1354–5. In a list of the penitentiaries appointed for the archdeaconry of Cornwall, one Brother John, of the Franciscan friary at Bodmin, was appointed for those who knew Cornish and English, and one Brother Roger Tyrel, one of the Dominican friary at Truro, for those who knew Cornish only. [*Grandisson Register*, II, 1145–6.]

6. 1542. Andrew Borde, *The Fyrst Boke of the Introduction of Knowledge* (published in 1547). In Chapter I the author writes: "In Englande, and vnder the dominion of England, be many sondry speches beside Englyshe: there is Frenche vsed in England, specyally at Calys, Gersey, and Jersey: In Englande, the Walshe tongue is in Wales, the Cornyshe tongue in Corne-wall, and Iryshe in Irlande ..." The Appendix to this chapter, "treatinge of Cornewall, and Cornyshe men", gives 26 lines of English dialect from Cornwall, which is clearly of an east Cornwall variety, including south-western dialectal forms such as *iche cham* 'I am', *dycke* 'thick', *dyn* 'thin', *dryn* 'therein', *vyshe* 'fish', *volke* 'folk'. This passage is reproduced, with a commentary, in my Appendix, pp. 206–10, below. At the end of the passage, Borde says: "In Cornwall is two speches: the one is naughty [i.e. poor, dialectal] Englyshe, and the other is Cornyshe. And there be many men and women the which cannot speake one worde of Englyshe, but all Cornyshe." He then proceeds to give specimens of Cornish speech, comprising the numerals and a number of phrases.[65] [F.J. Furnivall (ed.), *The Fyrst Boke of the Introduction of Knowledge*. EETS, ES 10 (1870). See pp. 120–5.]

7. 1572. Depositions of the Bishop's Consistory Court at Exeter. In a case of defamation, William Hawysh deposed that upon *dew whallon gwa metton in eglos de Lalant* (i.e. upon All Saints' day in Lelant church) one Agnes Davy was called "whore and whore bitch" in English "and not in Cornowok".[66]

8. 1595. *Ibid.* A girl at St Ewe mentioned that, while weeding in a garden, two of the witnesses were talking together both in Cornish and English.

9. 1602. Richard Carew, *The Survey of Cornwall* (probably complete in a first version by 1594, published in 1602).[67] Carew's remarks on the state of Cornish are in the First Book (pp. 125ff.). He discusses personal and

---

65. Printed in a regularized form by W. Stokes, 'Cornica', *Revue Celtique*, IV (1879–80), 262–4.
66. This and the following reference are quoted by A.L. Rowse, *Tudor Cornwall* (1941), 23, from Henderson MSS. X, pp. 124 and 176 respectively; and also by W.T. Hoblyn, 'In English and Not in Cornowok', *OC*, II.11 (1936), 11.
67. See Halliday's edition, 47ff.

place-names of the 'western Cornish', and gives examples of Cornish words and numerals. Then he goes on (p. 127):

> But the principal love and knowledge of this language lived in Dr. Kennall the civilian,[68] and with him lieth buried, for the English speech doth still encroach upon it and hath driven the same into the uttermost skirts of the shire. Most of the inhabitants can speak no word of Cornish, but very few are ignorant of the English; and yet some so affect their own to a stranger they will not speak it, for if meeting them by chance you inquire the way or any such matter, your answer shall be, *Meea navidna cowzasawzneck*, 'I can speak no Saxonage'.[69] The English which they speak is good and pure, as receiving it from the hands of their own gentry and the eastern merchants, but they disgrace it in part with a broad and rude accent, somewhat like the Somersetshire men, especially in pronouncing the names ...

Carew then goes on to list the "certain peculiar phrases" and "other rude terms", i.e. dialect words and phrases common to Cornwall, mentioned on p. 25, above. His book also has the distinction of being the only work to give a contemporary account of the 'gwary miracle' or mystery play (p. 144): "For representing it, they raise an earthen amphitheatre in some open field, having the diameter of his enclosed plain some forty or fifty foot. The country people flock from all sides, many miles off, to hear and see it, for they have therein devils and devices to delight as well the eye as the ear." [F.E. Halliday (ed.), *Richard Carew of Antony: The Survey of Cornwall*, 1953. See pp. 125ff., 144.]

10. 1610. John Norden, *Speculi Britanniae Pars: A Topographical and Historical Description of ¦Cornwall*. Norden, who may have made his visit to the county as early as 1584 (see *DNB*, s.v.), gives the following account:

> The Cornish people, for the moste parte, are descended of the Britishe stocke, thowgh muche entermixed since with the Saxon and Norman bloude; but vntill of late yeares retayned, the Britishe speache corrupted, as theirs is of Wales[70]. ... But of late the Cornishe men haue muche conformed themselues to the vse of the Englishe tounge, and their Englishe is equall to the beste, especially in the easterne partes; euen from *Truro eastwarde* it is in manner wholy Englishe. In the weste parte of the Countrye, as in the hundreds of *Penwith* and *Kerrier*, the Cornishe tounge is moste in vse amongste the inhabitantes, and yet (whiche is to be marueyled)

68. Vicar of Gwennap, *d.* 1592.
69. Correctly rendered, "I *will* speak no Saxonage".
70. Jenner, *Handbook*, 14, prints: "but untill of late years retayned the British speache uncorrupted as theirs of Wales is."

thowgh the husband and wife, parentes and children, Master and Seru-antes, doe mutually comunicate in their natiue language, yet ther is none of them in manner but is able to conuers with a *Straunger* in the Englishe tounge, vnless it be some obscure people, that seldome conferr with the better sorte: But it seemeth that in few yeares the Cornishe Language wilbe by litle and litle abandoned.

[Edn of 1728. See pp. 26–7.]

11. 1644. Richard Symonds, *Diary of the Marches of the Royal Army during the Great Civil War*. Symonds gives (p. 74) a short vocabulary of Cornish words, and four short sentences, and adds: "This language is spoken altogeather at Goon-hilly and about Pendennis, and at Land's-end they speake no English. All beyond Truro they speake the Cornish language." [C.E. Long (ed.), *Diary of the Marches of the Royal Army during the Great Civil War; kept by Richard Symonds.*[71] Camden Society, LXXIV, 1859.]

12. Mid-seventeenth century. William Jackman, vicar of Feock, custom-arily used a Cornish formula for the words of Administration at Holy Communion, because the older people did not understand English.[72]

13. 1662, 1667. John Ray, *Itinerary*. Ray mentions one 'Dickon Gwyn' (his real name was apparently Dick Angwin) of St Just-in-Penwith, as the only man who could write Cornish. Ray adds that few of the children could speak it, "so that the language is like in a short time to be quite lost".[73]

14. *c.* 1680. William Scawen, 'Observations on an Ancient Manuscript, entitled Passio Christi ...' (which includes an abridged version of the *Antiquities Cornu-Britannick*; see p. 23, above). Scawen states (p. 214): "'Tis observed also elsewhere in this county further west, where the Cornish hath been most spoken, that the English thereabouts is much better than the same is in Devon, or the places bordering on them, by being most remote from thence from whence the corruption proceeds." With reference to Devon, he notes (*loc. cit.*): "And there is the worst language commonly spoken, and spoken rudely too, which corrupts not only their own country tongue but ours also, in the places that are nearest to them, and those infect others nearest to them." Later (p. 216): "For we have some among these few [old folks] that do speak Cornish, who do not understand a word of English ... and those may be many in some of the western parts, to whom Mr. Francis Robinson, parson of Landawednack told me, he had preached a sermon not long since[74] in the Cornish tongue, only well understood by his

71. *Ibid.*, 15, erroneously cites the source of the work as BM Additional MS. 17052, instead of 17062.
72. Quoted by Jenner, *Handbook*, 16, from W. Hals, *The Compleat History of Cornwal* (1750), who apparently gives the Corn. formula.
73. Quoted by Jenner, *Handbook*, 16.
74. See A.S.D. Smith, *The Story of the Cornish Language* (2nd edn, rev. E.G. Retallack Hooper, 1969), 11.

auditory." [Printed as part of the appendixes to D. Gilbert, *The Parochial History of Cornwall* (1838). See IV, 214ff.]

15. 1695. William Camden, *Britannia*, translated and edited by E. Gibson. The following (p. 146) forms part of the additions to Camden's original (Latin) work of 1586:

> Their Language too, is the English; and (which is something surprizing) observ'd by Travellers to be more pure and refin'd than that of their neighbours, *Devonshire* and *Somersetshire*. The most probable reason whereof, seems to be this; that English is to them an introduc'd, not an original Language; and those who brought it in were the Gentry and Merchants, who imitated the Dialect of the Court, which is the most nice and accurate ... The old Cornish is almost quite driven out of the Country, being spoken only by the vulgar in two or three Parishes at the Lands-end; and they too understand the English. In other parts, the inhabitants know little or nothing of it; so that in all likelihood, a short time will destroy the small remains that are left of it. 'Tis a good while since, that only two men could write it, and one of them no Scholar or Grammarian, and then blind with age.

Gibson then gives the Lord's Prayer in Cornish, Welsh and Breton, and the Creed in Cornish, and suggests various reasons for the decline of Cornish. [E. Gibson, *Camden's Britannia, Newly Translated into English: with Large Additions and Improvements* (1695). See pp. 16–18.]

16. *c.* 1700. Nicholas Boson, *Nebbaz Gerriau dro tho Carnoack* (see also p. 23, above). According to Boson, the Cornish-speaking district was now:

> from ye Land's-End to the Mount, and towards St. Ives and Redruth, and again from the Lizard to Helston, and towards Falmouth ... within which little Extent also there is more of English spoken than Cornish, for here may be some found that can hardly speak or understand Cornish, but scarce any but both understand and speak English ... We find the young Men to speak it less and less, and worse and worse ...

[W.C. Borlase (ed.), 'Copy of a MS. in Cornish and English from the MSS. of Dr. Borlase', *JRIC*, XXI (1879), 182–3. R.M. Nance (ed.), 'Nicholas Boson's "Nebbaz Gerriau dro tho Carnoack"', *JRIC*, XXIII (1930), 336–7.]

17. 1707. Edward Lhuyd, *Archaeologia Britannica*. Lhuyd lists the following parishes in which Cornish was still spoken as a living language: St Just-in-Penwith, Paul, St Buryan, Sennen, St Levan, Sancreed, Morvah, Madron, Zennor, Towednack, St Ives, Lelant, Ludgvan, Gulval, and along the coast from Land's End to St Keverne. He adds that many of the inhabitants of these parishes, especially the gentry, do not understand Cornish, "there being no necessity thereof, in regard there's no Cornish Man but speaks good English". [E. Lhuyd, *Archaeologia Britannica* (1707). See p. 253.]

18. Eighteenth century. Various other records of the last speakers of Cornish, of whom the most celebrated is Mrs Dolly Pentraeth (*d.* 1777) of Mousehole. For these individuals, who are hardly central to our purpose, reference may be made to Jenner, pp. 20–3, and also to D. Barrington, 'On the Expiration of the Cornish Language', *Archaeologia*, III (1786), 279–84; J.H. Matthews, *History*, pp. 404–5; R.M. Nance, 'Cornish in 1756', *OC*, II no. 5 (1933), 44; and other works cited in the Bibliography, below.

It may be noted from the above writers that there was some dispute as to who were the last speakers of Cornish. Eighteenth-century claims were advanced for old people in Mousehole (especially Dolly Pentraeth), Marazion and even Truro. The observers, however, were often enthusiastic, but perhaps not always reliable, antiquaries, and their testimony is not very satisfactory. In any case, some of the last Cornish 'speakers', e.g. the nineteenth-century ones mentioned by Jenner,[75] probably knew only words and phrases, numerals, the Lord's Prayer, and other scraps and fragments handed on by their parents as quaint dialect pieces. Such relics do not constitute spoken Cornish. Our last safe testimony is probably that of Lhuyd in 1707. He states that St Buryan (*SED* locality 6) was one of the last places where the language was spoken, and "along the coast from Land's End to St Keverne" includes Mullion (*SED* locality 7), while Boson's description (*c.* 1700) of the Cornish-speaking area obviously includes Gwinear (*SED* locality 5). Note, too, that Cornish was reported as being spoken at St Ewe (*SED* locality 4) as late as 1595.

From the information given in these statements, unsatisfactory as it may be in some respects, one thing emerges with some clarity. That is, that from the beginning of the seventeenth century Cornish can be seen, generally speaking, to have been pushed as far west as Truro and beyond, i.e. it was current only in the two westernmost hundreds: the statements of Carew (1602), Norden (1610) and Symonds (1644) all testify to this. From there it was evidently pushed fairly quickly to the coast. We are thus able to establish a roughly-drawn isogloss running just to the west of Truro, and to compare it with Ellis's division between his Districts 11 and 12 (see pp. 28–9, above). How long before this the boundary between Cornish and English had been there, we cannot say from the evidence of the statements. If we take statement 1 at its face value, it would seem that it had been there for some considerable time.

Neither is there enough evidence of the same type for the establishment of an earlier isogloss further east. There are only five medieval references, and these are late – mid-fourteenth-century. The references to St Merryn (1339) and Minster (1349) in north-east Cornwall might suggest, as Jenner

75. pp. 21–3.

would have us believe, that Cornish was spoken over a large part of east Cornwall at this time,[76] but the place-name evidence does not agree with this by any means, and a more likely conclusion is that as Cornish receded down the peninsula pockets of Cornish-speaking people remained. This is probably the clue to the whole recession of Cornish – a general retreat, leaving small pockets here and there. An interesting parallel is that of the decline of the Greek language in southern Italy (the geographical shapes of Italy and Cornwall are worthy of comparison). The zones of southern Italy in which Greek was spoken during the later Middle Ages shrank more and more during the fifteenth and sixteenth centuries, but some small areas remained even after the Renaissance period; in the 1880s there were Greek speakers in Apulia and in the 1850s at places in Calabria, in some of which, in fact, it could still be heard in the 1930s.[77] If we require further evidence that Cornish had greatly receded by this time, it may be noted that John Trevisa, himself a Cornishman, makes no reference whatever to the language in his famous interpolations on the languages of Britain in his translation (1387) of Higden's *Polychronicon*, obviously feeling that it was not worthy of special mention. This perhaps suggests that Cornish was already the remote dialect of a minority group. Finally, the absence of any 'rounds' or playing-places, where the Cornish plays were staged, east of Truro, suggests that Cornish culture was already defunct in this area by the time of the plays, i.e. the end of the fourteenth century.

Very little evidence is forthcoming about the type of English used in Cornwall, but Carew (1602) says that the English in (? west) Cornwall is "good and pure", while both Scawen (*c.* 1680) and Gibson (1695) suggest that the English used in Cornwall is more refined than the (dialectal) English in use further east, i.e. in Devon and Somerset, Scawen explicitly referring to the English in use "where the Cornish hath been most spoken". Norden's statement (1610) that "their Englishe is equall to the beste, especially in the easterne partes" in the light of its context probably refers to the ease with which the Cornish had mastered the English language, and their fluency in it, rather than to its elegance or refinement as compared with the English of neighbouring counties.

This concludes our review of the evidence for the relative states of English and Cornish in Cornwall from the Middle Ages onwards. It remains to sum up all the evidence at our disposal of any type whatsoever, and to produce from this a coherent statement.

76. p. 11: "It is highly probable ... that until at least the fifteenth century the Tamar was the general boundary of English and Cornish." But this statement was withdrawn on Jenner's behalf by R.M. Nance. See below, p. 97.
77. See R. Weiss, 'The Greek Culture of South Italy in the Later Middle Ages', *Proceedings of the British Academy*, xxxvii (1951), 24–5.

Place-name evidence shows that at the end of the Anglo-Saxon period the River Ottery was probably still the main boundary between the English and the Cornish peoples, although scattered English settlements existed all the way down the peninsula. On the same evidence, it is also clear that English occupation was fairly complete all over south-east Cornwall. The conclusion reached in Chapter 3 was that, at the time of the Norman Conquest, the county was ruled by an English minority, who lived chiefly in east Cornwall, but had settlements and extended their authority throughout. The Norman Conquest, by subjugating both peoples to the same ruler, probably promoted the fusion which had already begun, and from this time on it was a matter not of conquest but of gradual mingling. Linguistically, the result of this mingling was that Cornish gradually ceased to be spoken, while English became at first the predominant, and, in the end, the only, language in the county.

At the time just after the Norman Conquest, we can state on place-name evidence that English was vastly predominant all over east Cornwall as far as Bodmin, and, in the north and south, roughly as far as, respectively, the rivers Camel and Fowey. This does not imply, however, that English was spoken by every inhabitant of this area: no doubt a certain amount of Cornish was still being used. West of this area there was no uniformity, Cornish being spoken in some places and English in others (and in some, of course, both Cornish and English).

We now have a dark period of almost 250 years of which we know nothing, and our next glimpse of the county's languages is in Grandisson's letter of 1328-9, written just after he had become bishop of Exeter, and describing his diocese – inhabited, he says, by a people speaking English at the tip of Cornwall. It is doubtful precisely how we can interpret *extremis,* but the letter suggests that even by this early date the area in which Cornish was generally spoken had receded to the far west. It may be significant that the 1354-5 list of penitentiaries for Cornwall mentions an appointment from Bodmin for those who knew both Cornish and English (and who presumably lived in the central and eastern parts of the county), while an appointment was made from Truro for those who knew Cornish only (and who no doubt lived chiefly in the west). It may be deduced from this that Brother John of Bodmin was a bilingual speaker, while Brother Roger of Truro may have spoken Cornish only – a bilingual speaker from east Cornwall and a speaker of Cornish from west Cornwall probably reflecting the general situation.

There is no doubt that during the Middle Ages Cornish was written and spoken by large numbers of people in the west of the county. Works of popular literature and entertainment exist from the fifteenth century onwards, and some of these are older in date of composition, but it must be repeated that all of them appear to be productions of west Cornwall, and that no

Cornish literature, as far as is known, was written in the east. And even on the Cornish literature itself, whose very form may in some instances have been copied or borrowed from English, it is obvious that from an early time English was having an enormous effect, lexically and phonologically. From this, we infer a certain amount of bilingualism, as well as that a marked English element was present in Cornish from an early date. Nevertheless, throughout and beyond the Middle Ages dramatic productions in Cornish remained popular, as both the existence of Jordan's *Creation*, 1611, and Carew's statements, 1602, testify. The existence of the Tregear Homilies suggests that the same is true of sermons.

Meanwhile, in east Cornwall the use of Cornish had ceased except in occasional pockets. The equivalent of the popular literature written in west Cornwall in Cornish was Canon Bowyer's poem on the Child Jesus, in English. And there are other documents in English which have no Cornish equivalent – a collection of legal documents, deeds and the like, many relating to Bodmin, whose existence testifies to the greater importance of east Cornwall administratively.

It thus looks as if there may have been an east–west cultural and linguistic division in Cornwall from quite an early date. It was not, of course, a stable, permanent division, but a fluctuating boundary, tending to recede further westward as the Middle Ages wore on, and due partly to the very remoteness of west Cornwall.

At the end of this period, as already noted, people in the west were still flocking to the Cornish *gwaries* or mystery plays, but from now on we have several testimonies, e.g. Norden's, that the language had definitely retreated beyond Truro. This accords with our place-name evidence of an earlier date that in some places west of the parishes of Veryan, Gerrans, Feock, Perranarworthal, Gwennap and Illogan Cornish was still being spoken after 1500, but that English was predominant up to this area.

From about 1600 onwards, we are reliant solely on the evidence of the statements listed above, and it is now simply a matter of recession and extinction as far as Cornish is concerned, and the use of English almost everywhere since 1700–50.

We should not conclude without making it clear that there is no evidence whatsoever that the Tamar was the boundary between Cornish and English as late as the fifteenth century,[78] or that Cornish was spoken east of the Tamar as late as the reign of Edward I or Elizabeth.[79] On the contrary, place-name evidence in Devon favours an early and fairly thorough settlement of that county,[80] notwithstanding pockets of British who remained, and Celtic

78. Jenner, *Handbook*, 11, followed by the *Encyclopaedia Britannica*, 14th edn, s.v. Celtic Languages: Cornish.
79. Jenner, *loc. cit.*   80. See *PND*, xixff.

dialects were certainly extinct here by the tenth century at the very latest. But, in any case, Jenner's statements on these points (and also his citation of a statement by Carew that Cornish was used liturgically *at Menheniot* in the reign of Henry VIII – a statement which I have been unable to trace, in fact) were withdrawn on his behalf by R.M. Nance, who had apparently discussed the matter with him.[81]

It remains for us to suggest reasons for the adoption of English in Cornwall and the decline and extinction of Cornish.

Cornish survived as long as it did only through geographical accident. The other Celtic dialects in England had in the main died out some hundreds of years before the Norman Conquest, but the remoteness of the county kept Cornish alive for a thousand years longer. However, when exposed to outside influences, Cornish, the dialect of a minority group, quickly showed signs of collapsing. This happened on several occasions.

The Anglo-Saxons were a ruling minority, administering the county from east Cornwall, and settling this area in some considerable numbers. It was natural, therefore, that Cornish should die in this area first. But their scattered settlements throughout the county helped to spread their language, and since they were the ruling class, speaking only English (as did, later, the gentry), their language was regarded as prestigious.[82] (Useful analogies may be made with English *vis-à-vis* French at the time of the Norman Conquest, and with the present-day regional dialects *vis-à-vis* Standard English.) The conquered people simply gradually adopted the language of their conquerors. Cornish was doomed from the moment the Anglo-Saxons crossed the Tamar, and it was only a matter of time before it succumbed completely.

As observed above, the Norman Conquest further helped to break down Cornwall's isolation by uniting English and Cornish people under a single ruler, and linking the county more firmly to England as a whole.

Between the Norman Conquest and the end of the Middle Ages, numerous small urban centres arose in Cornwall. These were partly the results of speculation of English feudal magnates and ecclesiastical landholders. The Cornish themselves were an agrarian people, not much given to urban dwelling. The towns housed a heterogeneous collection of peoples of many European nations,[83] and it may have been that English was in use as an urban lingua franca, and that this, together with the presence of so many

81. See Smith, *op. cit.* (1st edn, 1947), 9, where Nance is quoted (but unfortunately from an unspecified source).
82. Cf. L. Bloomfield, *Language* (1933), chap. XXVI.
83. In 1327, Penryn was equally divided between natives and foreigners, while in Tregoney and Grampound the foreign element still predominated. At Fowey in 1439, perhaps a third of the town, or at least of the property-holders, was foreign – Irish, French, Dutch. See Rowse, *op. cit.*, p. 95, and also W. Cunningham, *Alien Immigrants to England* (2nd edn, 1969), 122ff.

different languages, contributed to the disuse of Cornish. The most important towns would be those on the main roads, especially, during the Middle Ages, those en route to St Michael's Mount, and pilgrims from beyond the Tamar journeying to this venerable shrine no doubt helped to disseminate English throughout the whole length of the county. It was not, however, until the end of the Middle Ages that the Cornish people at last began to live in the towns, a time when the Reformation was adding its contribution to the influence of English.

The Tudor period saw the end of Cornwall's isolation, and, as Dr Rowse says, "the process of absorption into the life of the English people was in motion ... the disappearance of the [Cornish] language was a natural, an inevitable consequence."[84] Powerful factors were no doubt, as he says, "the increase in commerce, the rise in importance of the ports as opposed to the inland towns, consequent upon the naval developments of Elizabeth's reign and the war with Spain, by which Cornwall from being a remote, unimportant county was brought into the front line of the nation's offensive and defensive policy." But the Reformation also played a part, first of all by insisting, in the face of considerable opposition,[85] on an English liturgy and scriptures: it presumably did not seem worth while to translate these into an obviously moribund language for the benefit of an insignificant minority (the Prayer-Book and the Bible were, however, translated into Welsh).[86] One paragraph of the famous petition presented to Edward VI by the Cornwall and Devon insurgents reads significantly: "We will not receive the new service, because it is but like a Christmas game. We will have our old service of Matins, Mass, Evensong, and Procession as it was before; and we the Cornish, whereof certain of us understand no English, do utterly refuse the new service." Carew's statement[87] that "The Lord's Prayer, the Apostles' Creed, and the Ten Commandments have been much used in Cornish beyond all remembrance" presumably testifies to an obedient response by the local clergy to the official instructions to teach these items to the faithful in their own language, as in the rest of England: the use of English no doubt added to Cornish resentment with the new service of 1549, and the Cornish were by nature conservative in religious matters (the Roman mass was apparently celebrated in some churches in Cornwall as late as the seventeenth century).[88] The Reformation also meant the end of the mystery

84. *Op. cit.*, 23–4.
85. See Rowse, *op. cit.*, chap. XI, 262ff.
86. The question arises as to whether, in fact, any pre-Reformation translations had already been made in Cornish, as they were into ME. There is no evidence for such, but Jenner (*Handbook*, 17) suggests that the 'Matins' in Cornish, mentioned by Scawen, was a Primer, or Hours of Our Lady.
87. *Op. cit.*, 127.
88. See Jenner, *Handbook*, 12. The Reformation Church was, however, able to make some

plays, although it seems that the Cornish clung to these with considerable tenacity, as witness Carew. Nevertheless, their end, when it came, in the seventeenth century, must have also speeded the end of Cornish. Finally, the Reformation cut Cornwall off from Brittany, by severing the link of religion. Bretons comprised by far the largest foreign element in Cornish towns,[89] perhaps naturally, since their forebears had emigrated to Brittany from Devon and Cornwall about a thousand years previously, and they were of the same stock as the Cornish, culturally and linguistically as well as ethnologically, the two peoples almost certainly being mutually intelligible in language. They continued to settle in Cornwall in considerable numbers until the Reformation cut Cornwall off from Brittany, and they ceased to come over. Thus one more use of the Cornish language had gone.

Finally, the Civil War caused great social disruption in the county, and at the end of it conditions generally had undergone profound changes. What effect it had on the remnants of Cornish and those who spoke it is not clear, but involvement in the war must have meant one more break with the old ways and with isolated conditions.

The final 'invasions' of Cornwall came with the coaching era in the eighteenth century, but by this time Cornish was virtually defunct and beyond further damage. Likewise the tourist trade from the mid-nineteenth century onwards could affect only local English dialect.

From all accounts, it looks as though Cornish was given up early by the upper classes, and remained longest among the lower classes, so that at certain periods there would be in places of any size (e.g. Bodmin) a social stratification of languages, comparable with that which exists in present-day towns, where local regional dialect is largely correlated with lower to middle class residents, and Standard English (although to a lesser extent) with middle to upper class residents.[90] The question is not simply a geographical one, therefore, but also a social or sociolinguistic one (although in this book we are mainly concerned with its geographical aspects). Even as early as 1336, it was the principal parishioners of St Buryan who spoke English or French, while the last speakers of Cornish in the eighteenth century were fishermen and the like.[91] Among Scawen's 16 reasons for the decline of

---

concessions: note the article in BM Egerton MS. 2350 (f. 54a), one of a number drawn up *c.* 1560: "Item That it may be lawfull for such Welch or Cornish Children as can speake no English to learne the Promises in the Welsh Tongue or Cornish Language" (Jenner, *Handbook*, 13).

89. Rowse, *op. cit.*, 95–6.

90. Cf. B. Strang, *A History of English* (1970), 105; and 'The Tyneside Linguistic Survey', *Zeitschrift für Mundartforschung* (Beihefte, Neue Folge, Heft IV, 1968), 788–94; J.T. Wright, 'Urban Dialects: A Consideration of Method', *Zeitschrift f. M.*, xxxiii (1966), 232–46.

91. See D. Barrington, 'On the Expiration of the Cornish Language', *Archaeologia*, ii (1786), 279–84.

Cornish are several which attribute it to neglect of that language by the gentry.[92] There thus seems to be no doubt as to the low status of Cornish for at least the last 400 years of its history, and it is surprising, in view of this, that it lasted as long as it did.

Meanwhile, both the statements mentioned on pp. 89–92 above (Carew, Scawen, Gibson) and the present-day dialects of west Cornwall (see p. 21, above) appear to bear witness to the fact that the language in use in this area is somehow 'less dialectal', 'purer', more like Standard English, than in east Cornwall, Devon and Somerset. Earlier scholars have already borne witness to this, so that J. Bowring, writing in 1866, could say: "In the neighbouring county of Cornwall a rich vocabulary may be found of persons and places bearing British names, though even there many words have been Saxonized by time, and the English language has been universally introduced; not the local dialect of our own neighbouring county, but the English of the more educated classes."[93] O. Jespersen, writing more recently, gives comparable examples of languages used in greater 'purity' in districts originally outside their range: "In Cornwall and in the Scilly Islands, where Keltic was spoken till 150 years ago, I was struck by the 'pure' English talked by the peasantry, as compared for example with the dialect of the neighbouring county of Somerset."[94]

It will be argued that the English language in west Cornwall was introduced under the influence of education: speakers of Cornish in the Modern Cornish period would learn not the ancient Wessex dialects of east Cornwall, Devon and Somerset (although these nevertheless probably had some influence), but a version of English taught them in schools and by the upper classes and better-educated (note that it was the gentry who gave up Cornish and spoke English first), an English deliberately acquired, as distinct from a regional dialect passed on from generation to generation. In the next chapter, by taking specific examples, it is hoped to show what this means in phonological terms.

92. W. Scawen, *Antiquities Cornu-Britannick* (see pp. 23 and 91–2, above).
93. 'Language, with Special Reference to the Devonian Dialects', *TDA*, I.5 (1866), 32.
94. *Mankind, Nation and Individual* (1946), 53.

5 Phonological features of the dialects of Cornwall

In this chapter, four sets of features have been selected for consideration out of the full phonological inventory of the Cornish dialects. They have been chosen because they show phonological differences of a peculiar interest within the county, even though these differences occur only on a 'realizational' (i.e. phonetic) and not on a phonemic level, with the exception of 4, where there is a difference in phoneme distribution between areas. Moreover, the geographical distributions of these items have a special significance for the history of the English language in Cornwall. Items 2–4 have the further advantage of being well-known south-western dialectal problems which have exercised the ingenuity of scholars for some considerable time.

The items are as follows:
1. The reflexes of ME *a* (isolative and conditioned).
2. The reflexes of ME isolative *ǭ*, *u* and *iu*.
3. The reflexes of ME isolative *ū*.
4. The reflexes of ME initial *f*, *s*, *th*, *thr* and *sh*.

The material given in tabular form below, taken from vol. IV of *SED*, comprises data from the responses (rr.) given to the relevant phonological questions in the *Questionnaire* plus some other words. In addition, when useful, a certain amount of incidental material (i.m.) (which may or may not appear in the published vol. IV) is given in the tables, marked with a superior circle. When the word used is not an actual 'key-word' in *SED*, or at least part of a key-word, the latter is given in brackets following the word actually used, e.g. VI.11.9 matter (pus). 'Nr' means that the word under examination was for some reason not recorded.

In the Commentaries, the matter in smaller type relates to special phonological developments which require separate mention.

Spellings

Spellings of the ME and early MnE periods suggestive of sound-changes have not been widely sought as a substantiation for the theories proposed in this chapter. The weaknesses of the 'occasional spelling' theory and its application have been emphasized by E.J. Dobson[1] and are indeed widely recognized, especially those arising from the misprinting of manuscript readings and from misinterpretation of spellings. In any case, spellings of this type could be of only doubtful value as early representatives of the sounds under consideration here: what spellings could be unequivocally accepted as representing, for example, [æ] (see below), [y(:)] and [œy]? An attempt was made by W. Matthews in 'South Western Dialect in the Early Modern Period', *Neophilologus*, XXIV (1939), 193–209, to discover south-western spellings indicative of changing local pronunciations in the early MnE period, based on an examination of churchwardens' accounts and the like, chiefly of 1450–1500, from Bodmin, Stratton and St Ives. This is, however, neither of much use for present purposes (since spellings are not, in the main, adduced to support development of the sounds under consideration here), nor is it very satisfactory generally, for the usual reasons why occasional spellings generally speaking are not very satisfactory evidence – for example, it is very doubtful whether *e*-spellings would be used by native speakers for early MnE [æ] < ME *a* (cf. Dobson, 549). Early spellings of consonantal sounds, when available, seem from their very nature to offer more reliable evidence of actual pronunciations, and I have used these (for evidence of the voicing of ME *f*, *s*, etc.) more confidently.

The most important sources consulted by me are the place-name material in J.E.B. Gover, 'The Place-Names of Cornwall', and the English documents from Cornwall listed on pp. 86–7, above. I have also felt it reasonable to consult Devonshire material in cases where the reflexes of ME sounds are the same in Devon as in (part of) Cornwall (e.g. in that of ME ǭ), since here any significant spellings are obviously relevant to the whole area. In this connexion, I have noted no such spellings in the *Shillingford Letters* (ed. S.A. Moore [1871]) or in the records of the Exeter Gilds (ed. T. Smith, *English Gilds*, EETS, 40 [1870], 302–37). I have made use of *PND* and of B. Blomé, *The Place-Names of North Devonshire* (1929). Other, minor, sources, are mentioned in the Bibliography, below.

1. *English Pronunciation 1500–1700* (2nd edn, 2 vols, 1968), vol. I, viii–ix; vol. II, *passim*. (Hereafter cited as 'Dobson'.)

The reflexes of ME *a* (isolative and conditioned) (tables 1-8)

Table 1 ME isolative *a*

		1 Kilk	2 Alt	3 Egl	4 St E	5 Gw	6 St B	7 Mull
IV.9.4*	adder	a	a	a	a	a	a	æ
IV.8.7	apple- (wasps)	a	nr	a	a	a	a	æ
IV.11.8	apples	a	a	a	a	a	a	æ
V.4.4	ash	aι	aι	aι	aι	aι	æ	æ
V.1.14	ash-	aι	aι	aι	aι	nr	æ	æ
V.3.3	ash-	nr	nr	aι	aι	aι	æ	æ
V.4.5	ashes	aι	aι	aι	aι	aι	æ	æ
I.9.11	axle	a	a	a	a	æ	æ	æ
IX.1.7	backwards	a	a	a	a	æ	æ	a
V.7.11	bad	a	a	a	a	æ	æ	æ
IV.5.9	badger	æ	a	a	æ	æ	æ	æ
V.8.5†	bag	a	a	aι	æ	æ	æ	æ
VI.13.12	barrel	a	a	a	a	a	a	æ
IV.7.7	bat	a	a	a	nr °a	a	æ	æ
V.7.18	cabbage	a	a	a	a	æ	æ	æ
V.7.18	carrots	a	a	a	a	a	æ	æ
IX.3.8	catch	a °ε	æ °ε °a	æ °a	a	æ	æ	æ
VI.12.2	catching (infectious)	a	a	æ	a	æ	æ	æ
III.1.3	cattle	a	a	a	a	a	æ °a	æ
VI.14.16	flap	a	a	a	a (flat)	a	nr	æ
I.4.1	hay-rack	æ	a	a	æ	æ	æ	nr
VI.14.5	jacket	a	a	a	a	a	æ	æ
III.11.9	knacker	a	a	a	a	a	æ	æ
I.7.14	ladder	a	a	a	a	a	æ	æ
V.1.9	latch	æ	aˈ	nr	nr	æ	æ	æ
I.7.5	mallet	a	a	a	a	a	æ	æ
VIII.1.17	married	a	a	a	a	a	æ	a
IX.7.2	married	a	a	a	a	a	a	æ
VI.11.9	matter (pus)	a	a	a	a	a	a	æ
III.13.13	rabbits	a	a	a	a	a	a	æ

103

Table 1 (cont.)

		1 Kilk	2 Alt	3 Egl	4 St E	5 Gw	6 St B	7 Mull
IV.5.3	rat	a	a	a	a	a	a	æ
I.7.2	sack	a	a	a	æ	a	nr	æ
I.5.6	saddle	a	a	a	æ	a	a	æ
VII.4.5	Saturday	a	a	a	a	a	aᶠː	æ
III.4.4	stallion	a	a	a	a	a	æ	æ (stal)
VI.14.26	tag	aˡ	a	æ	aɩ	æ	æ	æ
VIII.8.6	that							
	(why)	a	a	a	a	a	nr	a
IX.10.1	that	a	a	a	a	a °æ	a °ɛ	a °æ
II.7.6	thatch	a	a	a	a	a	æ	æ
II.7.5	thatching	a	a	a	a	a	æ	æ
	thatcher	a	a	a	a	a	æ	æ

* *SED* reference numbers: the first numeral refers to the Book of the *SED* questionnaire in which the question eliciting the form given in the table appears, the second numeral to the relevant section of that Book, and the third to the question number. Thus IV.6.2 refers to Book IV, section 6, question 2.

† See also III.2.4:1 [aɩ] 2 [æ] 3 [a]; and III.5.2:3 [a] 5 [a].

Table 2 ME *a*+nasal

		1 Kilk	2 Alt	3 Egl	4 St E	5 Gw	6 St B	7 Mull
VI.10.7	ankle	a	a	a	a	a	æ	æ
VIII.4.10	anvil	a	a	a	æ	a	a	æ
VIII.1.12	aunt	a	a	a	a	a	æ	æ
IV.12.3	branch	a	a	a	a	a	æ	æ
II.2.10 (c)	dandelion	a	a	a	a	a	æ	a
IV.6.16	gander	a	a	a	a	æ	æ	æ
VIII.1.7	grandfather	a	a	a	a	a	a	a
	grandmother	a	a	a	a	a	a	a
VIII.1.8	grandfer (grand-dad)	a	a	a	a	a	a	a
	granny	a	a	a	a	a	a	a
I.7.13	hammer	a	a	a	a	a	æ	æ
VI.7.1	hand	a	a	a	a	a	æ	æ

Table 2 (cont.)

		1 Kilk	2 Alt	3 Egl	4 St E	5 Gw	6 St B	7 Mull
VI.7.13 (b)	-handed (right-h.)	a	a	a	a	a	æ	æ
VII.8.10	handful	a	a	a	a	a	æ	æ
I.3.16*	handle	nr	a	a	a	a	æ	a
I.8.2	handles	a	a	nr	a	a	a	a
II.9.8	hand-pins (handles)	a	a	a	a	nr	æ	æ
III.6.2/3	-lamb	a	a	a	a	æ	æ °a (v.)	æ
III.7.3	(-)lamb (pet-lamb)	a	a	a	a	æ	æ	æ
VIII.1.6	man	a	a	a	æ	æ	æ	æ
III.11.9	-man (knacker)	a	nr	a	æ	a	æ	æ
VIII.8.1	-man (bogey)	a	a	a	æ	æ	æ	æ
V.2.13	oil-lamp	a	a	a	a	a	æ	æ
VI.8.1	panting	a	a	a	a	a	æ	æ
V.2.7 (i.m.)	planch-	nr	nr	°a	°a	°a	°æ	°æ
III.6.7	ram	a	a	a	a	æ	æ	æ
III.6.2	ram-lamb (male lamb)	a	a	a	a	æ	æ	æ

* See also II.9.8:7 [æ].

Table 3 ME $a+f$, s, th

		1 Kilk	2 Alt	3 Egl	4 St E	5 Gw	6 St B	7 Mull
VII.3.11*	afternoon	a^r:	a^r:	$ɑ^r$: °a	a:	a: °æ: °æ	æ:	æ:
VII.3.14*	afternoon	a^r:	a^r:	°$ɑ^r$:	°a:	a:	æ:	æ:
IX.2.4†	ask	⁺a	a °a: °a	⁺a	a:	⁺æ °a: °æ:	⁺æ °æ: / °⁺a °⁺æ	⁺æ °a: / °⁺a °æ:
i.m.	cast	nr	nr	a:	æ:	a:	æ:	æ:
II.8.5	chaff	a:	a:	a:	a:	a:	æ:	æ:

Table 3 (cont.)

		1 Kilk	2 Alt	3 Egl	4 St E	5 Gw	6 St B	7 Mull
III.5.3	chaff	a:	a:	a:	a:	a	æ	æ:
VIII.9.3	daft (silly)	a:	a:	a:	æ:	æ:	æ:	æ:
VIII.9.4	daft (as)	a:	nr	a:	æ:	æ:	æ:	æ:
III.11.3	fasting- chamber	nr	nr	a:	a:	æ:	æ	æ:
II.9.1	grass	a:	a:	a:	a:	æ:	æ:	æ:
VII.2.2	last	a:	e:	a:	æ:	e: °a:	a: °æ:	æ:
VII.2.6	last	a:	e:	a:	æ:	e:	a:	æ:
VII.3.9	last	a:	e:	a:	æ: °a:	e:	æ:	æ:
VIII.1.25	master (my husband)	e:	e:	e:	nr	e:	nr	nr
IV.3.11	(-)path	a:	a:	a:	æ:	æ:	æ:	æ:

* Examples with *r*-colouring occur in forms such as [aᵗ:dn̥ʏ:n]. I.m. examples are of (unpublished) *after*.
† ⁺ denotes a metathesized form, i.e. *aks*.

Note also:
1 [a:] in nestle-draf 'weakling' III.8.4; staff-hook IV.2.5; past V.7.21. [a] in maskels 'caterpillars' (unpublished; in these cases no reference can be given).
2 [a:] in drafting III.11.2.
3 [a:] in cast p.p. [a] in passing II.6.10.
4 [a] in fasten.
5 [a:] in fast. [æ:] in draft-ewes III.6.6; fast; glass. [æ] in glasses.
6 [æ:] in pass.
7 [æ:] in draught (on plough); fast. [æ] in nasty.

Table 4 ME *al*+consonant or finally

		1 Kilk	2 Alt	3 Egl	4 St E	5 Gw	6 St B	7 Mull
i.m.	all	°ɔ:	°ɔ:	°ɔ:	°ɔ:	°ɔ:	°ɔ:	°ɔ:
VII.3.17	always	ɔ:	ɔ: °a	ɔ:	ɔ:	ɔ:	ɔ:	ɔ:
VI.2.3	bald(-)	a:	a	ɔ:	ɔ:	ɔ:	ɔ:	ɔ:
i.m.	ball	°a °a:	nr	nr	nr	nr	nr	°ɔ:
i.m.	call	°a: °ɔ:	°ɔ: °a °a:	°ɔ:	°ɔ:	°ɔ:	°ɔ:	°ɔ:
i.m.	fall	°a:	°ɔ: °a °a:	°ɔ:	°ɔ:	°ɔ:	°ɔ: e:	°ɔ:

Table 4 (cont.)

		1 Kilk	2 Alt	3 Egl	4 St E	5 Gw	6 St B	7 Mull
VI.11.4	gall (callosity)	a	a	ɔ:	ɔ:	ɔ:	nr	ɔ:
I.3.17	halter	a:	ɔ:	ɔ	ɔ	ɒ	ɒ	ɒ
I.4.2	halter (tethering-rope)	a:	ɔ:	ɒ	ɒ	ɒ	ɒ	ɒ
III.12.5	salt-	nr	°a °ɔ:	ɒ °ɔ:	°ɒ	°ɔ:	nr	nr
i.m.	small	°ɔ:	°ɔ:	°ɔ:	°ɔ:	°ɔ:	°o:	°ɔ:
i.m.	stalk	nr	°a	°ɒ	°ɒ	°⁺ɔ:	nr	°⁺ɔ:
I.3.1	stall	ɔ:	a	ɔ:	ɔ:	ɔ:	ɔ:	ɔ:
i.m.	talk	°a °⁺ɔ:	°a	°⁺ɔ:	°⁺ɔ:	°⁺ɒ °⁺ɔ:	°⁺ɔ:	°⁺ɔ:
VIII.7.10	walk	a	a ⁺ɔ:	ɒ	ɒ	⁺a: ⁺ɔ:	⁺ɔ:	⁺ɔ:

⁺ = l omitted.
Note also:
1 [ɒ] in palsy.
4 [ɔ:] in scald. [ɒ] in altered.
5 [ɔ:] in Cornwall; scald.
6 [a] in palsy. [a:] in spall 'break, hit' (of doubtful origin).
7 [ɔ:] in alter; scald.

Table 5 ME al+f, m

		1 Kilk	2 Alt	3 Egl	4 St E	5 Gw	6 St B	7 Mull
VI.9.7	calf (of leg)	a:	a:	a:	æ:	æ:	æ:	æ:
III.1.2	calf (the animal)	a:	a:	a: e:	æ:	æ:	æ:	e: °æ:
III.1.8	calf (the animal)	nr	a:	e:	æ:	æ:	æ:	e:
III.1.10	calf (the animal)	a:	a:	e:	æ:	æ:	æ:	e:ə

107

Table 5 (cont.)

	1 Kilk	2 Alt	3 Egl	4 St E	5 Gw	6 St B	7 Mull
III.1.11 calf (the animal)	a:	a:	e:	æ:	æ:	æ:	e:
III.1.2 calves (the animals)	a:	a:	a: e:	æ:	æ:	æ:	e: °æ:
VII.5.4* half	a:	a:	a:	a: °æ:	a: °e: °æ:	æ: °e:	æ:
VII.7.6 half-a- crown	a:	a:	e: °a:	a:	e:	æ:	æ:
VII.7.1 halfpenny	a	a	ɛ	ɛ:	ɛ:	e:	ɛ:
halfpenny- worth	a	a	ɛ	ɛ:	ɛ:	e:	ɛ:
VI.7.5 palm	a	a	æ	a	a	æ	æ:

Note: *l* is retained in *palm* except at loc. 7.
* See also IX.8.8:7 [e:ə].

Table 6 ME *a* following [(k)w]

		1 Kilk	2 Alt	3 Egl	4 St E	5 Gw	6 St B	7 Mull
i.m.	want	°ɒ	°ɒ	°ɒ	°ɒ	°ɒ °ɔ:	°ɒ	°ɒ
IV.5.4	want (mole)	a	a	a	a	ɒ	ɒ	ɒ
V.9.5	wash	aɩ	aɩ	aɩ °ɒɩ	ɒ	ɒ	ɒ	ɒ
IX.11.1	wash	aɩ	aɩ	ɒɩ	ɒ	ɒ	ɒ	ɒ
IV.8.7	wasps	ɒ	a	ɒ	ɒ	ɒ	ɒ	a
III.3.2	water	ɔ:	ɔ:	ɔ: °ɒ	ɔ:	ɔ:	ɔ:	ɔ:

Note also:
1 [a] in squat n.
2 [a] in squat n.
3 [ɒ] in watch n.
4 [ɒ] in straw-wad II.8.2.
5 [ɒ] in wattle- III.7.11.
7 [ɒ] in watch n.

Table 7 ME *a* following [(k)w] and before *r*

		1 Kilk	2 Alt	3 Egl	4 St E	5 Gw	6 St B	7 Mull
IV.4.6	quarry	nr	a	a	a	a	a	a
VII.8.1	quart	aʳː	aʳː	ɑʳː	aʳː	aʳː	ɔʳː	aʳː
VII.5.3*	quarter	aʳː	aʳː	ɑʳː	aʳː	aʳː	ɔʳː	aʳː
IX.2.9	warp	aʳː	aʳː	ɔʳː	aʳː	aʳː	aʳː	aʳː
VI.11.3	warts	əʳː	əʳː	əʳː	əʳː	əʳː	əʳː	əʳː

* See also VI.10.5:3 [aʳː].

Note also:
3 [aʳː] in warm.
7 [aʳː] in war.

Table 8 ME *ar* + consonant or finally (including ME *ar* < earlier *er*)

		1 Kilk	2 Alt	3 Egl	4 St E	5 Gw	6 St B	7 Mull
VI.6.8	arm	aʳː	aʳː	ɑːʳ	aʳː	aʳː	aʳː	aʳː
VII.8.10	armful	aʳː	aʳː	ɑʳː	aʳː	aʳː	aʳː	aʳː
VI.6.7	armpit	aʳː	aʳː	ɑʳː	aʳː	aʳː	aʳː	aʳː
VI.9.2	arse	a:	a:	a:	a:	æ: °a:	æ:	æ:
VIII.8.10	arse (beat)	a:	a:	a:	æ:	æ:	æ:	æ:
IX.1.10	arse (head over heels)	a:	a:	a:	a:	æ:	æ:	æ:
V.3.5	bar	aʳː	aʳː	ɑʳː	aʳː	aʳː	aʳː	aʳː
I.1.11	barn	aʳː	nr	nr °aʳː	aʳː	aʳː	aʳː	aʳː
I.9.3	cart	aʳː	aʳː °ɛəʳː	əʳː °ɑʳː	aʳː	əʳː	aʳː	aʳː
V.10.1	darning	aʳː	aʳː	ɑʳː	aʳː	aʳː	aʳː	aʳː
VIII.4.7	farmer	aʳː	aʳː	ɑʳː	aʳː	aʳː	aʳː	aʳː
I.1.2	farm-house (farmstead)	aʳː	aʳː	ɑʳː	aʳː	aʳː	aʳː	aʳː
VI.13.16	fart (to break wind)	aʳː	aʳː	ɑʳː	aʳː	aʳː	aʳː	aʳː

Table 8 (cont.)

		1 Kilk	2 Alt	3 Egl	4 St E	5 Gw	6 St B	7 Mull
i.m. I.5.1	hark harness	°aᵗ:	°aᵗ:	nr	°aᵗ:	°aᵗ:	°aᵗ:	°aᵗ:
	(to gear)	aᵗ:	aᵗ:	ɑᵗ:	aᵗ:	aᵗ:	aᵗ:	aᵗ:
VIII.6.2	start(s)							
	(begins)	aᵗ:	nr	ɑᵗ:	nr	aᵗ:	aᵗ:	nr
I.1.3	(-)yard	nr	nr	aᵗ:	aᵗ:	aᵗ:	aᵗ:	aᵗ:
I.1.9	-yard	aᵗ:	nr	nr	nr	aᵗ:	nr	aᵗ:

Note also:
2 [εᵗ:] in part.
3 [aᵗ:] in hard VIII.8.4; march. [ɔᵗ:] in shards.
4 [aᵗ:] in hard VIII.8.4.
5 [ɔᵗ:] in yard.
6 [aᵗ:] in hard VIII.8.4.
7 [aᵗ:] in hard VIII.8.4.

Note. In St Cleer the reflexes of ME isolative *a* and *a*+nasal are [a], [æ] and variants. N.C. approached or actually used [æ] more often than W.H.L., who usually (but by no means always) gave [ạ], [a], etc. For the reflexes of ME *a*+*f*, *s*, *th*, N.C. varies between an [a:] type, sometimes retracted or raised, and [æ:]. W.H.L. has an [a:] type, but [ɑ:] was heard in *daft* and *father*. [ɔ:] is invariable for ME *al*+consonant or finally except in *halter* ([ɒ·~ɒ]). There were no examples of unrounding in any words. ME *al*+*f*, *m* gave [æ:] in *calves*, [a:] in *half*, and [ɑ:] in *palm*. For ME *a* following [(k)w], [ɔ:] in *water* was the only example recorded. For ME *a* following [(k)w] and before *r*, [ɒ] was heard in *quarry* and [ɔᵗ·] in *quart* and *quarter*. For ME *ar*+consonant or finally, a large number of variants of two basic types were heard, namely of [ɑ:] and [ɒ:] (once [ɜ·]) followed by *r* or *r*-colouring. These two types were sometimes hard to distinguish, and intermediate types were recorded, e.g. [ɑ:] with rounding, and [ɒ:] with unrounding. [aᵗ] was recorded, but only as an infrequently occurring type.

In St Day, ME isolative *a* and *a*+nasal is [a], [ạ], and [æ] does not occur. Before *f*, *s*, *th*, ME *a* emerged as an [a:] type, sometimes retracted or raised. [ɑ:] was heard twice. [ɔ:] is invariable for ME *al*+consonant or finally. ME *al*+*f*, *m* gave [a:] and [ä:] in *half*. For ME *a* following [(k)w], no relevant words were recorded. For ME *a* following [(k)w] and before *r*, [ɒ·] was heard in *quarries* and [ɔᵗ:] in *quart* and *quarter*. For ME *ar*+consonant or finally, [aᵗ(:)] is the usual type; [æᵗ·] was recorded once, and [ɑᵗ:] once.

It will be part of our task throughout this chapter to compare the findings of *SED* in respect of the features under examination with material collected by A.J. Ellis in the only other survey of the phonology of dialectal English, namely *EEP*. Unfortunately Ellis (pp. 167–74) does not provide many examples of the reflexes of ME *a*, and since there are not enough of them to warrant a division into historical categories, I give Ellis's information simply as it appears in the recordings from his localities in Cornwall.

Millbrook   æ (IPA [æ]) is recorded in *bad, hath, past, as, call, asked.*
ar (IPA [ɑɹ]) is recorded in *farmer.*

Camelford   a (IPA [ɑ]) is recorded in *that, hand, chap.*
AA (IPA [ɔ:]) is recorded in *all.*
aR (IPA [ɑɾ]) is recorded in *larn* 'learn'.

Cardinham   æ is recorded in *hand, chance.*
oo (IPA [o:]) is recorded in *all.*

St Columb Major æ is recorded in *hand, chap.*
ee (IPA [e:]) is recorded in *chance.*
aa (IPA [ɑ:]) is recorded in *all.*

Marazion   æ is recorded in *Jacky, exactly, Samaritan, parish, as,*
tantrums, man, packman, cat.
a is recorded in *after.*
áɐ (IPA [ɑ·ə]) is recorded in *last.*
AA is recorded in *always, all.*
ææ (IPA [æ:]) is recorded in *laugh, half.*
ɔ (IPA [ɒ]) is recorded in *wasn't, what.*
éɐ (IPA [ɛ·ə]) is recorded in *-dancers, last.*
ee (IPA [ɛ:]) is recorded in *hall-* (cf. *fall*, table 4, above).

It is clear from the above that Ellis records [æ] in isolative position nearly always except in Camelford, a result partially in accord with the *SED* findings. Ellis's [ɑ] in Camelford (north-east Cornwall) corresponds with [a] in *SED* localities 1 and 2, but the rest of the county presents an over-simplification compared with the *SED* recordings for localities 3–7, which show both [a] and [æ]. Due allowance must, of course, be made for the possibly unreliable testimony of Ellis's informants, especially with regard to these two similar sounds.

With regard to the reflexes of ME *a* in combinative positions, we should note that:

A long vowel is recorded in *chance* at St Columb Major and in *-dancers* at Marazion. *SED* records no long vowels in such contexts.

ME *a+f, s, th* often remains short, as sometimes in the *SED* recordings.

[æ] is recorded in *call* at Millbrook; [ɑ:] in *all* at St Columb Major; and [ɛ:] in *hall-* and [æ:] in *half* at Marazion. The rest have an [ɔ:] type. Cf. the *SED* recordings for ME *al*+consonant or finally, and for ME *al*+*f*, *m*.

[ɒ] in *wasn't* and *what* at Marazion accords with the recordings at *SED* locality 7.

Again, we can say that these results are at least partially in accord with the *SED* findings, although not consistently so. But there is not enough data for a really adequate comparison.

Commentary

ME isolative *a*

There seems good reason for accepting [a] as the starting point of the development of early MnE *a* < ME *a*. According to both H.C. Wyld[2] and E.J. Dobson,[3] the later pronunciation [æ] (which, outside dialect, is now a feature only of older, careful Standard English, gradually being replaced by [a] and even [ɑ]) was an importation from dialectal speech. According to Dobson, ME *a* began to become [æ] in dialectal and vulgar speech in the fifteenth century. It became [æ] in "less careful" Standard English in the late sixteenth century, and was an accepted pronunciation by careful speakers *c.* 1670. Although partly based on 'occasional spellings' the evidence of which is doubtful, Wyld reaches more or less the same conclusions, but puts the full acceptance of [æ] towards the end of the sixteenth century. But, as Dobson suggests, both doubtless existed side by side in the sixteenth and seventeenth centuries.

The modern reflexes of ME isolative *a* in Cornwall are seen from the tables above to fall into two types, [a] and [æ]. ([aɪ], occurring before certain consonants, will be discussed below.) It will be noted that [a] is almost invariable in localities 1–3, that [a] and [æ] both occur in localities 4 and 5, although [a] is greatly predominant, and that [æ] is virtually invariable in localities 6 and 7. Summed up, [æ] becomes more prevalent as one goes towards the west, although it does, in fact, occur in varying degrees in all the localities with the virtual exception of 1 and 2. It is impossible, therefore, to draw a single isogloss separating the two types.[4]

From the accompanying map of *apples* (map 8), it will be seen that in the greater part of England ME *a* remains as [a], and that the pronunciation [æ] (sometimes raised to [ɛ]) is an eastern dialectal type, from which area we may infer that – as is the case with many other of the items mentioned below – it was adopted into Standard English as Dobson and Wyld suggest. Although

2. *A Short History of English* (3rd, rev. edn, 1927), §217.
3. *Op. cit.*, 545ff. and especially 547–8.
4. On the general inconsistency of isoglosses, see L. Bloomfield, *Language* (1933), §19.4.

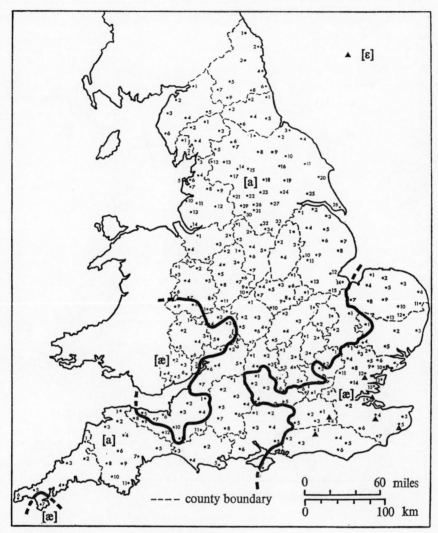

Map 8. The vowel in apples (SED *IV.11.8*).

certain other western areas beside Cornwall also have [æ] as the reflex of ME isolative *a* – notably an area to the north-west of the River Severn and a considerable part of Somerset – its occurrence in west Cornwall is separated from these by a large [a] area, and is consequently here regarded as an independent development. It will be argued that, in fact, [æ] in west Cornwall is not, strictly speaking, a 'development' (in the sense of a gradual progression

113

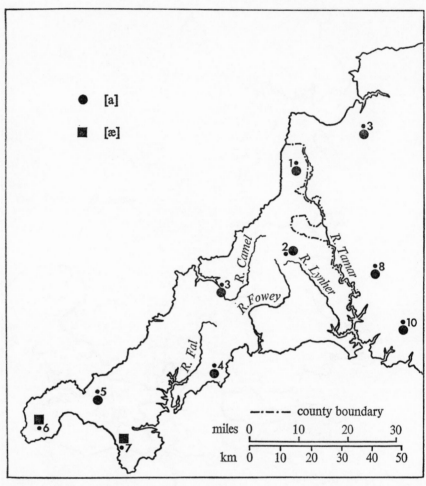

Map 9. The vowel in hand (SED *VI.7.1*).

from one sound to another) at all, but that it is the result of the adoption
of a Standard English sound after this eastern dialectal type had been introduced into Standard English, that in Cornwall [a] is the true south-western
dialectal type, as seen in localities 1 and 2, etc., while [æ] is an old Standard
English type, introduced into the county since the seventeenth century, and
still present there in varying degrees, but pre-eminently in places where the
English language was introduced late. We may legitimately expect the reflexes
to be mixed, due, perhaps, among other things, to the piecemeal adoption of
English in the west of the peninsula.

114

Diphthongized forms [aɪ] or [aˑ] occur in *ash*(-) (localities 1–5), *ashes* (1–5), *bag* (1, 3), *latch* (2), *tag* (1, 4), *old-fashioned* (2, additional material), *smashed* (3, additional material), and also in *wash* (see p. 123, below). This is a south-western palatalization, which takes place in [a], [ɛ] and [ɒ] before [ʃ],[5] [ʧ], [ʤ] and [g], cf. IV.6.4 *eggs*, *fresh* under V.7.8 (*insipid*), IX.8.7 *legs*, V.9.5 *wash*; and also IV.2.1 *hedge*. It will be noted that the diphthongal forms cited above are restricted to localities 1–5, and more especially 1–3.

Catch in localities 1 and 2 shows [ɛ] forms: these are widespread in dialect (cf. *SED*, IV, IX.3.8), and go back to a ME *e* type, *kecchen*.[6]

ME *a* before a nasal

The reflexes of ME *a* (which alternates with *o* in spelling) before a nasal follows the same general pattern as those of ME isolative *a*. No exception to this pattern is found in French words, e.g. *aunt*, *branch*, *glance*, *chance*, *plant(ed)*, (also unpublished), which throughout Cornwall, according to the *SED* transcriptions, have fallen in with the regular development of ME isolative *a*, giving [a] in localities 1–5, and [æ] in localities 6 and 7.

Short forms in French words of the *aunt*, *branch* class are generally assumed to derive from short forms in ME, which inherited them from continental French [a] as distinct from AN [aɔ].[7] Their presence in Cornwall is, however, puzzling, since they are chiefly characteristic of the north Midlands and north of England. It may be, therefore, that the [a~æ] of these words is simply the vowel sound of English words which for some reason has been extended to and has now overlaid an earlier sound developed from AN [aɔ], represented in the medieval Cornish documents by an *o* spelling (*donssye* 'dance', *chons* 'chance', *gronntye* 'grant', *plontye* 'plant') which presumably indicates an attempt at pronouncing the nasalized French sound.

ME *a* before *f*, *s*, *th*

In present-day Standard English, ME *a* before *f*, *s*, *th* appears as [ɑ:], except in the north and part of the Midlands, where [a] is retained. The traditional view of the development of ME *a* in these positions is exemplified by Wyld,[8] who proposes a series:

ME *a* > [æ] > [æ:] > [ɑ:]

Dobson suggests that ME *a* before *f*, *s*, *th* remained everywhere instead of being raised to [æ] as usual, and was then lengthened to [a:],[9] from which

5. Cf. the [i:] and [ʏ:] forms in *brush*, below.
6. See Dobson, 564, §70.
7. See J. and E.M. Wright, *An Elementary Historical New English Grammar* (1924), §85.
8. *Op. cit.*, §219.
9. §50. Lengthening is revealed by orthoepistic evidence only towards the end of the seventeenth century (in Cooper), but probably occurred much earlier than the time at which it was accepted into 'careful speech'.

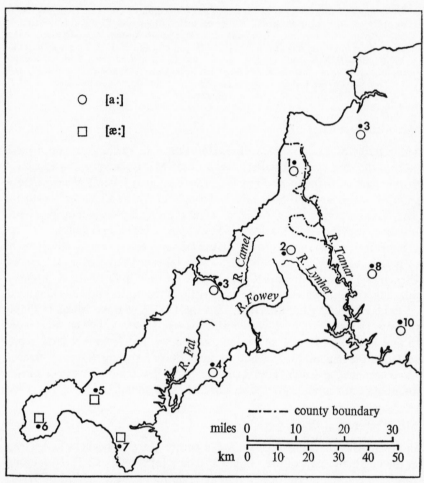

Map 10. The vowel in grass (SED *II.9.1*).

both dialectal [æ:] and Standard English [ɑ:] can easily develop, thus:

$$\text{ME } a > [\text{a:}] > \begin{cases} [\text{æ:}] \text{ dialectal} \\ [\text{ɑ:}] \text{ Standard English} \end{cases}$$

ME *a* before *f*, *s*, *th* in Cornwall follows a very similar pattern to that of ME isolative *a*, but with lengthened forms. [a:] alone (except for [e:]) is characteristic of localities 1–3, [æ:] is present in varying degrees in localities 4–7, and especially in 5–7. The metathesized forms in *ask* (i.e. *aks*) are not,

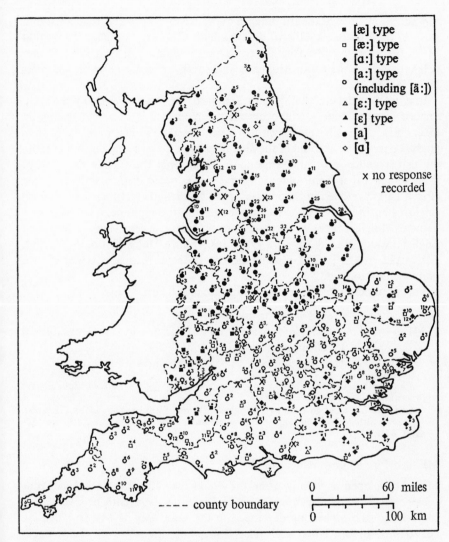

Map 11. *The vowel in* chaff (SED *II.8.5*).

of course, lengthened, but lengthening has also been resisted in some other cases, e.g. (unmetathesized) *ask* (2, i.m.), *chaff* (5, 6), *passing* (3, additional material), *fasten* (4, additional material). There appears to be no distributional pattern in the retention of these short forms, which occur sporadically in the south of England as well as regularly in the north (see map 11).

As in the case of ME isolative *a*, it will be argued here that [æ:] represents

117

the adoption of a Standard English type, while [a:] is the regular south-western (and indeed southern) development. (The map of *chaff* shows that ME *a* before a voiceless fricative consonant remains short in the north, but is lengthened in the south Midlands and south, its usual reflex in the latter being [a:].)

It is proposed here that [ɑ:] in Standard English is originally a south-eastern dialectal type – it appears on the map in this area – replacing an older [æ:] in the eighteenth century. (Replacement seems more likely than gradual change, on account of the dissimilarity of the two sounds, and because the usual tendency in modern English is towards the further fronting of front vowels.) It was this older [æ:] that was adopted in Cornwall sometime after it had developed in Standard English as a lengthened form of Standard English [æ]. Indeed, if we are to regard [æ:] in these phonetic contexts as a Standard English type, we are bound to postulate an [æ:] stage in Standard English, which would support Wyld (as against Dobson) up to a point, but would regard [ɑ:] as a south-eastern dialectal intrusion rather than a phonetic development.

This argument may be represented in tabular form:

$$\text{ME } a+f,\ s,\ th \begin{cases} \text{remains in the north} \\ > [\text{æ}] \text{ (from eastern dialect)} > [\text{æ:}],\ \text{and is replaced by } [\text{ɑ:}] \\ \quad \text{(from eastern dialect)} \\ \text{remains and} > [\text{a:}] \text{ in the south and south-west} \end{cases}$$

South-western dialectal forms such as [aᵗ:dɳʏ:n], [ɑᵗ:dəᵗ:] *after(noon)* are recorded in localities 1–3 only.

Last with [e:] must go back to an original ME long form, perhaps *lātest*, OE *latost*.

Master with [e:] is a widely-occurring variant of the Standard English type. See *SED*, VIII.1.25.

ME *al* before a consonant or finally

ME *al* developed a glide between the *a* and the following dark *l* and thus became [aɷɫ] in the fifteenth century.[10] Thereafter (sixteenth to seventeenth centuries),[11] the diphthong developed in the same way as ME isolative *au*, i.e. to [ɔ:]. Before labial and velar consonants the velar [ɫ] disappeared, giving, for example, [tɔ:k] and [tʃɔ:k] beside [ɔ:ɫ]. In certain phonetic circumstances,[12] however, there was a failure of diphthongization, either generally or occasionally, apparently because a dark [ɫ] did not regularly occur in the circumstances in question.

10. Dobson, §60 (suggests *c*. 1400). Wyld, *op. cit.*, §218, states that the diphthong, or some later development of it, "is fully established at least as early as the third quarter of the fifteenth century".

11. Dobson, §235.

12. Enumerated by Dobson, as shown by the orthoepists, *loc. cit.*

The examples in table 4 show a south-western failure to diphthongize and thus to become [ɔ:] in localities 1 and 2, once – in the case of *walk* – in locality 5, and twice (additional material *palsy*, *spall*) in locality 6. Diphthongization fails in *always* probably because of the following [w], and in *halter*, *salt-*, *stalk*, *talk* and *walk* apparently because of the following voiceless consonant. There seems to be no special reason why it should have failed in *bald*, *ball*, *call*, *fall*, *gall* and *stall*, also *palsy* and *spall*, especially since in this dialect *l* before a consonant and final *l* are consistently dark. Some of the [a] forms show lengthening to [a:], but this may be simply emphatic, or perhaps analogical with the long vowel in the equivalent Standard English forms.

It should be noted that these non-Standard English, south-western dialectal forms are with few exceptions confined to localities 1 and 2. It should also be noted that [ɫ] in *stalk*, *talk* and *walk* is sometimes retained, but only in localities 1–4.

Generally speaking, from this evidence it looks as if failure to diphthongize is a lot commoner in the south-western dialects than in Standard English. It also seems to fail in a variety of different phonetic contexts (e.g. finally) in addition to the more usual ones. This suggests that the diphthongization was a rather less universal feature than it appears to be when the Standard English development alone is considered.

Fall with [e:][13] must go back to an original form having ME *ā* < earlier *au*, as in the forms of *calf*, *half* (below). Dobson quotes a number of words in which late ME *ā* is shown before *l*, e.g. *all*, *small*, *balls*, *hall*, *tall*.[14] Cf. Ellis's Marazion *ee* (IPA [ɛ:]) in *hall-* (above).

Halter, *salt*, *stalk*, *walk* (also additional material *altered*, *palsy*) having [ɒɫ] are probably shortened variants of the ordinary Standard English form (i.e. [ɔ:ɫ] or [ɔ:]) shown in other words.[15] [tɒk] *talk* (locality 5) is a peculiarity not easily explained, showing both a shortened form and loss of *l*. The form [wa:k] *walk* (locality 5) presupposes failure of diphthongization, and the usual loss of *l* with compensatory lengthening (but on lengthening, cf. above).

ME *al* before *f, m*

In present-day Standard English, words such as *calf*, *half*, *palm* have [ɑ:]. Wyld proposes[16] a series:

ME *a* > [aɷ] > [ɑ:] > [æ:] > [ɑ:]

and states: "Thus the career of the vowel in *calf* was, after a certain point,

13. Cf. the transcriptions *fæl*, *væəl*, *vǣl* given for Wilts and Somerset in *EDG* (see Index *Fall*).
14. §104 (3) (b).
15. Cf. D. Jones, *An Outline of English Phonetics* (9th edn, 1962), §300.
16. *Op. cit.*, §260, following K. Luick, *Historische Grammatik der englischen Sprache* (1914–40), §521.

identical with that in *chaff*" (i.e. ME *a* > [æ] > [æ:] > [ɑ:]). Dobson proposes:[17]

ME *a* > [aɷ] > [a:]

[a:] then goes on to [ɑ:] or [æ:] (as in *chaff*, etc., cf. above) instead of to [ɔ:], the regular development (as in *bald*, *small*). He suggests that the development to [a:] is a Cockney or an eastern dialectal one, belonging perhaps to the late sixteenth century, and not making its way into Standard English until a century later.

After [aɷɫ] had lost the [ɫ] before labial consonants (in the sixteenth century), the normal development was to [ɔ:], but a special development, analogous to that of ME *sauven* > *sāven* > MnE [sɛɪv], took place in the southern dialects: the [ɷ] was assimilated to the following labial consonant, and the first element was lengthened to [a:], which became [æ:] in the late seventeenth century, and was adopted from the eastern dialects by Standard English, ousting the normal [ɔ:] (< [aɷ]). The [æ:] was itself later replaced by modern [ɑ:]. Thus in tabular form:

$$[aɫ] > [aɷɫ] > \begin{cases} [ɔ:] \text{ (normal development)} \\ [a:] \text{ (special southern development)} > [æ:], \text{ whence adopted} \\ \quad \text{into Standard English} \end{cases}$$

In Cornwall, *calf* and *half*, etc., show a very similar development to *chaff*, *grass*, etc., having [a:] in the east of the county and [æ:] (beside [e:], or [e:ə], see below, p. 122) in the centre and west. Except in locality 7, *palm* has a similar development to words containing ME isolative *a*, with retention of the *l*. In the south-west of England generally, [æ:] in *calf* (see map 12) occurs in 28 localities out of a total of 59 in Cornwall, Devon, Somerset, Dorset, Wilts, Hants and Gloucs, a dialectal type existing side by side with [a:], which latter is the regular development in most of the south, as distinct from [ɔ:] in the north and north Midlands. An [ɑ:] type seems either to have replaced or to have developed from an older sound in Standard English and parts of the east of the country (as shown on the map).

It should be noted that [æ:] occurs in *calf*, *half* only in central and west Cornwall: in localities 1–3 [a:] is recorded. It is possible to derive this [æ:] from a Standard English type which has now been replaced by [ɑ:], and of which a possible relic remains in north Norfolk (see the map). The fact that the remainder of the south-west of England often has [æ:], e.g. in Devon, Gloucs, etc. (above), is of no consequence: in these cases, the [æ:] may be either of a now archaic Standard English type (as is suggested for central and west Cornwall) or of a genuine south-western dialectal type. Which it is does not concern us here.

17. §238.

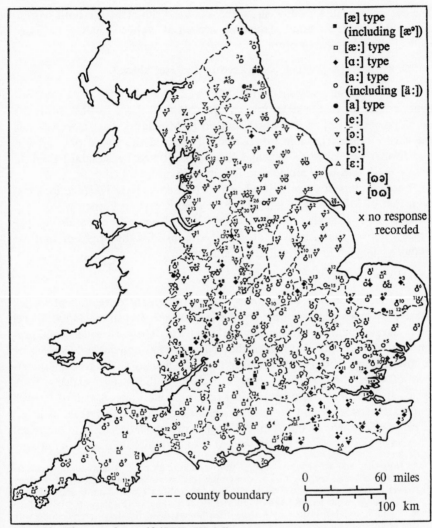

Map 12. The vowel in calf (SED *III.1.2*).

According to Wyld's theory mentioned above, the vowels in *chaff* and *calf* fell together at the [æ:] stage, and then went on to [ɑ:] together. The very similar distribution of the reflexes in the two types in Cornwall would seem to support this supposition up to a point. The localities show the following series:

	1	2	3	4	5	6	7	
chaff	a:	a:	a:	a:	a:	æ:	æ:	(II.8.5)
calf	a:	a:	a:	æ:	æ:	æ:	°æ:	(III.1.2)

121

The east Cornwall localities show the same development for both words, and so do localities 6 and 7. However, instead of Wyld's suggested development, I should prefer to propose for *chaff*, in Standard English:

ME *a* > [æ] > [æ:], which is replaced by [ɑ:] (see above)

We may summarize by saying that Cornwall, along with the other southern counties, shares in the development of [aɔł] to [a:] (as distinct from the development to [ɔ:] in the north and north Midlands). East Cornwall has the earlier type [a:], while west Cornwall received the sound only *after* it had further developed to [æ:] and had been adopted by Standard English, but *before* it had been replaced in Standard English by [ɑ:].

The development to [e:], [e:ə] in *calf* (the animal) and *half* is identical with that of ME *ā* and of late ME *ā* from *au* in certain French words, e.g. *chamber*, *safe*. It is also found in Dorset, and cf. *fall*, discussed above. The process here is the same as that described above for the origin of [æ:] (= Standard English [ɑ:]) in *calf*, *half*, namely:

[ał] > [aɔł] > [a:]

except that in the case of *calf*, *half* containing [e:] the development to [a:] must have taken place in time for the [a:] to take part in the Great Vowel Shift development to present-day [e:], [ɛɪ], etc. There is evidence of pronunciations of a ME *ā* origin in the orthoepists, as convincingly shown by Dobson,[18] and there is also evidence that this change was at first characteristic of vulgar or dialectal speech, especially of the eastern dialects, from which it made its way in some cases (e.g. *safe*, etc.) into Standard English during the sixteenth and seventeenth centuries. It looks, therefore, as if [e:] in *calf*, *half* could be an old Standard English pronunciation (this development does, in any case, account for the present Standard English sound in *ha'penny*).

Halfpenny and *halfpennyworth* show short and long forms. The short forms (localities 1–3) are dialectal, and are due to shortening (before a consonant cluster) of the long vowel at different stages of its development. Localities 1 and 2 show shortening at the [a:] stage, while locality 3 shows shortening at the final or [ɛ:] stage. [ɛ:] in localities 4, 5 and 7, and [e:] in locality 6 show (like Standard English [ɛɪ]) identification with the reflexes of ME *ā* (cf. above).[19]

ME *a* following [(k)w]

After [w] and [kw], ME *a* > [ɒ] in Standard English, as in *want*, *wash*, except before velar consonants, e.g. *wag*, *quack*. The rounding is probably again dialectal and vulgar in origin, starting in the eastern dialects in the fifteenth century, and not being finally accepted in Standard English until sometime

18. §104.
19. Cf. Dobson, 794.

in the eighteenth century.[20] In some dialects this rounding often did not take place at all. In Cornwall, as usual, there is a mixture of Standard English and dialectal types, the latter being mostly confined to localities 1–3:

Want v. and *water* show the Standard English type throughout, except that *want* shows lengthening at locality 5, and *water* has short [ɒ] at locality 3.

Want n. has the dialectal type in localities 1–4 and the Standard English type in localities 5–7.

Wash has the dialectal type in localities 1–3 and the Standard English type in localities 4–7. The dialectal type shows the usual diphthongization before [ʃ] (see p. 115, above).

Wasps shows the Standard English type except at localities 2 and 7.

ME *a* following [(k)w] and before *r*

Before a following *r*, ME *wa-* and *kwa-* > [wɔ:] and [kwɔ:] in Standard English, i.e. lengthening takes place. This is not so, however, when the *r* is followed by a vowel, e.g. in *warren*, *quarrel*. In the dialects, rounding and, therefore, lengthening often did not take place.

In Cornwall ME *a* following [(k)w] and before *r* shows a dialectal type throughout (usually [aᵉ:], but [ɑᵉ:] at locality 3, cf. below), except that the Standard English [ɔ:] (with *r*-colouring, however) occurs in *quarter* at locality 6 and in *warp* at locality 3. Raising and centralizing to [əᵉ:], presumably a further development from [aᵉ:] under the influence of the preceding [(k)w], was recorded in *quart* at locality 6 and in *warts* throughout.

ME *ar* before a consonant or finally

In present-day Standard English, ME *ar* appears as [ɑ:]. The *r* was first vocalized to [ə]-consonant, and then disappeared, the vowel preceding it meanwhile being lengthened and retracted, thus:

$$[a^r:] > [aə] > [ɑ:ə] > [ɑ:]^{21}$$

Whatever type of *r* ME is regarded as having had (it presumably varied dialectally), the southern dialects almost certainly had [ɹ] (from the OE West Saxon dialect) as they do today. In the south, then, [aᵉ:] descends from ME *ar* probably with little or no change.

According to *SED*, [aᵉ:] is the usual reflex of ME *ar* in Cornwall; [ɑᵉ:] occurs, but only in locality 3 (cf. above).[22]

20. See Dobson, §194, and especially n. 3.
21. According to Wyld, *op. cit.*, §222, ME *ar* > [ær] > [æ:r] (seventeenth century) > [ɑ:].
22. Lengthening of ME *a* regularly results in [a:] in the southern counties in all contexts (cf. ME *a+f, s, th*): [ɑ:] is a south-eastern and Standard English type. From my own listening to the tape-recordings from Cornwall, I have only been able to hear [aᵉ:] throughout, but this may have been an attempt at a Standard English pronunciation, adopted for the benefit of the investigators.

Arse shows no *r*-colouring throughout, but its vowel has fallen in with the development of ME *a* before *f*, *s*, *th*: localities 1–4 have [aː], and localities 5–7 [æː]. The loss of *r*-colouring and the subsequent development of the vowel are probably due to popular identification of the word with *ass*.[23]

[ɛəᵗ:] in *cart* and [ɛᵗ:] in (additional material) *part* at locality 2 may derive from ME lengthened types, as in *care*.

[əᵗ:] in *cart* at localities 3 and 5 and in *yard* at locality 5 (additional material) are centralized forms which are, however, difficult to account for. In *cart*, [əᵗ:] may be a further development from the lengthened form as shown in locality 2 (above); in *yard*, initial [j] may account for the centralization.

[əᵗ:] in (additional material) *shards* (< OE *sceard*, sg.), at locality 3, is the result of a retraction, over-rounding and raising ([aᵗ:] > [ɑᵗ:] > [ɒᵗ:] > [əᵗ:]) found in south-west England.[24]

Although marked differences of pronunciation occur in Cornwall, the *SED* transcriptions do not show any significant isoglosses in the distribution of the reflexes of ME *ar* (before a consonant or finally). It may be suggested, however, that the [ɑᵗ: ~ ɒᵗ:] type (with dialectal retraction and over-rounding) is probably mostly confined to east Cornwall, while [aᵗ:] predominates in the west.

Conclusion

The present-day reflexes of ME *a* in Cornwall, both isolative and conditioned, generally speaking fall into two types:

1. ME isolative *a* appears as [a] (localities 1–5).[25]

   ME *a* before a nasal appears as [a] (1–5).
   ME *a* before *f*, *s*, *th* appears as [aː] (1–4).
   ME *al* before a consonant or finally appears as [a(ː)] (1, 2).
   ME *al* before *f*, *m* appears as [aː] (1–3).
   ME *a* following [(k)w] varies between [ɒ]/[ɔː] and [a] (1–3).
   ME *a* following [(k)w] and before *r* appears as [aᵗ:], [əᵗ:], etc. (1–7).
   ME *ar* before a consonant or finally appears as [aᵗ:] (1–7).

2. ME isolative *a* appears as [æ] (localities 6, 7).
   ME *a* before a nasal appears as [æ] (6, 7).
   ME *a* before *f*, *s*, *th* appears as [æː] (5–7).
   ME *al* before a consonant or finally appears as [ɔː] or [ɒ] (3–7).
   ME *al* before *f*, *m* appears as [æː] (4–7).
   ME *a* following [(k)w] most frequently appears as [ɒ] or [ɔː] (4–7).

23. *Ass* is hardly current at all either in dialect or Standard English now. *r*-colouring in *arse* is regularly lost in the southern counties, but sometimes occurs in the south-east.
24. On this type and its early orthographic representation, see U. Jacobsson, *Phonological Dialect Constituents in the Vocabulary of Standard English* (1962), 191–4.
25. In my own listening to the available tape-recordings, I heard only [æ ~ ɐ] in locality 5 as the reflex of ME isolative *a* and *a*+ nasal.

ME *a* following [(k)w] and before *r* appears as [aᵗ:], [əᵗ:], etc. (1–7).
ME *ar* before a consonant or finally appears as [aᵗ:] (1–7).

This is a very general statement, not taking into account the numerous exceptions and the special developments described at various points above, but simply listing contrasting types as they appear in two areas.

The conclusions to be drawn from the data summarized above are, at least in some respects, plain. It must be more than mere chance that the reflexes of ME *a* are distributed as they are. Consideration of their distribution in the light of other phonological developments studied in detail below supports a conclusion that the sounds developing from ME *a* mainly in the western half of the county represent fairly consistently developments which can be identified with those of Standard English, while those in the eastern part are identical with south-western dialectal types.

A point which must be raised, though – for lack of evidence – it can hardly be adequately considered, is the possibility that [æ(:)], etc., in west Cornwall is the result of influence from a Cornish substratum. The difficulty is that it is not at all clear precisely how Cornish *a* was pronounced. It might be argued, perhaps, that British *a* had something of an [æ] quality, since it appears in early Anglo-Saxon names with substitution of OE *æ* except when followed by a back vowel in the next syllable, but this is simply adaptation to the OE sound-pattern. Later, British *a* may appear in OE as *a* in any circumstances,[26] and no inferences about the value of the (now Cornish) sound (i.e. whether [a] or [æ]) are possible.

The reflexes of ME isolative ọ̄ (table 9)

Table 9 ME isolative ọ̄

		1 Kilk	2 Alt	3 Egl	4 St E	5 Gw	6 St B	7 Mull
III.13.6	another, tother							
	(fight each other)	ʌ	ʌ	ʌ	ʌ	ʌ	ʌ	ʌ
VI.2.8	(an)other's, tother's							
	(pull each other's)	ʌ	ʌ	ʌ	ʌ	ʌ	ʌ	ʌ
VI.10.2	bare-footed							
	(barefoot)	Y	Y	ɷ	ɷ	ɷ	ɷ	ɷ
VI.14.23	boots	Y	Y	u:	u:	u:	u:	u:
IX.8.6	boots	Y:	Y	u:	u:	u:	u:	u:

26. See *LHEB*, §3.

Table 9 (cont.)

		1 Kilk	2 Alt	3 Egl	4 St E	5 Gw	6 St B	7 Mull
VIII.1.5	brother	ι	ε	ʌ	ʌ	ʌ	ʌ	ʌ
V.3.5 (b)	crook	ʏ	ʏ	ω	ω	ω	ω	ω
IV.1.4	flood(ed) (in flood)	nr	ʌ	ʌ	ʌ	ʌ	ʌ	ʌ
VI.10.1	foot	ʏ	ʏ	ω	ω	ω	ω	ω
VI.10.10	foot (feet)	ʏ	ʏ	nr	ω	ω	ω	ω
III.6.5	four/ two-tooth (gimmer)	ʌ	ʏ	u:	u:	u:	nr	u:
i.m.	good	°ʏ	°ʏ	°ω	°ω	°ω	°ω	°ω
VI.14.7	gloves	ʌ	ʌ	ʌ	ʌ	ʌ	ʌ	ʌ
IV.6.15	goose	ʏ:	ʏ:	u:	u:	u:	u:	u:
VI.5.10	gums	ʌ	ʌ	ʌ	ʌ	ʌ	ʌ	ʌ
III.2.8	hoof	ʏ	ʏ:	u:	u:	u:	u:	ʌ
III.4.10	hoofs	ʏ:	ʏ:	u:	u:	u:	u:	ʌ
VII.4.2	Monday	ʌ	ʌ	ʌ	ʌ	ʌ	ʌ	ʌ
VII.6.3	moon	ʏ:	ʏ:	u:	u:	u:	u:	u:
VIII.1.1	mother	ʌ	ʌ	ʌ	ə:	ə: °ʌ	ə: °ɒ °ʌ	ɒ °ʌ
IX.8.8	(t)other	ʌ	ε °ʌ °ι	ʌ	ʌ	ʌ	ʌ	ʌ
V.1.2	roof	ʏ:	ʏ:	u:	u:	u:	u:	u:
IV.12.1	root	ʏ:	ʏ:	u:	u:	u:	u:	u:
VIII.6.1	school	ʏ:	ʏ:	u:	u:	u:	u:	u:
VI.14.22	shoe(s)	ʏ:	ʏ:	u:	u:	u:	u:	u:
V.4.6	soot	ʏ	ʏ	u: °ʏ:	u: ιω	ω	ω	ω
V.9.1	(-)spoon (porridge-stick)	ʏ:	ʏ:	u:	u:	u:	u:	u:
III.3.3	(-)stool	ʏ:	ʏ:	u:ə	u:	u:	u:	u:
VI.5.6	tooth	ʏ:	ʏ	u:	u:	u:	u:	u:
VII.1.2	two	ʏ:	ʏ:	u:	u:	u:	u:	u:
VII.2.14	two	ʏ:	ʏ:	u:	u:	u:	u:	u:
VII.3.5	two	ʏ:	ʏ:	u:	u:	u:	u:	u:
IX.9.1	who	ʏ:	ʏ:	u:	u:	u:	u:	u:
IX.9.3	who	ʏ:	ʏ:	u:	u:	u:	u:	u:
IX.9.5	who	ʏ:	ʏ:	u:	u:	u:	u:	u:

Note also:
1 [ε] in shooting VI.5.4 (cf. [ʏ:] in shoots 'gutters' V.1.6).
2 [ʌ] in hoods 'eyebrows' VI.3.9.
3 [ʏ:] in spuke 'spoke' n. [u:] in cooking-board V.6.5.

126

Note. In St Cleer, the long reflexes of ME *ǭ* vary between [Y:] and [u:], most often being of the intermediate [y:~ü:] sounds. The short reflexes (few examples) are of the usual [ʌ] type and a [ɔ], [ö]/[Y] type.

In St Day, no [Y(:)] or [ü(:)] sounds were heard. The long reflexes of ME *ǭ* result in [ʉ:~u:], usually slightly lowered or preceded by an [ɔ] glide, thus [°u:~ɔu:]. The short reflexes are of an [ɔ] type and (in words like *gloves, other*) [ʌ] or [ǫ~ӟ], a sound which seems to oscillate between [ǫ] and [ʌ].

Commentary

ME *ǭ* had become [u:] before 1500.[27] In some words this [u:] was shortened, certainly by the end of the sixteenth century, and probably by the middle of that century.[28] Then the shortened form fell in with the development of ME *u* (< OE *u*), and with it regularly became [ʌ] in normal circumstances. Standard English [ɔ] in words like *cook, foot, good* is the result of a later shortening of the [u:], apparently in the mid-seventeenth century.[29] Three types thus survive in present-day Standard English, namely: 1. Those with [u:], e.g. *boot, spoon*; 2. Those with [ʌ], e.g. *blood, brother*; 3. Those with [ɔ], e.g. *cook, good*. These three types find their dialectal counterparts in the development of ME *ǭ* in Cornwall, and are discussed below in their several categories.

1. In Cornwall, words with Standard English [u:] < ME *ǭ* regularly have [Y:] in localities 1 and 2 and [u:] in localities 3–7. In localities 1 and 2, [Y:] coalesces with [Y:] from ME *iu*, but this latter sound has a different development in localities 3–7.

> *Boots* in localities 1 and 2 shows shortening to [Y] (presumably on account of the following [t]), like the short forms in Standard English *foot, soot* (cf. the similar examples at Somerset 13, Wilts 7, Devon 2, Dorset 5, Hants 7, and cf. also Hants 1). [Y] in *hoof* at locality 1 and in (-)*tooth* at locality 2 are similar cases (cf. VI.5.6 Somerset 2, 8, Wilts 1–4, etc.). *Four/two-tooth* at locality 1 and *hoof(s)* at locality 7 have fallen in with the *gloves, Monday* type. For [ɛ] in *shooting*, see 2, below.
> *Spuke* (additional material) at locality 3 may be a variant of *spoke*, and thus contain ME *ǫ* and not *ǭ* (see *EDD*, s.v. Spuke sb. 1). But it is in any case noteworthy in that it shows [Y:], which is rare in this locality.
> *Stool* at locality 3 shows a schwa-glide produced by the following [ɫ].

2. Except for *mother*, words having Standard English [ʌ] from ME *ǭ* regularly have [ʌ] throughout Cornwall. A south-western dialectal development, however, is observable in localities 1 and 2, which occasionally show

27. Luick, *op. cit.*, §581.2; Dobson, 681.
28. The orthoepist John Hart has the spelling *u* (presumably [ɔ]) in 18 words. See B. Danielsson, *John Hart's Works on English Orthography and Pronunciation 1551 . 1569 . 1570, Part II: Phonology* (1963), §131.
29. See Wyld, *op. cit.*, §237; Dobson, §§35 (it appears in Standard English c. 1640), 38.

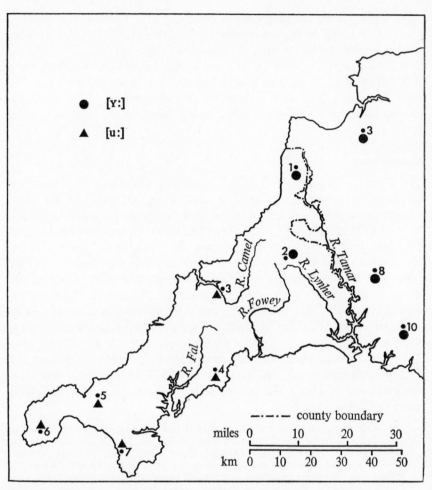

Map 13. The vowel in moon *(SED VII.6.3).*

[ɪ] or [ɛ] before [ð] (in *brother*, *(t)other*). The path of this development is presumably:

ǭ > [uː] > [ɷ] > [ɪ] (> [ɛ])

Examples of fronting of [ɷ] (to [ɪ]) of another origin may be noted from table 10, showing the development of ME *u*, below.

Shooting (< OE *scēotan*), recorded with [ɛ] in the additional material at locality 1, seems to have fallen in with the regular development of the south-western (Devon, and Cornwall localities 1 and 2) vowel in *shut* (< OE *scyttan*), which shows [ɪ] and [ɛ] as well as [ʌ] forms. See *SED*, IX.2.8.

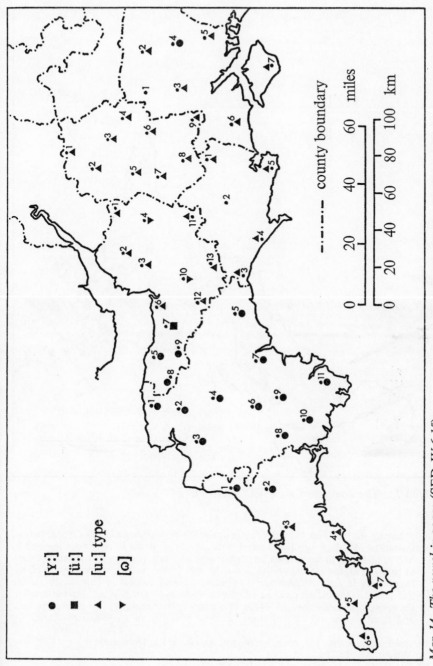

Map 14. The vowel in goose (SED IV.6.15).

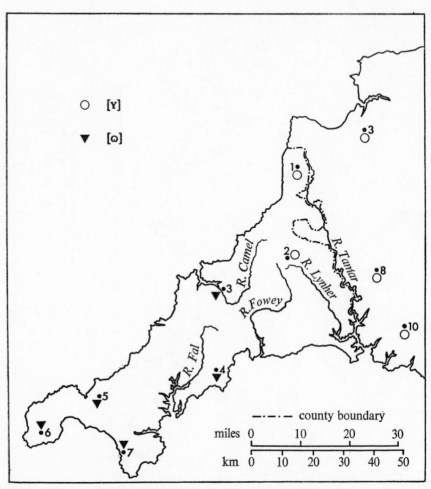

Map 15. The vowel in foot *(SED VI.10.1).*

Mother. In localities 4–7 a development to [ɔ: ~ ɒ] is evidenced in this word; that is, instead of ME ǭ > ū > u > [ʌ] as usual, ME u (< ū < ǭ) seems to have been lowered to ME o, and then in some cases lengthened again to [ɔ:], perhaps by the same process as [ɒ] > [ɔ:] in, for example, *broth, cross, off*, etc., in the seventeenth century;[30] cf. the lengthening in *father*.[31] *Mawther* is apparently chiefly current in East Anglia, where this form has the dialect meaning of 'wench, great awkward girl', etc. (first attested in the *Promptorium Parvulorum*,[32] 1440). This seems to be the result of first of all a phonetic and then a semantic differentiation, current primarily in south-eastern dialect. In

30. See Luick, *op. cit.*, 707, Anm. 1; Wright, *op. cit.*, §93.2; Dobson, §51.
31. Wright, *op. cit.*, §94.
32. See *OED*, s.v. *Mauther*, and cf. *EDD*, s.v. *Mawther*.

Cornwall, localities 4–7 have the phonetically different type, but do not show the semantic shift, and this suggests that *mawther* became an acceptable pronunciation in early Standard English, which was adopted in west Cornwall, but which in south-eastern dialects also underwent a shift in meaning. The sound-change is obviously not a general one, since it is entirely restricted to *mother* (cf. *brother, other*).[33]

3. Words having Standard English [ɔ] < ME ǭ regularly have [ʏ] in localities 1 and 2 and [ɔ] in 3–7. In localities 1 and 2, [ʏ] coalesces with [ʏ] from ME *u*, and in 3–7 [ɔ] coalesces with [ɔ] from ME *u*. As noted above, *boots, hoof* and *(-)tooth* also show the shortened type.

Soot shows the usual developments in localities 1 and 2 and 5–7, but localities 3 and 4 have some peculiarities: locality 3 has the lengthened type, as in *shoe, spoon*, etc., but also has [ʏ:] in an i.m. example. Locality 4 also has [u:], beside [tɔ], which is unique in ME ǭ words, the vowel having fallen in here with the reflexes of ME *iu*. For east and central Cornwall there were probably originally two types in this word. namely [u:] (in localities 3 and 4) and [ɔ] (in 1 and 2, and throughout Devon and west Somerset), the latter being the result of the seventeenth-century shortening, the former being the older type. A south-western dialectal fronting then took place, affecting the vowels in localities 1 and 2 and partly in 3: in 1 and 2 the short [ɔ] became [ʏ], but in 3, when fronted the long [u:] became [ʏ:] (i.m.); otherwise, in locality 3 it remained.
Cooking- (additional material) at locality 3 has retained the long type.
Hoods (additional material) at locality 1 has fallen in with the development of ME ǭ in the words of type 2, above; cf. Standard English *blood, flood*.

The reflexes of ME isolative *u* (table 10)

Table 10 ME isolative *u* (including *u* shortened from ME *ū*)

		1 Kilk	2 Alt	3 Egl	4 St E	5 Gw	6 St B	7 Mull
III.5.5*	(-)brush	ι	ι	ι	ι	ι	ɔ	nr
V.2.14	brush	ι °i:	ʏ	ι	ι	ɔ	ə\u1d3f:	nr
V.9.11	brush	i:	ʏ:	ι	ι	ɔ	ə\u1d3f:	ɔ
III.1.14	bull	ʏ	ɔ	ɔ °ʏ	ɔ	ɔ	ɔ	ɔ
III.1.6	bulling, bullward (on heat)	ɔ	ɔ	ɔ	ɔ	ɔ	ɔ	ɔ
IV.10.5	bushes	ʏ	ʏ	ɔ	ɔ	ɔ	ɔ	ɔ
III.11.1	butcher	ʏ	ʏ	ɔ	ɔ	ɔ	ɔ	ɔ
V.5.4	butter	ʌ	ʌ	ʌ	ʌ	ʌ	ʌ	ʌ
VIII.1.15	cousins	ʌ	ʌ	ʌ	ʌ	ʌ	ʌ	ʌ
V.2.10	cushion	ʏ	ʏ	ɔ	ɔ	ɔ	ɔ	ɔ
IV.7.4	doves	ʌ	ʌ	ʌ	ʌ	ʌ	ʌ	ʌ
VII.1.10	dozen	ι	ι	ʌ	ʌ	ʌ	ʌ	ʌ

33. Cf. Dobson, §97, n. 3.

Table 10 (cont.)

		1 Kilk	2 Alt	3 Egl	4 St E	5 Gw	6 St B	7 Mull
VI.13.11	drunk	ʌ	ʌ	ʌ	ʌ	ʌ	ʌ	ɔ
IV.6.14	ducks	ʌ	ʌ	ʌ	ʌ	ʌ	ɔ	ʌ
VII.6.18	dust	ι	ι °æ̈	ι	ʌ	ɔ	ʌ	ʌ
VII.1.15	hundred	ʌ	ʌ	ʌ	ʌ	ʌ	ʌ	ʌ
II.2.11	mushrooms	ʌ	ʌ	ʌ	ʌ	ʌ	ʌ	ʌ
V.7.15	onion	ʌ	ʌ	ʌ	ʌ	ʌ	ʌ	ʌ
V.6.6	oven	ʌ	o: °o:	ʌ	ʌ	ʌ	ʌ	ʌ
VI.2.8	pull	Y	ɔ	ɔ	ɔ	ɔ	ɔ	nr °ɔ
IX.3.3	put	ʌ	ʌ	ɔ °ʌ	ɔ	ʌ °ɔ	ɔ	ʌ °ɔ
III.3.8	put							
	(to hire pasturage)	ʌ	ʌ	ɔ	ɔ	ɔ	ɔ	ɔ
I.7.17	saw-dust	ι	æ̈	æ̈	ʌ	ʌ	ι	ʌ
V.3.9	shovel	+Y:	+æ̈	ʌ	ʌ +æ̈	ʌ	+æ̈	ʌ °+æ̈
VII.6.16	slush	ʌ	æ̈	ʌ	ʌ	ʌ	ɔ	ɔ
III.7.1	suck	Y	ʌ	ɔ °Y	ɔ	ɔ	ɔ	ɔ
V.8.10	sugar	Y	Y	ɔ	ɔ	ɔ	ɔ	ɔ
IX.2.3	sun	ʌ	ι	ι	ʌ	ʌ	ʌ	ʌ
VI.7.6	thumb	ʌ	ʌ	ʌ	ʌ	ʌ	ʌ	ʌ
VII.6.21	thunder	ʌ	ι	ε	ʌ	ʌ	ʌ	ʌ
VI.5.4	tongue	ʌ	ʌ	ʌ	ʌ	ʌ	ʌ	ʌ
VIII.1.12	uncle	ʌ	ʌ	ʌ	ʌ	ʌ	ʌ	ʌ
IX.9.6	uncle	ʌ	ʌ	ʌ	ʌ	ʌ	ʌ	ʌ
VIII.1.6	woman	ɔ	ɔ	ɔ	ɔ	ɔ	ɔ	ɔ
III.7.5	wool	ɔ	ɔ	ɔ	ɔ	ɔ	ɔ	ɔ

+ = [v] has disappeared.
* See also I.3.14:4 [ʌ]; and VIII.9.4:6 [ι] 7 [ɔ].

Note. In St Cleer, the reflexes of ME *u* are nearly always [ʌ] or (in the *bull*, *push* type) [ɔ] or their variants. But [Y] was heard once in *put* (beside [ʌ ~ ɔ ~ ǫ]); [ö] was heard in *bush(es)*.

In St Day, ME *u* results in [ǫ ~ ä], a sound which seems to oscillate between [ǫ] and [ʌ], or in [ɔ] (as in *bull, push*, etc.); [ɒ] was heard in *hundred*.

Commentary

Excepting its appearance in special circumstances as [ɔ] (chiefly in the context of labial consonants), ME *u* has usually given Standard English [ʌ], a stage which it probably reached in the sixteenth century or even earlier in some dialects (see p. 141, below).

1. In Cornwall, words with Standard English [ʌ] usually have [ʌ] throughout, falling in with [ʌ] < ME ǭ in words like *brother, gloves*.

[ɔ] occurs in *brush* (localities 5–7), *drunk(en)* (7), *ducks* (6), *dust* (5), *slush* (6 and 7), *suck* (3–7). [ɔ] in *brush* is perhaps accounted for by the influence of a preceding labial (+ [ɾ]), as in Standard English *push, bush*; [ɾ] may have had the same influence in *drunk(en)*. [ɔ] in *ducks, dust*, (possibly in) *slush*, and *suck* is the result of shortening of ME *ū*, without subsequent development to [ʌ]. For further comment on *brush* and *suck*, see below. *Dust* and *slush* also have a lengthened form in some localities (see below).

Localities 1–3, and, in one case, 6, show the south-western dialectal development to [ɪ] in *dozen* (localities 1 and 2), (-)*dust* (1–3, 6), *sun* (2 and 3), *thunder* (2, also [ɛ] in 3, cf. p. 145, below). *Brush* also has [ɪ] in localities 1–6.[34] Cf. pp. 127–8, above.

Localities 2–7 show a different south-western development, namely to [æˇ] (on the phonetic values of this notation, see pp. 147–8, below). This sound occurs in (-)*dust* (localities 2 and 3, beside [ɪ]), *slush* (2), and, with loss of [v], in *shovel* (2, 4, 6, 7). It also occurs in IV.3.9 *ruts* (i.e. cart-tracks), of obscure origin, in localities 1–4, and cf. *croust* (< OF *crouste*), p. 189, below. In *dust* (< OE *dūst*), [æˇ] merely represents a retention of the long vowel, instead of ME shortening before [st] which occurs in Standard English. The long form also appears in Cornish as *dowst*. The other words must also go back to ME forms with *ū*. *Shovel* is discussed separately below.

Brush, with its many phonetic variants, deserves separate consideration. These fall into four types:

(a) Those having [ɪ], the result of unrounding and fronting of [ɔ]. These are chiefly restricted to localities 1–5, but an additional example occurs in 6. [iː] is presumably a lengthened form of this, probably because [ʃ] follows, cf. p. 115, above.

(b) Those having [ɔ], possibly on account of the [bɾ]. These occur only in localities 5–7.

(c) [ʏ] in locality 2, representing the usual fronting of ME *u*[35] in words like *bull, bush*. [ʏː], also at locality 2, is presumably a lengthened form of this, probably because [ʃ] follows; cf. p. 115, above.

(d) A metathesized form in locality 6.

The above are standard south-western dialectal forms, all except (b) and the short form at (c) being represented in Devon.

Oven shows the Standard English forms except at locality 2, where a lengthened vowel is registered. Presumably OE *ofen* > ME *ǭfen* ([ɔːvn̩]) > [oːvn̩], instead of the usual raising of ME *o* to *u* and further development to [ʌ]. This is a well-attested dialectal form in the south-west (and also elsewhere).[36]

Shovel (< OE *scofl*) also has ME *o* which is raised to *u* and becomes [ʌ] in Standard English, perhaps being influenced by *shove*, v. The Standard English type occurs in Cornwall in localities 3–5 and 7, but the other localities show [ʏː] (locality 1) or [æˇ] (2, 6, also 4 and (i.m.) 7 beside [ʌ]), in all these latter cases the [v] being lost. Both of these are well-attested south-western dialectal types: when *f* ([v]) is lost early with compensatory lengthening of the vowel, *o* > *ǭ* > [ʏː], in accordance with the regular development of *ǭ* in this area. When *f* is lost later – after *o* has been raised to *u* – compensatory lengthening gives *ū*, and then [æˇ], in accordance with the usual result of the diphthonging of ME *ū* in this area.

34. Cf. Wright, *EDG*, §100.
35. It is also possible that [ʏ] is the rounding of [ɪ] following [bɾ], not the fronting of [ɔ]: cf. [ʏ] in *pitcher* at II.6.7, locality 1.
36. See *EDG*, Index, s.v.

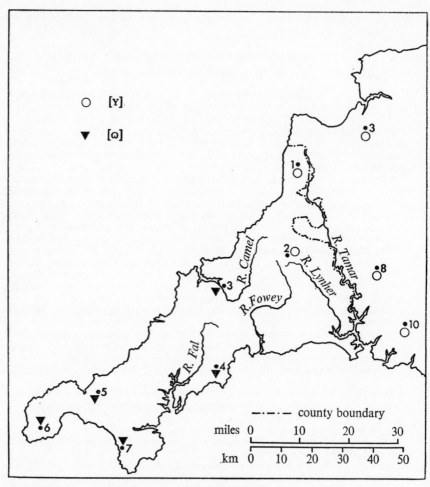

Map 16. The vowel in butcher (SED *III.11.1*).

Suck (< OE *sūcan*). The ME shortened vowel *u* has progressed to the [ʌ] stage in locality 2 only. Elsewhere it has remained at the [ʊ] stage, becoming [ʏ] at localities 1 and (i.m.) 3.

2. In Cornwall, words with Standard English [ʊ] have [ʏ] beside [ʊ] in localities 1 and 2, and [ʊ] in 3–7, thus falling in, generally speaking, with the pattern of the reflexes of ME *ọ̄* in words like *crook* and *foot*. The sound-change [ʊ] > [ʏ] in localities 1 and 2 is thus only sparingly evidenced, doubt-less because of the difficulty of pronouncing the front vowel [ʏ] after a

labial consonant such as [b], [p] or [w]. It will be noted, for example, that *woman* and *wool* have [ɷ] throughout.

IX.3.3 *put* shows variation between [ʌ] and [ɷ] in localities 3–7,[37] but this word has only [ʌ] in 1 and 2. There was variation in *put* in the seventeenth century, when the [ʌ] pronunciation first arose, and this is reflected in dialectal development throughout the south-western counties.

37. The variation reflects Dobson's words, §196, p. 721: "The rounding influence acted sporadically and produced inconsistent results, as is evident from the common words *put, but, butcher*, and *butter*."

The reflexes of ME isolative *iu* (table 11)

Table 11 ME isolative *iu* (< early ME *eu, iu*, AN *ü*)

		1 Kilk	2 Alt	3 Egl	4 St E	5 Gw	6 St B	7 Mull
V.10.7	blue	Y:	Y:	u:	u:	ɩɷ	u:	ɩɷ
VII.6.7	dew	Y:	Y:	ɩɷ	ɛɷ	ɩɷ	ɩɷ	ɩɷ
III.6.6	ewe	Y:°jo:	jo:	jɔ:	jɔ:	jɔ:	jɔ:	jɔ:
III.6.3	ewe-lamb	Y:	jo:	jɔ:	jɔ:	jɔ:	jɔ:	jɔ:
VII.1.19	few	Y:	Y:	ɩɷ°ju:°u:	ɩɷ	ɩɷ°ju:	ɩɷ	ɩɷ
VII.8.21	few	Y:	jY:	ɩɷ	ɩɷ	ɩɷ	ɩɷ	ɩɷ
V.7.2	gruel	Y:	Y:	u:ə	u:ə	u:ə	u:ə	ɩɷɩ
VI.14.24	-new	Y:	Y:	ɩɷ	ɩɷ	ɩɷ°ju:	ɩɷ	ɩɷ
VII.4.8	New Year's Day	Y:	Y:	ɩɷ	ɩɷ	ɩɷ	ɩɷ	ɩɷ
VIII.3.5	news- (gossip)	Y:	Y:	nr	nr	nr	ɩɷ	ɩɷ
IX.1.3	skew(-) (askew)	Y:	Y:	ɩɷ	ɩɷ	ɩɷ	ɩɷ	ɩɷ
VI.13.14	spew (to vomit)	Y:	Y:	ɩɷ	ɩɷ	ɩɷ	ɩɷ	ɩɷ
V.7.6	suet	Y:ə	Y:ɩ	ɩɷɩ	ɩɷə	ɩɷə	ɩɷə	ɩɷɩ
VI.14.2	suit v.	Y:	Y:	u:	u:	ɩɷ	ɩɷ	ɩɷ
VI.14.21	suit n.	Y:	Y:	ɩɷ	ɛɷ	ɩɷ	ɩɷ	ɩɷ
VII.4.2	Tuesday	Y:	Y:	ɩɷ	ɛɷ	ɩɷ	ɩɷ	ɩɷ
VI.5.19	tune	Y:	Y:	u:	ɛɷ	ɩɷ	ɩɷ	ɩɷ

Table 11 (cont.)

		1 Kilk	2 Alt	3 Egl	4 St E	5 Gw	6 St B	7 Mull
IX.4.15	used to	jʏ:	jʏ:	ju:°jʏ:	jɩɷ°ju:	ju:	jɩɷ°ɩɷ °ju:	ɩɷ°ju:°jɩ
V.1.16	useful	jʏ:	jʏ:	ju:	ju:	ju:	jɩɷ	jɩɷ
V.1.17	useful	jʏ:	jʏ:	ju:	ju:	ju:	jɩɷ	jɩɷ

Note also:
1 [ʏ:] in mule VIII.9.4.
3 [ɩɷ] in stew-pot.
4 [ɩɷ] in humour ([ɩɷmərt:]) VI.11.9.
6 [u:] in rule n. [ɩɷ] in flue V.1.3, screw.
7 [ɩɷ] in beauty, bruised, (a)buse. [ʏ:] in Newton (place-name).

Note. In St Cleer, as with the long reflexes of ME *ǭ*, the reflexes of ME *iu* vary between [ʏ:] and [u:], quite often reaching [ʏ:], and being recorded only infrequently as [u:].

In St Day, there seems to be a tendency towards [ɩu] or the like: [ju:] was heard in *dew, few, new, pupils,* ['u:] in *funerals* and *New Year's Day.* But [u̜:] was heard in *suits.*

Commentary

ME *iu* has given either [ju:] or [u:] in present-day Standard English, as in *dew* and *blue* respectively, the type depending on the phonetic context. Early ME *iu* and *ęu* and AN *ü* all eventually merged in *iu* at about the end of the thirteenth century,[38] ultimately giving [ju:] or [u:]. Later – probably in the sixteenth century in 'advanced' Standard English, and between *c.* 1640 and *c.* 1670 in 'careful' Standard English – ME *ęu* also merged with this sound.[39] It is not known for certain how long AN *ü* retained its separate identity or in what (if any) parts of the country. Perhaps both *ü* and *iu* were co-existent for some time. The grammarians' evidence appears to be inconclusive.[40] ME *iu* was evidently a falling diphthong at first, but there is early evidence for its development into a rising diphthong.[41]

In Cornwall, ME *iu* of all origins usually appears as [ʏ:] in localities 1 and 2, falling in with [ʏ:] from ME *ǭ* in words like *moon, stool.* This is prefixed by [j] in *used to* and *useful,* and in VII.8.21 *few,* locality 2 only. In localities

38. Cf. Luick, *op. cit.*, §§399.2, 407.3; Wright, *op. cit.*, §86.
39. Dobson, §243.
40. See Dobson, §§180 (summarizing theories of development) ff.
41. Dobson, §185.

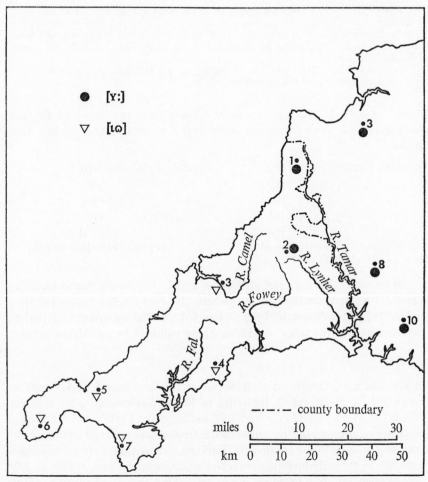

Map 17. The vowel in -new. Note: *i.m.* [nju:] *was also recorded at locality 5* (SED *VI.14.24*).

3–7, ME *iu* usually appears as [u:] or [ιω] (with an occasional variant [εω] in locality 4, for which see p. 145, below; note, however, [jʏ:] in *used to*, locality 3, and [ʏ:] in *Newton* at 7, additional material), probably depending to a certain extent upon the nature of the preceding consonant, e.g. *blue* and *gruel* have mainly [u:], whereas *dew* and *tune* usually have [ιω] (cf. Standard English [u:] in *blue, gruel,* [ju:] in *dew, tune*). There is usually a [j] on-glide in *use, useful.* [u:] falls in with [u:] from ME *ǭ* in words like *moon, stool,* but [ιω] does not occur in words of other origins except in *soot* at locality 4 (see p. 131, above).

137

Ewe (< OE *eowu*) is recorded simply as [Y:] at locality 1, by the side of i.m. [jo:]. Locality 2 has [jo:] and all the other localities have [jɔ:]. [jo:], [jɔ:] are presumably to be explained by shift of stress, giving ME *yowe* (< OE *eówu*).[42] This is a very widespread dialectal form, and is not restricted to the south-west or even to the south: see *SED*, III.6.6.[43]

[vju:] *few* at localities 3 and 5 (i.m.) and [nju:] *-new* at locality 5 (i.m.) may be due to present-day Standard English influence.

It may now be helpful to set out in tabular form the Standard English and regular (i.e. most frequently occurring) Cornwall reflexes of ME $\bar{\varrho}$, *u* and *iu*.

Standard English: $\bar{\varrho}$ gives [u:]   Cornwall: $\bar{\varrho}$ gives [Y:]~[u:]
                  [ʌ]   [ʌ]
                  [ʊ]   [Y]~[ʊ]
       u gives [ʌ]   *u* gives   [ʌ]
                  [ʊ]   [Y]~[ʊ]
     iu gives [ju:]   *iu* gives [Y:]~[u:] or [ɪʊ]
                  [u:]

It will be noted that the chief differences are: 1. The occurrence in localities 1 and 2, very occasionally 3, of [Y:] where Standard English has [u:] or [ju:] and of [Y] where Standard English has [ʊ]; 2. The occurrence of [ɪʊ] in localities 3–7 for the reflex of ME *iu*. These will now be considered in turn.

[Y(:)]

In the whole of Devon, in west Somerset (i.e. localities 5, 7–9)[44] and in north-east Cornwall, [Y(:)], the reflex of ME $\bar{\varrho}$, has usually fallen together with [Y] from ME *u* and [Y:] from ME *iu* (see maps 13–17). There has been much speculation about the origin of the front-rounded vowel sounds in the present-day dialects of south-west England,[45] and they gave considerable difficulty to the early investigators, chief among whom was A.J. Ellis in *EEP* (and elsewhere). For example, when describing the characteristics of his District 10 (see p. 28, above), he says:

The vowels (ə[1], yy[1], əə[1]) sharply distinguish the dialect from D 4 [to the

42. Dobson, §245 and n. 2.
43. Cf. Danielsson, *op. cit.*, §101 (iii): Hart has the spelling *yowe* once.
44. Somerset locality 7, Stogumber, just to the west of the Quantock Hills, seems to be the eastern boundary of this area. Here ME $\bar{\varrho}$ (long reflexes – the short ones give [ʊ]) and *iu* result in [ü:] (as distinct from Devon and Cornwall [Y:]) according to the *SED* fieldworker; ME *u* gives [ʊ]. It has, however, been reasonably suggested that this boundary may at one time have been situated further to the east. See R.E. Palmer, *Thomas Whythorne's Speech* (1969), 33–4, and n. 58, below.
45. Similar sounds in words of all three origins are recorded in parts of north-west England and East Anglia: see the relevant words in *SED*, vols. I–III. It is assumed here, however, that the fronting in each area arose independently.

east]. They are very difficult even to appreciate ... The vowels (yy$_1$ y$_1$, ǝǝ$_1$ ǝ$_1$) are quite as difficult to utter [as (ǝ^1)], but easier to recognise. They are usually both called "French u," but they decidedly reminded me of (y, ǝ) or Fr. pu, peu, from which, however, they were clearly distinct, and apparently 'lowered.' To say (tyy$_1$ bǝǝ$_1$ts) two boots, is a most difficult problem to a stranger, and one he is not very likely to solve.[46]

Later he says:
The sounds (y$_1$ ǝ$_1$ ǝ^1) were distinctly recognised [by me], as different from (y ǝ ǝ), although I failed in imitating and cannot analyse them.[47]

In one of the Districts most relevant to the present book, namely District 11 (see p. 29, above), Ellis uses the symbols (y), (y$_1$) in words of ME $\bar{o}$, u and iu origins, as will be noted from the citation of his examples on p. 147, below, and before going any further it will be necessary to state, as precisely as possible, what he means by these symbols.

(y) is described (p. 87*) as French u, German $\ddot{u}$, "lying intermediate between (i) and (u)." This is presumably IPA [y], though Ellis states that "perhaps pure (y) does not occur in our dialects."

(y$_1$) is (*loc. cit.*) "a modification of Fr. u in a direction not precisely ascertained," but note (*loc. cit.*) that ($_1$) attached to a symbol indicates a sound articulated "with a lower tongue, or appreciated as a deeper sound".

With this rather vague terminology, certainty is impossible, but it may be said with some confidence that both of these symbols represent a sound that is obviously very close to IPA [ʏ]. (When written double, such a symbol indicates a long form.)

Although these sounds, as recorded by *EEP*, are regular for District 10 and the larger part of District 11, they are recorded by *EEP* only as far west as Millbrook (Cornwall). Ellis's dialect tests for Camelford, Cardinham and St Columb Major are almost free of the [ʏ(:)] sounds, and his Marazion specimen, the only representative of his District 12, is completely free of them. The relevant recordings of Ellis are given in full at the end of this section to show his contrast between the two types recorded by him, and to parallel this contrast with that which emerges in the *SED* recordings. From these, it will be noted that, even in District 11, fronting is not invariable in Ellis's recordings, and that (u) (IPA [u]), (*u*) (IPA [ʊ]) and other sounds are also recorded, perhaps representing non-dialectal influence (but cf. pp. 134–5, above). On the basis of the *SED* recordings, we might perhaps have expected Ellis to have recorded [ʏ(:)] from Camelford ($7\frac{1}{2}$ miles west-north-west of Altarnun, the nearest *SED* locality, number 2) as well as from Millbrook.

46. p. 146. Cf. *SED*, IV, 10: "Further, to [our fieldworkers'] northern ears ... many of the vernacular sounds of the south seem strange and phonetically complicated."
47. p. 147.

His failure to do so (except in the case of (sku^{y}l) – see below) suggests either that his informant at Camelford was not reliable or that the western boundary of the [Y(:)] area (which, as the *SED* recordings show, is somewhere between Altarnun (locality 2) and Egloshayle (3), with very few examples of it west of Altarnun) occurrred in his day between Altarnun and Camelford, or (perhaps most likely) that the area just to the west of Altarnun is a 'fringe' area, in which the feature occurs only in sporadic examples. On the whole, I am inclined to trust Ellis's information here (his informant was a native, it must be noted). There is no *SED* locality near Millbrook, but St Cleer (15 miles north-west of Millbrook), which I visited separately, yields examples of the [Y(:)] type. Although the above considerations might seem to add up to a somewhat confused picture, we can at least say with some degree of certainty that the present-day [Y(:)] area, with one or two exceptions, ends at a line drawn between Egloshayle and Altarnun, probably passing to the west of St Cleer. The western edge of Bodmin Moor and the rivers Camel (in its upper reaches) and Fowey suggest themselves as likely natural boundaries. An investigation of this feature carried out over a closer network of localities in this border region would probably establish for certain exactly where the boundary lies.

We next have to consider the origin of the [Y(:)] sounds in the south-west. As shown above, these go back to the following ME sounds:

Long:	ME	$\bar{\rho}$	*goose, root*
		iu	*blue, tune*
Short:	ME	*u*	*bull, sugar*
		$\bar{\rho}$	*foot, good*

The evidence for the origin of the fronting of ME $\bar{\rho}$, *iu* and *u* to [Y(:)] is very sparse indeed. There are no early spellings comparable to those which show the early fronting of ME $\bar{\rho}$ in the north,[48] and there are no statements on the subject from grammarians or orthoepists. We can, however, make certain deductions based on the known or partially known chronology of the normal development of the ME sounds in question. (It could, of course, be objected that the south-western dialects need not have taken part in the 'normal' (i.e. Standard English) development of these ME sounds, perhaps reaching [u:], [ju:], etc., earlier, and indeed there may be a certain amount of evidence for this, e.g. the progress of ME *ī* to monophthongal [ɑ:] and of ME $\bar{\rho}$ to [Y:] (see n. 60, below), but it is not evident from such examples whether they represent an earlier starting-point of the sound-changes in question or a swifter passage through the various subsequent stages, or both. In the absence of any reliable chronology for these dialectal

48. See p. 102, above.

developments, it is safer to use that of the Standard English developments, for which at least we have rough datings based on evidence (statements, etc.) commanding some sort of acceptance.)

1. ME $\bar{\varrho}$ had reached [u:] by, at the latest, c. 1500 (see p. 127, above), and the fronting to [ʏ:] could not have taken place before the [u:] stage was reached.

2. ME *iu* had begun to develop to [ju:] probably as early as c. 1560 (although in careful speech [iu] was preferred for another hundred years or so),[49] and then became [u:] in some phonetic contexts perhaps in the seventeenth century.[50] Since [ʏ(:)] presumably arises either from [jʏ:][51] (<[ju:]) or from [u:], the earliest it could have arisen here is after the [iu] stage had developed into something else, either [ju:] or later [u:]. (It is not, of course, impossible that, in some cases, [ʏ:] arose from [iu], via a stage [iʏ], with absorption of the first element (and [iu]>[iʏ] would be a parallel with [ɛɷ] (<ME *ū*)>[ɛʏ]; see below). In this case, the process could have begun any time after the end of the thirteenth century (see p. 136, above). But at least in *use* and *useful*, fronting must have taken place after [iu] had become [ju:], since a [j] element is present. Cf. also *few*, locality 2. On the whole, the simplest explanation of [ʏ:] in all the ME *iu* words is a derivation either from [ju:] or from [u:].)

3. ME *u* (<shortened *ū*<OE $\bar{\varrho}$, and <OE *u*) is recognized by the orthoepists as [ʌ] only from c. 1640, but on other evidence it can probably be said to have existed in Standard English from c. 1550, in Cockney dialect from c. 1525, and in scattered dialects (perhaps first northern and then eastern) from as early as the fifteenth century.[52] Fronting could not have taken place before ME *u* had become [ʌ], otherwise words like *brother*, *butter* would now have not [ʌ] but [ʏ].[53]

4. The late shortening in ME $\bar{\varrho}$ words (e.g. *foot*, *good*) apparently took place about the middle of the seventeenth century (see p. 127, n. 29, above). Now, since $\bar{\varrho}$ words which contain the fronted sound in Cornwall usually have 'normal' quantity, e.g. *foot*, *good* have [ʏ], while *moon* has [ʏ:], in words of this origin at least the fronting would seem not to have taken place until after the second shortening, i.e. until the middle of the seventeenth century. Exceptions to this (e.g. *boots*, *tooth* have [ʏ]) are noted above, and are presumably simply due to occasional quantitative differences between south-western dialect and Standard English.

49. Dobson, §187. Cf. H.C. Wyld, *A History of Modern Colloquial English* (2nd edn, 1921), 244.   50. Dobson, 712.
51. Cf. [j] absorbed before a front vowel in VII.3.4/5/18 *year*, VIII.8.13 *yes*, and outside Cornwall (e.g. Devon, Somerset) in V.6.2 *yeast*, VII.3.8 *yesterday*.
52. Dobson, 586–7. Cf. Luick, *op. cit.*, §§529ff., Wyld, *Colloquial English*, 232–4.
53. Ellis, *EEP*, 157, records (dyᵢn) *done* p.p. from Iddesleigh (Devon), but this may be an analogical form based on the local pronunciation of *do*.

As far as the words of $\bar{\varrho}$ origin are concerned, the argument under 3 seems conclusive: if $\bar{u} < \bar{\varrho}$ had immediately gone on to [Y:] *c.* 1500, words with shortened vowels like *brother* would have [Y]. Since they have not, the inference to be made is that in $\bar{\varrho}$ words fronting did not take place until after this stage had been reached, i.e. (excluding Cockney, northern and eastern dialects) in the mid-sixteenth century. The same applies to words of *u* (< OE *u*) origin. In words of ME *iu* origin, I have suggested above that [Y:] could not have arisen until [iu] had developed to [ju:] or [u:]. The earliest this could have happened was apparently in the sixteenth century (Dobson suggests *c.* 1560; see p. 136, above). Whether words of all these origins had fronting first and extended it to words of Class 4 later, or whether the [ju:], [u:], [ɷ] sounds were fronted all together as they existed in the seventeenth century, cannot be established with certainty. But we are safe in the supposition that the [Y(:)] sounds originated not earlier than the middle of the sixteenth century, and that some words could not have had fronted vowel sounds until the middle of the seventeenth century.

This view of the comparatively late origin of [Y(:)] is supported by negative evidence in the lack of significant early spellings. No examples are reported by Matthews under ME *u* (see n. 48, above); Mr Gover's 'Place-Names of Cornwall' yields nothing; *PND* yields only Slew, Horrislew and Slewton, all containing OE *slōh* 'slough, mire'.[54] The *-ew-* spellings, possibly indicating [Y:], are modern in all cases: Slew has no significant early forms at all; Horrislew is *Horyslow* as late as 1718, and Slewton is *Slowe Towne* as late as 1665. None of them therefore give evidence of fronting at an early date. It may be noted, too, that Andrew Borde, in his *Fyrst Boke of the Introduction of Knowledge*, 1547, makes no mention of this sound. It is true that his imitations of dialect sounds are meagre and rough, but in his characterization of Scottish speech[55] he spells *good* as *gewd* in order to give some idea of an [Y:] or [y:] sound. If a similar sound had existed in east Cornwall at the time of his visit, he might have been expected to make some comment. Finally, Professor M.L. Samuels, who, together with Professor A. McIntosh, is engaged upon a large-scale survey of ME dialects, has informed me privately that he knows of no spellings from south-western sources testifying to the [Y(:)] sounds. In the spelling *oy* in words like *moon*,

54. See pp. 28, 91 and 580 respectively. The spellings of the place-names Laployd (p. 423) and Floyte (p. 452), both of which contain OE *flōd*, suggest a long sound as the reflex of ME $\bar{\varrho}$ in these examples. Since no sound-change $\bar{\varrho} > oi$ is attested in this part of the country, *oy* may represent [o:], as it does in some medieval south-western documents (see below), although the *oy* spellings are very late (Laployd has in fact no early spellings in *oy*, and, it should be noted, is now pronounced [læpləd]; Floyte is *Floydway* in 1717). There is evidence that the vowel was retained long in this word (as in others) in the seventeenth century; see Dobson, §37.
55. p. 138.

y is not indicative of phonetic quality, but merely shows that the vowel is long. *y* is used similarly in the Cornish language of *Meriasek*, e.g. *moys* (for *mōs* 'go'), *tays* (for *tās* 'father').[56]

The most likely conclusion, on consideration of all the available evidence, therefore, seems to be that fronting to [ʏ(:)] was something later imposed upon the [ju:], [u:], [o] sounds as they existed in the sixteenth to seventeenth centuries, a further and later local development of the Great Vowel Shift.[57]

Finally, the question must be considered whether this palatalization to [ʏ(:)] (and, at the same time, the development of ME *ū* to [œʏ], etc., for which see below) owes anything to a Celtic substratum.[58] Similar origins have been suggested for French *ü* ([y]) from Latin *u*: "It is, however, possible ... that the tendency to form rounded front vowels, which is common to Celtic and French, may be a 'heritage from the Celtic Speech of Gaul'."[59] There is an obvious parallel.

It is not a complete parallel, however. The impulses (if any) which might have produced [y] in French *lune* from Latin *luna*, for example, were presumably at work during the earliest period of Old French,[60] affecting the language (i.e. Old French) which immediately replaced the substratum. This can hardly be the case with English, for, to take an example, if Celtic *ū* had had a similar effect on the English which immediately replaced it, i.e. OE, OE *ū* would have become [y:] (written *y*), and its further development would have been, like *ȳ*, the umlaut of Primitive OE *ū*, to ME *ī*, MnE [aɪ], as, for example, in *fire* (< OE *fȳr*). But, in fact, there is no evidence that this happened, and the only hope for the substratum theory would lie in showing

56. On the basis of some rather flimsy indirect evidence, R.E. Palmer, in *Thomas Why-thorne's Speech*, postulates a coalescence of ME *ǭ* and *eu* in /y:/ in Whythorne's autobiography (*c.* 1576). Whythorne was a native of Ilminster, in south-central Somerset, born in 1528, who, however, moved to Oxfordshire when he was ten, and to London at 17. The coalescence, if genuine, would therefore have to have been present in Somerset dialect by 1528–38. But Palmer's argument (mainly in §5.32) depends on too many doubtful factors to convince, in particular that Whythorne identified London [u:]<ME *ǭ* with his own – presumably native – [u:]<ME *ǭ* and *ou*, suggesting that this was a different sound from that normally developed from ME *ǭ* in his native dialect, which may therefore have been [ʏ:], an argument which seems to fall down on a good many counts.
57. A partially parallel example of this south-western tendency to fronting (and also to raising) is afforded by *road* (< OE *rād*, ME *rǭd*), *SED* IV.3.12, in whose forms all the stages by which ME *ǭ* reached [ʏ:] in this area are illustrated: having reached an [o:] stage (e.g. Cornwall 5), instead of diphthongizing to [ɔə], it rises to [u:] and [u:ə] (e.g. Cornwall 1–4, 7). In Somerset 8 it has even become [ʏ:ə] (in *road-men*; note also [ʏ:] in *frozed* at VI.13.19, Cornwall 2). The same fronting and raising tendency in Standard English accounts for the Great Vowel Shift, but the south-western dialects have, in some cases, taken the process one step further.
58. Cf. H. Wiegert, *"Jim an' Nell" von W.F. Rock: Eine Studie zum Dialekt von Devonshire*, Palaestra, 137 (Berlin, 1921), §207.
59. M.K. Pope, *From Latin to Modern French* (1934), §9, and see also §§8 and 183. See also W.D. Elcock, *The Romance Languages* (1960), 192–3.
60. Pope, *op. cit.*, §183.

that an hereditary palatalizing tendency, Celtic in origin, could persist in operating over so long a period as to be able to affect all later [u(:)] sounds brought into existence over the course of the history of the English language, including, for example, the [u:] which developed from ME ǭ c. 1500. This is an example of the mystical or atavistic version of the substratum theory, condemned by Bloomfield.[61] But, in any case, it might well be asked why, if a Celtic palatalizing tendency had no effect on OE ū, when the Celtic and OE languages were in intimate contact, it should have had an effect a thousand years later: at the earliest time that [y(:)] could have arisen, this area of Cornwall had been English-speaking for at least 450 years, since c. 1100. There seems to me to be no evidence in favour of influence by a Celtic substratum.

We can now postulate the following series, concluding either that: 1. Fronting began to take place not long before c. 1550–60 in any case, and possibly not until the middle of the seventeenth century; or that 2. Fronting took place from c. 1550–60 in the long reflexes of ME ǭ, in the reflexes of ME u and perhaps iu, but not until the middle of the seventeenth century in the short reflexes of ME ǭ.

ME ǭ   > [u:] (by c. 1500)   > [y:] *goose, root*
    iu   > [ju:] (c. 1560) > [jy:]   > [y:]
           (or: > [ju:] (c. 1560) > [u:]*   > [y:]) *blue, tune*
u after labial
   consonants
   remains as   [ɷ].   After c. 1550 > [y]   *bull, sugar*
ǭ > [u:], then by late shortening
            > [ɷ] (mid-17th century) > [y]   *foot, good*

* Seventeenth century.

[ιɷ]

This transcription, representing the reflex of ME *iu* (and in one case only, namely *soot*, ME ǭ), appears to denote either a falling diphthong or one with more or less equal stress on both elements.[62] Whatever the precise sound, however, the important thing is the difference between this diphthong and the (usually) monophthongal [y:] of localities 1 and 2. What I suggest happened is that the Standard English reflex of ME *iu* was present in at least part of the central area of the county (the west was still Cornish-speaking to some extent) from the first stages of its development, and that

61. *Op. cit.*, 386, 469.
62. I have not heard precisely [ιɷ] in my own examination of this sound from tape-recordings, but it may well be that what I heard as ['u:], ['ʉ:], etc., with a rather slight first element, was heard by the *SED* field-worker as [ιɷ].

at first it was a falling diphthong; this has since become or almost become a rising one in some cases, and one with almost equal stress in others.[63] In some cases, the diphthong has virtually lost its first element [ɪ] or [j].

The development in Standard English was presumably [íu] > [iǘ:] > [ju:] (> [u:] in certain phonetic contexts):[64] all but the first of these stages seem to be represented (taking into account my transcriptions, see n.63, below) in localities 3–7. A lowering of the first element of the diphthong to [ɛ] in locality 4 occurs after a front consonant (although there are unfortunately only four examples), and is unattested elsewhere, as far as I know. The [ɛɷ] forms were given by one informant only, namely F.J.L., and I did not identify any such forms on the tape-recording he made in 1963. There is, however, probably no special significance in the lowered first element, which coincides with the traditional dialectal lowering of isolative [ɪ] to [ɛ] (cf. *SED*, IV, VII.5.12 *dinner* (under *a meal out*), III.8.1 *pigs*, V.10.9 *thimble*, V.7.19 *vinegar*, I.8.3 *whip* (under *swingletree*).

Again, we must consider whether or not the central and west Cornwall reflexes of ME *iu* could be the result of influence from a Cornish sound (cf. Welsh *iw* ([iu]), used by Welshmen in their pronunciation of English words such as *new*, *tune*). As usual, the difficulty is to decide exactly how any comparable Cornish sound was pronounced. For one of the values of late Cornish *u* (from earlier [ü(:)]), Lhuyd gives *iu̯* (approximately IPA [iu]), as in *bugh* 'cow', *huhelder* 'height',[65] transcribed, however, by Jenner[66] as *ew* "as in the English word *few*". But even admitting [iu] (or the like) in such Cornish words, it is more probable, as suggested above, that its articulation was influenced by English and not *vice versa*. The late Cornish group of diphthongs *eu*, *ew*, *yu*, *yw* all ended up, according to Jenner, with "the sound of *ew* in the English word *dew*".[67] But the same applies here as to Cornish *u*.

The influence of a Cornish sound [iu] could only be postulated if it could be shown that this sound developed in Cornish too early to have been influenced itself by the English sound (i.e. the reflex of ME *iu*). Even then, there would be no certainty, since it is quite possible that this sound and the Standard English [iu] (> [ju:]) arose independently, and that mere accident brought a Standard English [iu] type into an area once characterized by a very similar Cornish sound.[68]

63. Cf. my hearing of *blue* in locality 6 as having the diphthong [ɪ̆ú:], a sound which seems to lie half-way between [ju:] and [ɪɷ], and also *EEP true* (from St Columb Major) (triú) – IPA [trɪ̆u:] – p. 147, below.
64. Dobson, §185.   65. *Op. cit.*, 229.
66. p. 59.   67. p. 57.
68. It is worth noting that [ɪɷ], [ɪu] < ME *iu* are fairly widespread in dialect in places where Cornish influence is impossible, as witness, for example, [ɪɷ] – V.10.7 *blue*, Somerset 4; VI.14.21 *suit*, Somerset 2; [ɪu] – VI.14.24 *brand-new*, Kent 7, Hants 4, Sussex 6.

Conclusion

In conclusion, we may say that [ɣ(:)] is a dialectal representative of several ME sounds, the result of a fronting which took place in the early MnE period throughout the whole of Devon, in west Somerset and in east Cornwall. [u:], [o] and [ɪo], found in central and west Cornwall, are, on the other hand, Standard English representatives of the ME sounds in question. A clear isogloss, with only occasional exceptions, separating these two types, occurs between localities 2 and 3. The western edge of Bodmin Moor and the rivers Camel (in its upper reaches) and Fowey may be significant natural boundaries here, coinciding with one of the lateral hundred divisions.

The English language east of the division just mentioned was introduced early into Cornwall from the neighbouring county of Devon, and appears to have formed, with Devon and west Somerset, a discrete linguistic type, in an area bounded on the west by both natural and administrative boundaries. Thus, the relevant sounds in east Cornwall took part in the dialectal fronting described above when this sound-change took place over the whole area. But in the rest of Cornwall, the English language mostly remained unaffected by this change. In central Cornwall, [u:] and [o] remained unaltered, and an early version (i.e. [ɪo]) of the reflex of ME *iu* was retained. The west was still Cornish-speaking in parts, but ultimately adopted the type prevalent in central Cornwall.

Finally, attention must again be drawn to the sporadic south-western forms which, in addition to [ɣ(:)], penetrate the county from the east, e.g. [ɪ~ɛ] in localities 1–3, the reflex of ME *ǭ* and *u*. These show a significant divergence between what is dialect and what is something else. On the other hand, there may, in the central and western localities, be evidence of an archaic Standard English type in *mother* (with [ɔ:~ɒ]).

Ellis's transcriptions

The following are A.J. Ellis's transcriptions of words containing the reflexes of ME isolative *ǭ*, *u* and *iu* in Cornwall, Districts 11 and 12. The words are given in the order in which they occur in Ellis's passages, but identical second and subsequent occurrences are not given. For explanation of the symbols (y), (y₁), see p. 139, above. A superior '5' indicates that the sound preceding it is articulated with protruded lips. Explanation of the other symbols will be found either below or in *EEP* itself, chiefly on pp. 76*–88* and in the notes accompanying the individual passages.

District 11

Devonport by Plymouth dialect test (given here for the purposes of comparison), *EEP*, p. 166.

ʃíy₁⁵, skúɐl [skyy₁⁵1] (from another informant), thr,yy₁⁵ ('through'), ty₁⁵ ('to'), dr,ɜqkin, sy₁⁵n, dyy₁⁵ ('do'), lyy₁⁵k, tr,yy₁⁵ *Note.* (u)=IPA [u]; ɜ=IPA [ʌ].

Millbrook, Co, p. 167. (*Note.* "The pron. is thorough s.Dv., and Mr. Rundell [who gave the information] states that having had occasion to visit Padstow in Co., he was surprised to find the speech practically the same.")[69]

gy₁d, ty₁ ('to'), ʃy₁, zy₁n, ʃyy₁, ɐty₁k ('a-took'), ly₁kt, kry₁l, ky₁d'n

Camelford dialect test, p. 168

ʃu, skuʸl, thruu ('through'), drɜqk'n, zun ('soon'), du, lʉk, trʉʉ *Note.* (*u*)= IPA [ʊ].

Cardinham dialect test, p. 169

ʃéy₁, skuul, thru ('through'), drɔqken, sini ('sonny'), séʉn, déy₁, lɜk ('look'), truu *Note.* The equivalent IPA transcriptions of *you*, *soon*, *do* and *look*, above, would be: [jey], [sɛɔn], [dey], [lʌk]. [ɔ]=IPA [ɒ]; (*i*)=IPA [ɩ].

St Columb Major dialect test, pp. 169–70

sʟkúul, druu ('through'), dʀɜqkin, sʟzuun, duu, lʉk, triú

District 12

Marazion, comparative specimen, pp. 171–3

rɜnd ('runned', i.e. ran), tu ('to'), drɜqk, tu ('too'), ɜqk'l, klɜb, sɜm, fʉd·'ld ('fuddled'), wʉd'n ('wouldn't'), mɜn·de, gɜz'l, wʉd'nt, trɜs ('trust'), lɜmp, shʉg·ɐ

West Cornwall classified word list (items from "the Land's End and adjacent districts"), p. 174

dʉl ('dull'), huuk, huud, frɜnt

69. *EEP*'s nearest locality to Padstow is St Columb Major, *SED*'s is locality 3. There does not seem to be any evidence to support Mr Rundell's statement from either, certainly not with regard to the sounds under investigation here.

The reflexes of ME isolative $\bar{u}$ (table 12)

Table 12 ME isolative $\bar{u}$

Note. For the present-day reflex of ME $\bar{u}$, the *SED* field-worker recorded, in the main, [æÿ] throughout the whole of Cornwall and Devon (but [œÿ] in localities 8–11) and in west Somerset (cf. *SED*, IV, 10–11, 15ff.). The Editors (Professor H. Orton and I) were not satisfied either that this was an accurate transcription or that the sound was, in any case, uniform throughout this area. The transcriptions given below are, therefore, taken from tape-recordings of the responses to the relevant questions in the *Questionnaire*

Table 12 (cont.)

(plus as much free, unrehearsed conversation with the informant as could be obtained) which were made by Mr S. Ellis and myself in Spring 1963, subsequent to the original *SED* programme.

For the purposes of the present book, the original transcriptions made from these recordings by Professor Orton and myself have been slightly modified by the removal of the diacritic indicating unrounding of the lips, and, very occasionally, others.

		1 Kilk	2 Alt	3 Egl	4 St E	5 Gw	6 St B	7 Mull
VII.2.8	about	nr	œɥ	ӓω	ɛǫ	nr	nr	nr
IV.12.2	boughs	nr	nr	ɛǫ ɛɥ	ɛǫ	ɛ̈ö ɛ̈ω	ɛǫ	ɛö̈
VII.6.2	clouds	ɛ̈ω	ɛ̈ɥ	ɔ̃ǫ	ɛ̱ǫ	ɛǫ	ɔ̇ǫ	ɛ̈ω
III.1.1	cow	ɛ̈ω	ɛ̈ɥ	ɔ̇ǫ̇	æω	ɛǫ	ɛǫ	ɛ̱ǫ
III.1.1	cows	ɛ̈ω	ɛ̈ÿ	ɔ̇ǫ̇	ɛǫ	ɛǫ	ɛǫ	nr
VI.3.9	eyebrows	əω	ӓ·ɥ	ɛω	æǫ	ɛǫ	ɛ̈ö̈	æǫ
IV.4.1	ground	ə·ɥ	əɥ	ɔ̈ö̈	æǫ	æǫ	ᵟǫ	ɛǫ
V.1.1	house	ʔœɥ	nr	ɛö̈	ɛö	ɛǫ	ɛö̈	ɛǫ
IV.8.1	louse	nr	ᵒɥ:	ɛ̈ö̈	ɛ̈ǫ	ɛ̈ǫ	ɛ̈ö̈	ɛ̱ǫ
IV.5.1	mouse	əɥ or ʔœɥ	œɥ	ɛö̈	ɛ̈ö	ɛ̱ǫ	ɛ̱ǫ	ᵒü: ɛǫ
VII.8.5	ounce	ɛ̈ǫ	ɛ̈ǫ	ɛ̱ǫ	ɛö̈	ɛǫ	ɛǫ	ɛǫ
IV.7.6	owl	ɛ̈ɥᵒ	əɥω ӓɥω	ɛǫᵒ	ӓǫ	ɛ·ö̈ ɛö̈	ɛω	ɛ̱ǫ
I.8.1	plough	nr	nr	ɛǫ	æǫ	ɛǫ	ӓǫ	ɛǫ
VII.7.8	pound (£)	ɛ̈ω	ɛ̈ǫ	æǫ	æǫ	ɛ̈ǫ	nr	ɛǫ
VII.8.2	pound (lb)	ɛ̈ɥ	nr	ɛǫ	æǫ	ӓǫ	ɛǫ	nr
IX.1.1	round	œɥ	ɛ̈ɥ	ɛ̃ǫ	æǫ	æǫ	ӓω	ɛǫ
III.9.1	snout	œÿ	ӓɥ	ɛ̈ǫ	ɛ̈ö	ɛǫ	ɛ̈ǫ	ɛ̱ǫ
VII.6.25	south	ɛ̈ɥ	œy	æǫ	ӓ̈ǫ	ɛǫ	ɛ̈ǫ	ɛ̈ǫ
III.8.6	sow n.	nr	ӓ·ɥ	æǫ	æǫ	ɛǫ	ɛ̈ǫ	ɛ̈ǫ
VII.1.16	thousand	nr	nr	ɛ̱ǫ	æǫ	əǫ	ɛ̈ǫ	ɛ̈ǫ

Note I later decided that [ω] as the second element in the diphthong at locality 1 should be emended to [ȯ] or [ʏ].

Further examples of the reflexes of ME *ū* heard on the tape-recordings:

1 ? [ɛ̈ɥ] in out
[ɛɥ] or ? [ɛʏ] in out
[ɛɥ] in down, out

[ɛʉ] in round
[ɛ̈ʉ] (or ? [œʉ]) in around
[ɛ̈ʉ] in about, down
[ɛʏ] in house
[ɛ̈ʏ̈] in out
[œʏ] in now
[æ̈ʏ] in now
[æǫ] in down
[ɛʉ] in around
[æʉ] in down
? [œʉ] in round
2 [ᵒʉ:] in now
[ɛʉ] in now
[ɛ̈ʉ] in ploughing
[œʉ] in about, out
[əʉ] in down, now
[œʏ] in out
[ɛ̈ʏ] in about
[ɛω] in down
[œʉ] in down
[œʏ] in out
? [əʉ] in down
[ɛ̈ω] in down
3 [ɛω] in council houses, out
[ɛω] in out
[ɛ̦ω] in out
[ɛ̦ω] in down
[ɛ̈ω] in about
4 [ɛω] in now, pounds
[ɛ̦ω] in house, now
[æω] in now
[æ̦ω] in about
[ɛ̦ω] in cows, houses, plough, thousands
[ɛ̈ω] in plough
5 [ɛω] in down, now
[ɛ̦ω] in out
[ɛ̈ω] in out
[ɛ̦ω] in down, out
[əω] in down
6 [ɛω] in down, now, ounce, pound, round
[æω] in down, now, pound
[ɛ̦ω] in pound

149

[ɛ̞ɷ] in out
[ɛ̠̈ɷ] in out
[ɛ̞ɷ] in cows, thousands
7 [ɛ̠̈ɷ] in down
[ɛɷ] in out
[ɛ̞ɷ] in now
[ɛɷ̞] in now
[ɛɷ̞] in round

Note. In St Cleer, the first element of the diphthong could be either un-rounded, showing degrees of variation between [ɛ] and [a], and often central-ized or retracted, or it could be rounded, i.e. [œ]. The second element seemed basically to be [ʏ], but was frequently heard as [ʏ̠] and [ʉ] or [ö].

In St Day, the first element is basically [ɛ] (never rounded), sometimes raised to [ɛ̞] or even [e]. The occasional centralization very rarely reaches an [ə] position. The second element is [ɷ].

Commentary

Beginning to diphthongize soon after 1400,[70] ME *ū* > present-day Standard English [aɷ], probably via the stages [ɔu] and (sixteenth–seventeenth centuries) [əu] (and possibly [ɛu], see below), the modern pronunciation being adopted as standard in the eighteenth century, and being only dialectal – especially northern – up to about 1700.[71]

I have thought it useful to give here the following data from Devon[72] (all localities) and Somerset localities 5, 7–9 (i.e. west Somerset), which consists of the broad types of the diphthongs heard by the Editors of *SED* during their listening to the relevant tape-recordings (see Note, above), simply to show the extent of the south-western distribution of the distinctive [œʏ] reflex outside east Cornwall. (See *SED*, IV, 18–21, 51–9, where the field-worker's transcriptions are also summarized.)

Somerset

5 [ɛ̈ʏ ~ ɛ̈ö] mainly, [œʏ] very frequently.

7 [ɛ̈ɷ] mainly, [əʉ ~ əɷ] occasionally, [æ̈ɷ] occasionally, [aɷ] once.
(As noted above (n.44), this locality probably represents the eastern boundary of the area in which ME *ọ̄*, *u* and *iu* result in reflexes of a fronted type. The

70. Luick, *op. cit.*, §483 and Anm. 1.
71. Dobson, 685, suggests via [ɔu] and [ʌu], but [ʌu] seems inherently unlikely in view of the latter development of the diphthong to Standard English [aɷ] and dialectal [ɛɷ], etc. (with front first elements). Wyld, *Short History*, §246, giving the more traditional theory of development, proposes a series *ū* > [uːⁿ] > [ou] > [au].
72. Comparison should also be made with that of Wiegert, *op. cit.*; see §§58–9, 209.

absence of a fronted second element in the reflexes of ME *ū* need not therefore surprise us here. The field-worker records here [æɒ], etc., as distinct from his [æŸ] further west in Somerset, see *SED*, IV, 20.)

    8 [œʏ~œɥ~œö~œɒ] usually, [ëʏ~ëɥ] infrequently, [æɥ~æö] infrequently, [əɥ] once.

    9 [œʏ] usually, [ɛʏ] occasionally.

Devon

    1 [œʏ~œɥ~œö].

    2 [œʏ] and [ëʏ] mainly, [æʏ] once, [°ü] once, [əʏ] once.

    3 [œʏ] usually, [ëʏ] occasionally, [ʏ:] once.

    4 [œʏ] usually, [ɛʏ] frequently.

    5 [œʏ~œö].

    6 [œʏ].

    7 [œʏ] usually, [ëʏ] once.

    8 [œʏ~œɥ~œö~œɒ] mainly, [ëɒ] rarely, [äɒ] rarely, [ëʏ] once.

    9 [œʏ~œö] mainly, [ëö~ëɒ] frequently, [°ɒ·] once.

   10 [œʏ] mainly, [ɛʏ~ɛö] frequently, [æʏ~æö] frequently, [aʏ~aö] occasionally.

   11 [œʏ~œö] mainly, [ɛʏ] once, [æʏ] once.

All the information tabulated above clearly shows that in Devon, west Somerset and Cornwall localities 1 and 2 (plus St Cleer) the reflexes of ME *ū* are quite different from those of Cornwall localities 3–7 (plus St Day), the differences consisting generally in a rounding of the first element and centralizing or fronting of the second element of the diphthong in the first area mentioned, and the absence of such rounding and centralization or fronting in the second area. This statement is a simplification, and applies to a different extent in different cases. In Devon, west Somerset and northeast Cornwall, in cases in which rounding does *not* occur in the first element, there is often heavy centralization, but allowances must be made for the fact that rounding ([œ]) and centralization ([ə] or [ë]) are not always easy to distinguish on a tape-recording, where no lip-movement can be observed, and that, although intensive programmes of listening were undertaken by both Professor Orton and myself, it might not always be agreed by other listeners that we were correct in every case.[73]

The recordings made by A.J. Ellis in *EEP* are as follows (for his use of the acute accent, see p. 77*):

73. Cf. *EEP*, 167, n. 2 on Millbrook: "*down town house*, at first hearing this diphthong sounded to me as (ə′u) and it was not till after close examination and continual repetition that I was convinced the sound was (œy₁⁵)." ((ə′u)=IPA? [ʌ̈ɒ]; (œy₁⁵)=IPA? [œʏ].) Cf. also Ellis's doubts on his transcriptions (above), and Wyld, *Colloquial English*, 234 (on *cur* and *cœur*).

In District 10[74] (west Somerset and part of north-east Devon), for the reflexes of ME $\bar{u}$ Ellis has (ɛ'u) (IPA [ɛɷ]): "It is quite distinct from the Dv. (ɷ'y₁)" (=IPA ? [əʏ]).

In District 11[75] (most of Devon, east and central Cornwall), Ellis records (ɷ'y₁⁵) – "as well as I can analyse it ... Prince L.-L. Bonaparte heard it as French *œu* in *cœur*, followed by French *u*, that is (œ'y), which it certainly resembles. How far does this extend? It is certainly in n.Dv. Mr. Baird (Nathan Hogg) acknowledges it in e.Dv., Mr. Shelley (Plymouth) in s.Dv. In Co. I have not been able to trace it, with certainty, further than Millbrook, just on the e.b. of Co., not even in the vv. [viva-voce] specimen from Camelford. But I suspect that it really pervades Co. as well as Dv. The diphthong is not unlike the Dutch *ui* in *huis*, or the French *œi* in *œil*." There can be little doubt that Ellis is referring to an [œʏ] type.[76]

For Millbrook, Ellis records (ɷ'y₁⁵), as described above.

For Camelford, Ellis records (ə'u) (IPA ? [ʌɷ]; probably approximately equivalent to the transcriptions given by me above as [ëɷ]), but confesses (in n.1) that he is not at all certain "that it was not (ɷ'y₁⁵), here and at St Columb Major".

For Cardinham, Ellis records (*éu*) (IPA ? [ɛɷ] or ? [eɷ]), and (ɛ'u) (IPA [ɛɷ]), (ɛ'u) (IPA [ɛu]).

For St Columb Major, Ellis records (ɔóo) (IPA ? [ɒou] approximately), but thinks (n.1) that this is "certainly wrong, and that (ə'u) ... is more correct."

In his two localities Millbrook and Camelford, Ellis records something that might well be an approximate equivalent to *SED* [œʏ], etc. At Cardinham, [ɛɷ], etc., corresponds to similar diphthongs recorded in the tables above, and the recording from St Columb Major should be compared with the diphthongs in *clouds*, *cow*, *cows* and *ground*, recorded at Egloshayle (locality 3) in the tables above (St Columb Major is 7½ miles south-west of Egloshayle). There thus seems to be a striking similarity between our recordings and those of Ellis.

In District 12[77] (west Cornwall), Ellis gives (áu) (IPA [ɑu]).

[œʏ] and its variants

The second element of the diphthong ending in [ʏ] (or its variants [ʏ], etc.) is more or less identical with the short reflex of ME $\bar{ǫ}$ and u[78] (as in the

74. See p. 146.
75. pp. 156–70.
76. pp. 156–7. For a long and detailed description of the articulation of Ellis's (ɷ'y₁⁵), see his note on *doubt*, p. 158.
77. pp. 171–4.
78. Cf. *EEP*, note on *doubt*, p. 158: "The last element of the diphthong in this word is precisely the same as for (tyy₁)=two."

parallel case in Standard English, [aɷ] < ME $\bar{u}$ and [ɷ] < ME $\bar{ǫ}$, u); the same phonetic process, i.e. fronting of u to [ʏ], etc., operates here too, except that in this case the u is the second element of a diphthong. This in turn implies the previous existence of a diphthong ending in [ɷ]. The [œʏ] is entirely exclusive to this south-western area, and apparently occurs nowhere else in England.[79] Its nearest neighbours geographically – at Somerset localities 6, 12, 13, Dorset 3, Cornwall 3–7 – are [ɛ̈ɷ], [ɛɷ], and we may perhaps therefore postulate an earlier diphthong of this type from ME $\bar{u}$, in which the second element became [ʏ] at the same time as the fronting of [ɷ] from ME $\bar{ǫ}$, u (above), and which in turn could produce a front-rounded sound [œ] as the *first* element, thus:

$$\text{ME } \bar{u} > [\text{əu}] > \begin{cases} [\text{ɛ̈ɷ}] > [\text{ɛ̈ʏ}] \\ \quad\text{or} \\ [\text{ɛɷ}] > [\text{ɛʏ}] \end{cases} > [\text{œʏ}]$$

The above argument suggests a late (early MnE) origin for this diphthong and its variants, and indeed there is no evidence for its early existence in the spelling of place-names (in Cornwall or Devon) or in any other documents examined. Modern Colehays ("the modern form is corrupt")[80] is *Colehouse* 1596, perhaps suggesting that an [œʏ] in -*house* has in modern times been mistaken for -*hays*, but this is only a vague possibility. No significant early spellings are given by Matthews (see p. 102, above). We have put the date of the fronting of ME $\bar{ǫ}$, u as sixteenth–seventeenth centuries, so the present diphthong probably did not arise before that, and in any case a previous stage [ɛ̈ɷ] or [ɛɷ] could hardly have been in existence before this date (see p. 150, above). For discussion of possible Celtic influence in the fronting of the second element of this diphthong (and, by implication, its subsequent effect on the first element), see pp. 143–4, above.

[ɛɷ], etc. (localities 3–7)

The [ɛɷ] which appears in Cornwall localities 3–7 sometimes has a centralized first element, but not to the extent of the other south-western counties, e.g. (parts of) Somerset, Dorset, Wilts, where it is, or approaches, [əɷ], [ʌɷ] (see *SED*, IV, 15ff.). It is, in fact, more like the south-eastern and Standard English variety of the diphthong, and never has a front-rounded first element. The possibility that it represents the same dialectal type as found in Somerset, Dorset and Wilts, however, must not be discounted.

79. But cf. [əü] in Ulster English: see J. Braidwood, 'Ulster and Elizabethan English' in *Ulster Dialects* (1964), 65.
80. *PND*, 469. Cf. the remarkable statement by A.H. Marckwardt, *American English* (1958): "At the present time . . . a word such as *about* will be pronounced with the stressed vowel of *bite* in Devon . . ." (p. 14). This clearly shows that the author has confused [œʏ] with [æɪ] or the like, and indeed they can sound very similar, especially if the [ʏ] is slightly unrounded, as it sometimes is.

Distribution

The geographical distribution of these types is virtually identical with that of the reflexes of ME *ō̭*, *u*, *iu*, above: again, the western edge of Bodmin Moor, and the rivers Camel (in its upper reaches) and Fowey seem to be significant natural boundaries, coinciding with one of the lateral hundred divisions.

The English language east of this division was introduced early into Cornwall from the neighbouring county of Devon, and appears to have formed, with Devon and west Somerset, a discrete linguistic type, in an area bounded on the west by both natural and administrative boundaries. Thus, ME *ū* in east Cornwall took part in the dialectal development of the diphthong [œʏ] when this took place over the whole area. But in the rest of Cornwall, no such fronting and rounding took place, and the sound remained at an [ĕɷ], [ɛɷ] stage. In any case, west Cornwall was still Cornish-speaking in parts, but ultimately adopted the type prevalent in central Cornwall. Two general theories, therefore, present themselves for consideration:

1. South-western ME *ū* > [əu] > [ĕɷ], [ɛɷ]. At some period, this developed in Devon, north-east Cornwall and west Somerset into an [œʏ] (or [ĕʏ], etc.) diphthong, leaving the rest of Cornwall and Somerset with the old types, [ĕɷ], [ɛɷ], etc.

2. [œʏ] developed perhaps from an earlier [ĕɷ], [ɛɷ], but the [ɛɷ] in central and west Cornwall may be not this older form but an independent, different type, perhaps from an older stratum of Standard English (in which ME *ū* > [ɷu] > [əu] > [ɛu] > [aɷ]).

The reflexes of ME initial *f*, *s*, *th*, *thr* and *sh* (tables 13-17)

Table 13 ME initial *f*

Note. In this and the following tables, a superior letter ᶠ marks words of French origin.

		1 Kilk	2 Alt	3 Egl	4 St E	5 Gw	6 St B	7 Mull
V.4.2	faggot (-wood)ᶠ (kindling-wood)	nr	f	f	f	f	f	f
VI.13.7	faintᶠ	f	f	f	f	f	nr	f
VII.4.11*	fair/feastᶠ (festival)	f	nr	f	f	f	f	f

Table 13 (cont.)

		1 Kilk	2 Alt	3 Egl	4 St E	5 Gw	6 St B	7 Mull
II.1.1	fallow (f.-land)	v	v	v	nr	f	nr	f
VIII.4.7	farmer^f	v	v	v	f	f	f	f
I.1.2	farmhouse^f (farmstead)	v	v	v	f	f	f	f
III.8.10	farrow	v	v	v	v	v	nr	nr
VI.13.16	fart (to break wind)	v	f	v	f	f	f	f
VII.7.2	farthings	v	v	v	v	f	f	f
VIII.1.1	father	v	v	v	f	f	f	f
VIII.9.6	fault^f	v	v	v	f	f	v	f
III.3.1	feed	v	v	v	nr °f	v °f	f	nr °f
III.5.1	feeding	v	v	nr	nr	nr	f	nr
VI.10.1	feet	v	v	v	v	v	f	f
VI.10.10†	feet	v	v	v	v	v	f	f
I.9.9	fellies	v	v	v	v	f	v	v
IV.10.13	fern	v	v	v	f	v	f	f
VI.11.8	fester^f	v	v	v	f	v	f	f
VII.1.19	few	v	v	v	f	f °v	f	f
VII.8.21	few	v	v	v	v °f	f	f	f
I.1.1	fields	v	v	v	f	f °v	f	f
VII.2.5	fifth	v	v	v	v	f	f	f
III.13.6	fight	v	f	v	f	v	f	f
III.4.2	filly	f	f	f	f	f	f	f
IX.3.2	find	v	v	v	f	f °v	f	f
VI.7.7	finger	v	v	v	v	v	f	f
V.7.21	finished^f	nr	f	nr	nr	nr	nr	nr
VIII.6.2	finishes^f	nr	nr	nr	nr °f	f	nr	nr
V.3.1	fire	v	v	v	f	v	f	f
VII.2.1	first	v	v	v	f °v	f °v	f	f
VI.7.4	fist	v	v	v	f	v	v	v
IV.5.7	fitchew^f, etc. (pole-cat)	v	v	v	f	v	f	f
VII.5.6	five	v	v	v	f	f	f	f
VI.14.16	flap	f	f	f	f	f	nr	f
V.9.7	flasket^f (clothes-basket)	f	f	f	f	f	f	f

155

Table 13 (cont.)

		1 Kilk	2 Alt	3 Egl	4 St E	5 Gw	6 St B	7 Mull
IV.8.4	fleas	v	v	v	f	v	f	f
IV.7.2	fledged	f	nr	f	f	f	f	f
IV.8.5	flies	v	v	v °f	f	f	f	f
III.12.3	flitch	v	v	f	f	v	f	f
IV.1.4	flood(ed)							
	(in flood)	nr	f	f	f	f	f	f
V.2.7	floor	v	v	v	f	f	f	f
V.6.1	flourᶠ	v	v	v	f	f	f	f
VIII.5.13	flowersᶠ	v	v	f	f	f	f	f
III.4.1	foal	v	f °v	v	f	v	f	f
VII.6.9	fog	v	v	v	v	f	f	f
VII.4.10	foolᶠ	f	f	f	v	f	f	f
VI.10.1	foot	v	v	v	v	v	f	f
VIII.8.6	for							
	(why)	v	v	v	f	f	nr	f
IV.1.3	ford	v	v	v	f	f	f	f
VI.1.7	forehead	v	v	v	v	v	f	f
III.4.8	forelock	v	v	v	v	v	f	f
I.7.9	forks	v	f	f	f	f	f	f
VII.3.2	fortnight	v	v	v	f	f	f	f
VII.1.14	forty	v	v	v	f	f	f	f
IX.1.7	forwards	v	v	v	f	f; v in forth	f	f
IX.3.2	found	v	v	v	f	f	f	f
VII.1.4	four	v	v	v	f	f °v	f	f
IV.6.2	fowls							
	(keep hens)	v	v	v	f	v	f	f
IV.5.11	fox	v	v	v	f	v	f	f
VI.11.1	freckles	nr	v	v	f	nr	nr	nr
VII.4.4	Friday	v	v	v	v	f	v	f
VIII.2.7	friends	f	v	v	f	f	f	f
IV.9.6	frogs	v	v	v	f	v	f	f
VIII.2.11	from	v	v	v	v	f	f	f
IX.2.6	frontᶠ	v	v	v	f	f	f	f
VII.6.6	(-)frost	v	v	v	v	f	f	f
II.3.1	furrow	v	v	v	v	v	v	v
IX.2.1	further	v	v	v	f	f	f	f

Table 13 (cont.)

		1 Kilk	2 Alt	3 Egl	4 St E	5 Gw	6 St B	7 Mull
IV.10.11	furze (gorse)	v	v	v	f	v	f	f
IV.7.8	pheasants[f]	f	f	v	f	f	f	f

* Localities 1, 3 and 4 have *fair*, 5–7 *feast*.
† *Foot* is actually recorded, except at locality 3.

Table 14 ME initial *s*

		1 Kilk	2 Alt	3 Egl	4 St E	5 Gw	6 St B	7 Mull
V.4.3	cinders	z	z	z	s	s	s	s
I.7.2	sack	z	z	z	s	s	nr	s
I.5.6	saddle	z	z	z	s	s	s	s
III.12.5	salt (i.m.)	nr	°z	°z	°s	°s	nr	nr
VII.4.5	Saturday	z	z	z	z	z	s	s
I.7.17	saw-dust	z	z	z	s	s	s	s
I.7.16	sawing-horse	z	z	z	s	s	s	nr
II.9.6	scythe	z	z	z	s	z	s	s
IV.7.5	sea-gull (gull)	z	z	z	nr	z	s	s
VII.2.3	second[f] adj.	z	z	z	s	s	s	s
VI.3.2	see	z	z	z	z °s	z °s	s	s
VIII.2.5	seed, seen (saw)	z	z	z	s °z	s °z	s	s
II.3.6	seedlip (sowing-basket)	z	z	z	s	z	s	s
VIII.7.2	seesaw	z	z	z	nr	s	nr	s
VII.1.6	seven	z	z	z	s	s	s	s
VII.5.4	seven	z	z	z	z	s	s	s
V.10.3	sew	z	z	z	s	s	s	s
VIII.5.4	sexton[f]	z	z	z	s	s	s	s
VI.13.14	sick (to vomit)	s	z	z	s	s	s	s
VIII.2.9	sight	z	z	z	s	s	s	s
VII.7.7	silver	z	z	z	s	s	s	s
VIII.3.3	sit	z	z	z	s °z	s °z	s	s
VII.1.5	six	z	z	z	z	z	s	s
VII.7.4	sixpence	z	z	z	z	s	s	s

Table 14 (cont.)

		1 Kilk	2 Alt	3 Egl	4 St E	5 Gw	6 St B	7 Mull
III.11.4	slaughter-house	s	s	nr	s	nr	nr	s
I.9.1	sledge	s	s	s	s	s	s	s
V.6.10	slice^f	s	s	s	s	s	nr	s
III.1.11	slip	s	nr	nr	nr	s	s	nr
III.4.6	slip	s	s	s	nr	s	s	nr
VII.6.14	slipper(y)	s	s	s	s	s	s	s
IV.1.10	slope	s	s	s	s	s	s	s
IV.9.2	slugs	s	s	s	s	s	s	s
VII.6.16	slush	s	s	s	s	s	s	s
V.1.4	smoke	z	s	s	s	s	s	s
IV.9.3	snails	s	s	s	s	s	nr	s
II.9.7	snead (shaft)	s	s	s	s	s	s	s
VI.5.14	snoring	s	s	s	s	s	s	s
III.9.1	snout	s	s	s	s	s	s	s
VII.6.13	snow	s	z	s	s	s	s	s
VIII.1.22	so	s	s	s	s	s	s	s
V.8.4	some	z °s	z	z °s	s	s °z	s °z	s
VII.8.15	something (incl. somewhat)	z	z	z	s	s	s °z	s
VIII.1.4	son	z	z	z	s	s	s	s
V.4.6	soot	z	z	z	s z	s	s	s
VII.8.16	sort^f (kind)	z	z	z	nr	s	s	s
VII.8.17	sort^f (kind)	z	z	z	nr	s	s	s
VII.6.25	south	z	z	z	s	s	s	s
III.8.6	sow n.	z	z	z	s	z	s	s
VIII.9.7	such	z	z	z	s	s	s	s
III.7.1	suck	z	z	z	z	z	z	s
V.7.6	suet^f	z	z	z	s	s	s	s
VI.14.21	suit^f	z	z	s	s	s	s	s
VI.14.2	suits^f v.	s	s	s	s	s	s	s
IX.2.3	sun	z	z	z	s	s	s	s
II.9.4	swath	z	z	z	s	nr	s	nr
VIII.8.9	swearing	z	z	z	s	s	s	s
VI.13.5	sweat	z	z	z	s	z	s	s
V.9.12	sweep	z °s	z	z	s	s	s	s
V.8.4	sweets	s	z	s	s	s	nr	s

Table 15 ME initial *th*

		1 Kilk	2 Alt	3 Egl	4 St E	5 Gw	6 St B	7 Mull
II.7.6	thatch	d	d	d	d	ð	θ	θ
II.7.5	thatching							
	thatcher	d d	d d	d d	d d	ð ð	θ θ	θ θ
VII.6.15	thawing	ð	ð	ð	θ	θ	θ	θ
V.7.7	thicken	ð	ð	ð	θ	θ	θ	θ
VI.9.3	thigh	ð	ð	ð	θ	θ	θ	θ
V.10.9	thimble	ð	ð	ð	θ	ð	ð	θ
VII.2.4	third	ð	ð	ð	θ	θ	θ	θ
VI.13.9	thirl(y) (hungry)	ð	ð	ð	ð	nr	θ	ð
VI.13.10	thirsty	ð	ð	ð	θ	ð	θ	θ
VII.1.11	thirteen	ð	ð	ð	θ	θ	θ	θ
VII.1.13	thirty	ð	ð	ð	θ	θ	θ	θ
II.2.2	thistle	d	d	d	d	d	θ	θ
VII.1.16	thousand	ð	ð	ð	θ	θ	θ	θ
VI.7.6	thumb	ð	ð	ð	ð	ð	θ	θ
VII.6.21	thunder	ð	ð	ð	ð	θ	θ	θ
VII.4.3	Thursday	ð	ð	ð	ð	θ	θ	θ
IX.1.8	thwart(-ways) (diagonally)	ð	ð	ð	ð	θ	θ	θ

Table 16 ME initial *thr*

		1 Kilk	2 Alt	3 Egl	4 St E	5 Gw	6 St B	7 Mull
II.8.3	thrashels							
	(flails)	dɾ	dɾ	dɾ	dɾ	nr	nr	θɾ
V.10.2	thread	dɾ	dɾ	dɾ	θɾ	θɾ	θɾ	θɾ
VII.1.3	three	dɾ	dɾ	dɾ	θɾ	θɾ °dɾ	θɾ	θɾ
VII.7.3	threepence	dɾ	dɾ	dɾ	dɾ	θɾ	θɾ	θɾ
VII.7.3	threepenny-							
	bit	dɾ	dɾ	dɾ	dɾ	θɾ	θɾ	θɾ
II.8.1	thresh	dɾ	dɾ	dɾ	dɾ	θɾ	θɾ	θɾ
VI.6.3	throat	dɾ	dɾ	dɾ	dɾ °θɾ	θɾ	nr	θɾ
VIII.7.7	throwing	dɾ	dɾ	nr °dɾ	nr	θɾ	θɾ	θɾ

Table 17 ME initial *sh*

		1 Kilk	2 Alt	3 Egl	4 St E	5 Gw	6 St B	7 Mull
V.11.1	chemise[f]	ʃ	ʃ	ʃ	ʃ	ʃ	ʃ	ʃ
I.6.2	shaft-horse (incl. sharp-h., shafter, sharper)	ʃ	ʃ	ʃ	ʃ	ʃ	ʃ	ʃ
I.9.4	shaft(s) (incl. sharp(s))	ʃʃ	ʃʃ	ʃʃ	ʃʃ	ʃʃ	ʃʃ	ʃʃ
IX.4.2	shall	ʃ	ʃ	ʃ	ʃ	ʃ	nr	ʃ
IX.4.4	shan't	ʃ	ʃ	ʃ	ʃ	ʃ	ʃ	ʃ
I.8.7	share n.	ʃ	ʃ	ʃ	ʃ	ʃ	ʃ	ʃ
II.6.3	sheaf, -ves	ʃʃ	ʃʃ	ʃʃ	ʃʃ	ʃʃ	ʃʃ	ʃʃ
III.7.6	shearing	ʃ	ʃ	ʃ	ʃ	ʃ	ʃ	ʃ
III.7.7	shears	ʃ	ʃ	ʃ	ʃ	ʃ	ʃ	ʃ
III.6.1	sheep	ʃ	ʃ	ʃ	ʃ	ʃ	ʃ	ʃ
III.11.8	sheepskin	ʃ	ʃ	ʃ	ʃ	ʃ	ʃ	ʃ
V.9.4	shelf	ʃ	ʃ	ʃ	ʃ	ʃ	ʃ	ʃ
V.7.14	shelling	ʃ	ʃ	ʃ	ʃ	ʃ	ʃ	ʃ
I.2.1	shepherd	ʃ	ʃ	ʃ	ʃ	ʃ	ʃ	ʃ
VII.7.5	shilling	3	3	3	ʃ	ʃ	ʃ	ʃ
VI.14.8	shirt	ʃ	ʃ	ʃ	ʃ	ʃ	ʃ	ʃ
VI.14.22	shoe(s)	ʃʃ	ʃʃ	ʃʃ	ʃʃ	ʃʃ	ʃʃ	ʃʃ
IX.4.8	should(n't)	ʃʃ	ʃʃ	ʃʃ	ʃʃ	ʃʃ	ʃʃ	ʃʃ
IX.4.9	shouldn't have	ʃ	ʃ	ʃ	ʃ	ʃ	ʃ	ʃ
VI.6.6	shoulder	ʃ	ʃ	ʃ	ʃ	ʃ	ʃ	ʃ
V.3.9	shovel	ʃ	ʃ	ʃ	ʃ	ʃ	ʃ	ʃ
IX.2.8	shut	ʃ	ʃ	ʃ	ʃ	ʃ	ʃ	ʃ
VIII.9.2	shy	ʃ	ʃ	ʃ	ʃ	ʃ	ʃ	ʃ
V.8.10	sugar[f]	3	ʃ	3	ʃ	ʃ	ʃ	ʃ

Note. In St Cleer, hardly any voicing in initial position was heard from N.C., but W.H.L. occasionally voiced all four initial fricative consonants, and also admitted to [dɹ] in *three*. In this locality, voiced initial fricatives were referred to as "old", or, in one case, as "slang", and it looks as if they were once a feature of the area but have now vanished.

No initial voicing was heard in St Day or anywhere in the district.

Commentary

From the data given in *SED*, vols. II[81] and IV, it is clear that Cornwall is only part of a much larger area in the south and west of England in which initial fricative consonants are voiced.

The rise of the voicing of initial fricatives is obscure, and dates for its origin both before and during the OE period have been suggested.[82] It has been widely held[83] that initial voicing was present before the large influx of French words in the eleventh century and subsequently, since these have apparently taken part only to a limited extent in the process. The spelling evidence is unsatisfactory since no conclusions can be drawn from OE orthography in this respect, and ME has special spellings only for [v] and [z], namely *v* and *z* respectively; [ð] and [ʒ] were spelled in the same way as [θ] and [ʃ], namely with *th* and *sh* (and their variants) respectively.

From what ME evidence there is, however, combined with that of modern dialects, we can be reasonably certain that in the ME period an area in which ME *f-*, *s-*, *th-* and *sh-* were voiced, generally or sporadically, extended from Kent (and, on the evidence of place-names, even into Essex) to Shropshire, south of a line approximating to Watling Street, except perhaps in west Cornwall. The occasional occurrences of voicing in the modern dialects in the north and east of this area are no doubt relic forms.[84]

Attention must be drawn to the occurrence of initial [d] in the words *thatch*(-) and *thistle*. This feature is not restricted to east and central Cornwall: [d] in *thatch*(-) occurs in south Devon and east and central Cornwall, and in *thistle* in Devon, east and central Cornwall, west Somerset, and Wilts locality 6. ME *th* in these words presumably became [d] via an intermediate stage [ð],[85] but all dialectal evidence of this development, save in these two

---

81. Ed. H. Orton and M.V. Barry (1969–71).
82. For a recent theory proposing a pre-OE date, see W.H. Bennett, 'The Southern English Development of Germanic Initial [f s þ]', *Language*, XXXI (1955), 367–71.
83. See R. Jordan, *Handbuch der Mittelenglischen Grammatik, Erster Teil, Lautlehre* (2nd, rev. edn, 1934), §§208, 215; Luick, *op. cit.*, §703; Brunner, *op. cit.*, §36, n. 1; Ellis, *EEP*, 38; Wright, *EDG*, §§278, 320; J. Kjederqvist, *The Dialect of Pewsey* (1903), 94–6. B. Widén, *Studies on the Dorset Dialect* (1949), 79 (note), however, believes that the sound-change [f] > [v] was still operating at the time of the borrowing from Anglo-Norman. See also F.T. Elworthy, *The Dialect of West Somerset* (1875), 68–74.
84. For a discussion of the extent of the area, and the other matters mentioned in this paragraph, see M.F. Wakelin and M.V. Barry, 'The Voicing of Initial Consonants in Present-Day Dialectal English', *Leeds Studies in English*, N.S.II (1968), 47–64.
85. The possibility of Low Dutch influence cannot perhaps be entirely discounted in these words: cf. Middle Dutch *decken* v., *dac* n., Dutch *distel*.

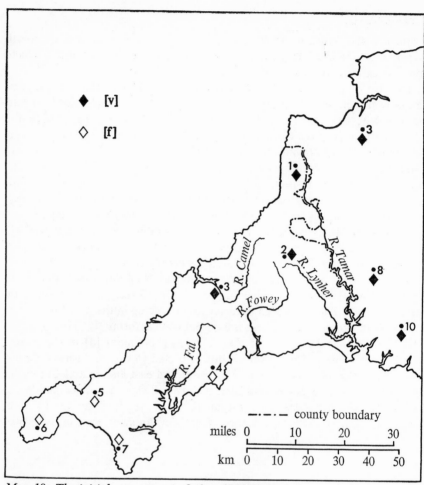

Map 18. The initial consonant in father (SED VIII.1.1).

words, seems to have disappeared. *SED* records no other traces of this phenomenon.[86]

Parts of the south-west, including east and central Cornwall, show [dɽ] as the reflex of ME *thr-*, presumably from an earlier stage [ðɽ], after which, [ð] was pulled back by the following [ɽ] to a retroflex [ɖ] position, closure of the fricative being effected at the same time.

It is clear from the tables above that in Cornwall there is a very marked fading of the feature under consideration after locality 3, i.e. in the centre

86. The south-eastern sound-change by which words with Standard English [ð] (< [θ]) > [d], e.g. in *this, they, there,* although phonetically the same, is of a different origin.

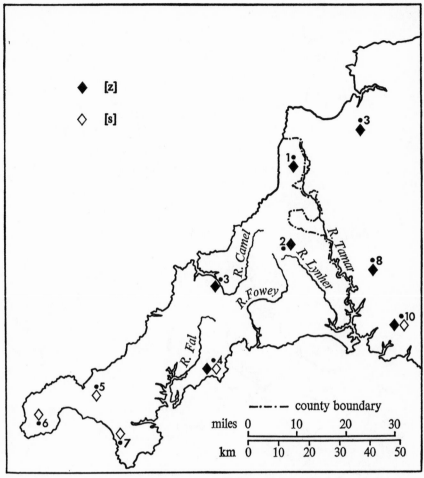

Map 19. The initial consonant in seven (SED *VII.1.6, VII.5.4*).

and west of the county. On numerical evidence alone, and not counting incidental material, the following summaries show this strikingly.

ME initial *f*. Out of 70 words:
Locality 1 has 56 with initial [v]

2	54
3	55
4	17
5	23
6	5
7	3

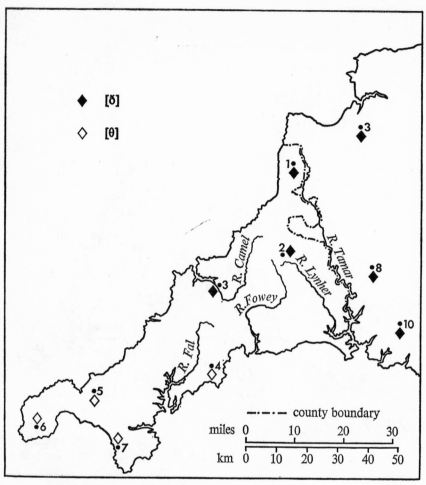

Map 20. The initial consonant in thigh (SED *VI.9.3*).

ME initial *s*. Out of 59 words:
Locality 1 has 40 with initial [z]
            2   42
            3   39
            4   7
            5   9
            6   1
            7   0

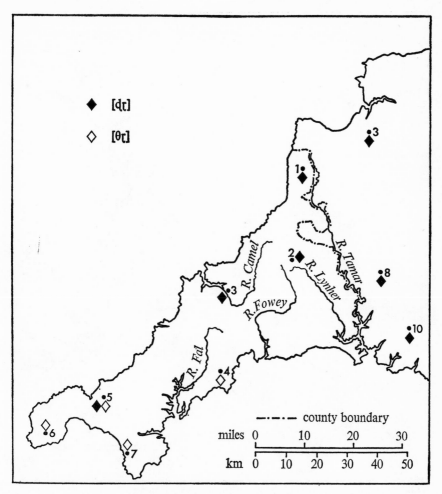

Map 21. The initial consonant in three (SED *VII.1.3*).

ME initial *th*. Out of 18 words:
Locality 1 has 14 with initial [ð] and 4 with initial [d]

2	14	4
3	14	4
4	5	4
5	6	1
6	1	0
7	1	0

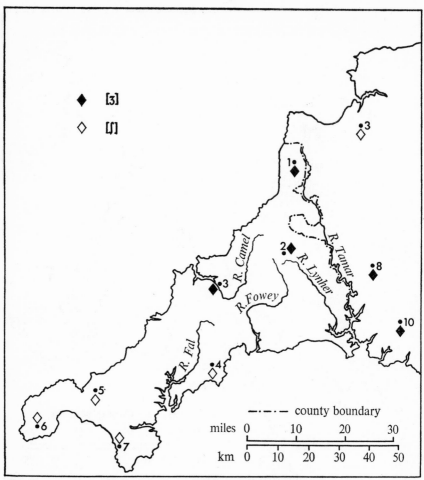

Map 22. The initial consonant in shilling (SED *VII.7.5*).

The words with initial [d] are, in all localities, *thatch, thatching, thatcher, thistle* (locality 5, *thistle* only).

ME initial *thr*. Out of 8 words:
Locality 1 has 8 with initial [dr]
        2   8
        3   7
        4   5
        5   0 (but note i.m. *three*)
        6   0
        7   0

ME initial *sh*. Out of 28 words:
Locality 1 has 2 with initial [ʒ]

2	1
3	2
4	0
5	0
6	0
7	0

It will be noted that [ʒ] is by far the least frequently occurring of [v], [z], [ð] ([d̯ɾ]) and [ʒ], having, for example, in locality 1, 2 out of 28 examples, while there are in the same locality 56 out of 70 examples of [v]. Localities 4–7 have no examples of [ʒ] at all.

A.J. Ellis, in *EEP*, does not present sufficient evidence for Cornwall to allow very definite conclusions to be drawn. His data may be summarized as follows:

District 11

Millbrook   [f] and [s] are always voiced, except for [sw] in *swipes*.

Camelford   [f] is never voiced, [s] is usually voiced. [ð] occurs in *thing* (no other examples).

Cardinham   [f] and [s] are sometimes voiced and sometimes not (more or less equal examples).

St Columb
Major   [f] is voiced one out of three times, [s] is always voiced.[87]

District 12

Marazion. No voicing.

The data, and therefore the conclusions, are not very satisfactory, but the important thing is that District 11 (=*SED* localities 1–4) shows voicing, albeit inconsistently, while District 12 (=*SED* localities 5–7) shows none, thus to a limited extent agreeing with the data presented by *SED*. (It should also be remembered that Ellis has only one locality in his District 12, namely Marazion. If this is regarded as roughly equivalent to *SED* locality 6 (the nearest locality), the similarities between the two areas (*EEP* District 12 and *SED* localities 5–7) appear more obvious.) Cf. Ellis's earlier quotation from 'Tregellas' (see p. 30, above): "'No sooner have you passed Cranstock [sic]

87. Or, perhaps, half-voiced. They are transcribed sʟz, and Ellis states (p. 170, n. 1): "These were said to begin with (s) followed by a faint sound of (z), in that case they would form the transitional sound from (z) to (s)."

(8 wsw. St. Columb Major) and Cubert (2 s. Cr.), and entered into St. Columb's,' than you begin to hear (z-) for (s-), in first to a small and then to a large extent."

As would be expected, Ellis shows voicing in his other southern and western Districts.

Evidence of spellings

Only spellings for [v] and [z] (with a few in *d*) are available from early sources,[88] and these are all from place-name material, excerpted from 'The Place-Names of Cornwall'. The situation is complicated by the fact that a late analogical lenition or mutation affected Cornish initial *f* and *s*, having the same phonetic effect as 'voicing', but occurring in written form only in the late anglicized spellings of place-names.[89] This was in all probability not a grammatical change, for which a special context was necessary, but more likely took place in any and all contexts.[90]

The evidence is unsatisfactory also in that it is very sparse, and spellings in *v* are, as usual, the only ones represented at all fully. An examination of all the English and Cornish names beginning with [f ~ v] shows that spellings with *v* are actually very rare: even when the modern form has *v*, earlier forms often do not. (In Cornish names, including those with the element *fenten* (see below), this is due to the lateness of the mutation mentioned above.)

In east Cornwall, some English place-names occur with initial *v*, many containing the element OE *fenn*, e.g. Venn in Launcells, Vendown in Minster, Viverdon (? < OE *fīf* + *beorg* + *dūn*) in St Mellion. *Fenten ~ venten* ('spring, well', < Latin *fontana*) also occurs here, e.g. Fentervean in St Gennys, northeast Cornwall, and it is possible that in east Cornwall *v* occurring in this element is due not to lenition but to (English) dialectal voicing.[91] But in place-names of English (as distinct from Cornish) origin, apart from the isolated example of Viscar in Wendron (west Cornwall), the westernmost examples of *v* are Varley (only *probably* English) Point in St Endellion, and a small group comprising Venn in Cardinham, the Voxen in Helland, Varewash in Bodmin, and Le Virses in Lanhydrock. Forsaken Land in St Winnow appears as *Varsakenlond* 1390. These names occur within an

88. What is really needed is a survey of *present-day* place-name pronunciations, which would provide us with a map of voiced initial fricative consonants in such names in addition to the few examples which happen to have been preserved in early sources.
89. See Jenner, *A Handbook of the Cornish Language* (1904), 71; R.M. Nance, *A Guide to Cornish Place-Names with a List of Words Contained in them* (1951) 2; idem, *A Cornish-English Dictionary* (1955), vi.
90. Cf. Jenner, *op. cit.*, 177 (final sentence).
91. In any case, some of these eastern place-names may be, as in Devon, from OE *fenn* + *tūn*, rather than Corn. *fenten*.

eastern area roughly approximating to *SED* localities 1–3 (and St Cleer), and comprising the old hundreds of Trigg (in the north) and Wivel (in the south).

In central and west Cornwall, *fenten ~ venten* and one or two other Cornish words comprise the majority of the names having voiced *f* initially (those which have [v] arising from lenition of [b] or [m] are, of course, not taken into account in this investigation). This is partly because the majority of place-names in this area are, in any case, Cornish, *fenten* being an especially common component, and there is thus little to compare them with. However, one would expect the *ventens* to have *f* if the English sound-change alone were operating, since this change would hardly be expected to affect Cornish names in an area which must have been predominantly Cornish-speaking at the time the names originated: the fact that many of them have *v* suggests that there was the additional impetus of a similar impulse – the phonetically similar sound-change known as lenition or mutation – within Cornish. The evidence, although poor, is sufficient to warrant such a conclusion. This impulse in Cornish does not seem to have affected English place-names in central and west Cornwall, which usually retain their voiceless initials, e.g. Foxhole (cf. Ventonwyn) in St Stephen-in-Brannel, Fair Moor (cf. Venton-ladock) in Ladock, Frogmore (cf. Ventonglinnick) in St Clement, Forest (cf. Venton Race) in Illogan. The evidence is not, of course, 100 per cent consistent, and some Cornish names are also spelled and pronounced with initial *f*.

To sum up, with regard to the English place-names, we may state that the dialectal change by which [f] > [v] is reflected in the spellings, but that this voicing seems to die out in the centre and west of the county. Conversely, some Cornish names in central and west Cornwall, especially those containing *fenten*, have a voiced initial, but this is to be ascribed to Cornish lenition. Although there is not very much place-name evidence, as far as it goes we may claim that it supports the dialectal evidence.

The theory of two similar impulses at work – an English sound-change in English names and a Cornish sound-change in Cornish names – is supported by the evidence of spellings of words beginning with *s*. In these, *z* is extremely rare, except in the case of the element *sawn* (<Corn. *saun* 'cleft', etc., Welsh *safn*), in which, apart from an isolated example in the parish of St Teath (north-east Cornwall), it is usually restricted to the far west of the county. English names spelled with *z* are limited to Zaggy (i.e. 'soggy', with dialectal unrounding of the vowel) Lane in Callington and Zelah (?<OE *sele* 'hall') in St Allen (but the latter is perhaps doubtful). Perranzabuloe appears as *Saincte Piran in zandes* in 1564.

In east Cornwall only, there are a certain number of place-name spellings with initial *d* in words which had ME *th*. Such are Dunderhole (<OE *þunor-*)

169

Point in Tintagel and Dupath (*Thewpath alias Dewpath* 1706; < OE *þeofa pæþ*) in Callington. It is assumed here that these spellings genuinely represent [d] and not [ð], a conclusion which is substantiated by Andrew Borde's spelling (1547) of *thick, thin, therein*, etc., with initial *d* in his imitation of Cornish dialect (see Appendix below). Such spellings, though reflecting genuine phonetic developments, find no counterparts in the present-day dialects of Cornwall except in *thatch*(-) and *thistle* (above).

As noted above, ME *th+r* usually > [dɽ] (presumably via an intermediate stage [ðɽ]) in Cornwall localities 1–4. Place-name evidence of this change is found in Druckham in Lawhitton (*Throcombe* 1377, 1464; *West Drocombe* 1445; *Drokeham* 1512), east Cornwall. There are no other certain examples.

As far as it goes, place-name evidence supports the conclusion from present-day dialectal evidence that [d] for ME initial *th* and [dɽ] for ME initial *thr* are south-western dialectal features occurring (apart from the other south-western counties) only in east and central Cornwall.

Voicing in words of French origin

There is little evidence from the data presented here to show that ME initial *f, s, th* and *sh* assume a voiced quality less readily in French words than in native words. In the tables above, words of French origin are marked with a superior letter [f]. Of the 70 words beginning with *f*, 16 are of French or probable French origin. Of these, *faggot-wood, faint, fair/feast, finished, finishes, flasket, fool* and *pheasants* have a negligible incidence of initial [v], while *farmer, farm-house, fault, fester, fitchew* (probably French, see *OED*, s.v. *Fitch, Fitchew*), *flour, flowers* and *front* have a more or less average or 'normal' incidence.

Of the 59 words beginning with *s*, seven are of French origin. Of these, *slice* and *suit* v. have a negligible incidence of initial [z] (but cf. *so* and the English words beginning with *sl*), while *second, sexton, sort, suet* and *suit* n. have a more or less average or 'normal' incidence.

There are no French words beginning with *th* or *thr*.

Of the 28 words beginning with *sh*, two are of French origin. Of these, *chemise* has no examples of initial [ʒ], while *sugar* has a more or less average or 'normal' incidence.

Generally speaking, however, it does seem that voiced initial consonants in native words have a slightly wider and more concentrated distribution than those in French words over the whole area; loan-words, especially the later ones, perhaps had initial voicing extended to them by analogy (e.g. a man who pronounces [v] in *furrow* will presumably also do so in *fête* – first recorded in 1745, according to *OED*), until the tendency to voicing was no longer strong enough to compel the initial consonants of new words to conform.[92] It must be remembered, however, that here we are dealing with Cornwall alone, which has a very different historical background from the rest of the south-west, and we may well have to seek an answer different from any which could account for the situation elsewhere. There is not, in any case, enough evidence to allow any statement to be made on a purely numerical basis, and the dates of the first recorded occurrences of the French words in English do not seem to help, for example *pheasants* (negligible incidence) is first recorded in 1299, and *farm-* (normal incidence) in 1297.

To sum up, in Cornwall voicing tails off in the initial consonants of any words, English or French, after locality 3. In localities 4 and 5 it is moderate, in 6 and 7 it is negligible. In addition to an inexplicable north–south distribution, localities 1–3, 5, and even 6, having more examples of voicing than localities 4 and 7 (note that voicing was heard at St Cleer, though not to any great extent), there is the usual east–west distribution, the county falling into three areas, namely those represented by localities 1–3, 4 and 5, 6 and 7. It thus seems that ME *f*, *s*, and *sh* became voiced predominantly in the eastern part of Cornwall, i.e. in the same territory which, as we have seen, formed, together with Devon and west Somerset, a 'discrete linguistic type' in respect of other features, in an area bounded on the west by both natural and administrative boundaries. To this extent, therefore, east Cornwall forms part of the larger south-western area of England in which voicing is traditional. Voicing has, however, extended further down the county than has the fronting of the sounds discussed earlier, even appearing, outside the main eastern area, in the far west.

It should finally be stated that the only evidence of the converse use of [f] for [v] (e.g. in *vinegar*, *vicar*, cited by Alexander Gil[93] as a south-western feature, and found very occasionally by *SED* in the other south-western counties) is in *verdigris*, heard by me twice with initial [f] on the tape-recording from Cornwall locality 2.

Conclusion

We have now reached the stage at which we must sum up and draw conclusions. The material may be summarized as follows:

1. ME *a* reflexes in isolative and combinative positions
A consideration of the evidence allows the general conclusion that apparently south-western dialectal types of reflex ([a(:)], etc.) are present in varying degrees in localities 1–5, that apparently Standard English types ([æ(:)], etc.)

92. See Wakelin and Barry, *op. cit.*, 61.
93. *Logonomia Anglica* (1621), ed. O.L. Jiriczek (1903), 32.

are present in varying degrees in localities 3–7, and that localities 3–5 vary to a greater extent than the others, often having both types.

2. ME ǭ, u and iu reflexes

Apart from the [ʌ] from ME ǭ and u, which does not vary to any great extent, these reflexes fall with some precision into two types, which, for convenience, we may classify in general terms as [ʏ(:)] and others ([u:], [ɷ] and [ɩɷ]). With few exceptions, [ʏ(:)] is restricted to localities 1 and 2.

3. ME ū reflexes

These are distributed in almost the same way as those of ME ǭ, u and iu: localities 1 and 2 have an [œʏ] type, and 3–7 [ɛɷ] types.

4. ME initial f, s, th, thr, sh reflexes

Localities 1–3 have most voicing, 4 and 5 much less, and 6 and 7 hardly any.

Thus:

ME ǭ, u, iu; ME ū	Localities 1 and 2 versus 3–7 have [ʏ(:)]; [œʏ].
ME f-, s-, th-, sh-	Localities 1–3 versus 4–7 have [v, z, ð, ʒ].
ME a	Localities 3–7 versus 1–5 have [æ(:)], etc.

This generalized statement aims only to list the localities in which the sounds predominate, e.g. [ʏ(:)] is listed for localities 1 and 2, but also occurs once in 7, initial [v] occurs in every locality, but predominates in 1–3.

On the phonological evidence, it seems possible to distinguish three areas, namely localities 1 and 2 (or 1–3); 6 and 7 (or 5–7); and the intervening area. Localities 1 and 2 (or 1–3), in east Cornwall, represent the area in which English was earliest introduced and Cornish earliest given up. In this area, dialectal characteristics predominate, thus:

1. [a] < ME isolative a and a + nasal.
   [a:] < ME a + f, s, th.
   [a(:)] < ME al + consonant or finally.
   [a:] < ME al + f, m.
   [a] < ME a following [(k)w].
   Special developments: [aɩ] or [aˈ] < ME a + [ʃ], [ʧ], [g]; [ɛ] in *catch*; [aʳ:ɖ-] forms in *after(-)*; retention of [ɫ] in *stalk, talk, walk*; short forms in *halfpenny(worth)*; dialectal forms in *cart, part, shards*.

2. [ʏ(:)] < ME ǭ.
   [ʏ] < ME u (rounded).
   [ʏ:] < ME iu.
   Special developments: [ɩ] or [ɛ] < ME ǭ + [ð]; [ɛ] in *shooting*; [ɩ] or [ɛ] <

ME *u*; various dialectal forms of *brush*; [o:] in *oven*; [ʏ:], [æÿ] in *shovel*, with loss of [v].

3. [œʏ], etc., from ME *ū*.

4. [v, z, ð, ʒ] < ME initial *f, s, th, sh*; [dʈ] < ME initial *thr*.
   Special developments: [d] < ME *th* in *thatch*(-) and *thistle*.

Localities 6 and 7 (or 5–7) represent the area in which Cornish was abandoned last, and here the ME sounds give rise to reflexes more like those of (present-day or earlier) Standard English, thus (the dates refer to the Standard English developments):

1. [æ] < ME isolative *a* and *a*+nasal (ME *a* > [æ] in the sixteenth to seventeenth centuries).
   [æ:] < ME *a*+*f, s, th* (ME *a*+*f, s, th* is lengthened in the seventeenth century).
   [ɔ:] or [ɒ] < ME *al*+consonant or finally (ME *aul* > [ɔ:ɫ] in the sixteenth to seventeenth centuries).
   [æ:] < ME *al*+*f, m* ([æ:] arises in the seventeenth century).
   [ɒ] or [ɔ:] < ME *a* following [(k)w] ([ɒ] was fully accepted in Standard English by the eighteenth century).

2. [u:] < ME *ǭ* (ME *ǭ* had become [u:] before 1500).
   [ʌ] < ME *ǭ* ([ʌ] probably existed in Standard English from *c.* 1550).
   [ɷ] < ME *ǭ* ([ɷ] probably arose about the middle of the seventeenth century).
   [ʌ] < ME *u* (as above).
   [ɷ] < ME *u* (rounded) remains.
   [ɩɷ] or [u:] < ME *iu* (the diphthong did not become a rising one until the later sixteenth century).

3. [ɛɷ] < ME *ū* (ME *ū* had reached a preceding [əu] stage by the sixteenth to seventeenth centuries).

4. [f, s, θ, ʃ] < ME initial *f, s, th, sh* remain.

It may be seen from the summaries immediately above that nearly all the sounds concerned came into existence in the sixteenth to seventeenth centuries, and it is at this period and subsequently that we assume them to have been introduced into west (and central) Cornwall, since we have tentatively postulated a date of *c.* 1500 (based on place-name evidence) as the date at which English was predominantly spoken in the peninsula as far west as Truro. West of Truro, as Cornish was given up, so English was adopted, and the phonological system which prevailed was probably one which approximated to the Standard English of the time. It is suggested here that the features cited above were characteristic of this mode of speech.

As might be expected, the central area of Cornwall sometimes shows the dialectal type and sometimes the other type, e.g. [a] (beside [æ]) as the reflex of ME isolative *a*, but (with very few exceptions) [uː] as the long reflex of ME *ǭ*. This is consonant with the theory that English was adopted in the peninsula gradually, leaving pockets of Cornish speakers behind. We should not expect uniformity here (if, indeed, anywhere).

While pockets of Cornish speakers may account for the presence of Standard English types in east and central Cornwall, English settlements made early in west Cornwall must often account for the presence of the older dialectal features there, e.g. of [v, z, ð, ʒ]. Such settlements have been mentioned already: they have names like Bejowsa, Tresawson, and Alverton, the only completely English compound name in the west of Cornwall recorded in Domesday Book. But the presence of other extraneous elements in either area, e.g. [yː] in locality 7, [æ] in localities 1 and 2, must no doubt be accounted for by simple contamination one way or the other.

At any rate, it appears that by working back from the evidence of present-day English in Cornwall, we are able to deduce successive strata of languages and dialects. Underlying present-day dialectal English in east Cornwall is, of course (apart from that dialect's ME and OE ancestors), only Cornish itself, but underlying the English of west Cornwall there is presumably a much earlier south-western dialectal form of speech, ultimately replaced by an early MnE form corresponding more closely to the incipient 'Standard English', and underlying this, Cornish again. Whether or not there is evidence of a yet further stratum (a non-Indo-European language?) is open to question, but is not within the ambit of the present discussion.[94]

The ME documents from Cornwall have not so far been fully analysed, but when this is done one of their main contributions will be to reveal whether or not the manuscripts from western Cornwall show characteristic south-western features – e.g. the presence of a rounded vowel as the reflex of OE *ĕo* and the voicing of initial fricative consonants. If they do, then it will be clear that a 'south-western' type of speech *was* at first typical of the whole peninsula, west as well as east, and that this type was overlaid in the early MnE period by the more 'Standard' type, much as the Kentish dialect of Dan Michel's *Aʒenbite of Inwyt* (1340) has now been overlaid by a different type of English. If they do not, but on the other hand display features that we associate with early London dialect, then we may perhaps assume that even at this early period the English dialect of west Cornwall was showing traces of the more 'Standard' type of speech to which we have been referring.

94. See W.B. Lockwood, *Indo-European Philology* (1969), 42; R.M. Nance, *A Guide to Cornish Place-Names* (1951), 1.

6 Morphological features

The small collection of morphological examples from *SED* assembled under several headings in this chapter is intended to support the phonological material in the preceding chapter and the lexical material in that following. The examples are specially selected to emphasize yet again that dialectal forms have penetrated the east of the county and predominate there, and that Standard English forms (or ones identical with them) predominate in the west. There is not always a clear distinction, the material admits of many exceptions, and thus isoglosses are inconsistent, as usual. Nevertheless, a picture may be said to emerge which coincides in general terms with that shown by other material examined in the present book. The omissions of any treatment of, for example, the pronoun *I* under section 1 is because no differences in usage are registered throughout the county, while *you* shows a confused and complicated distribution (cf. IX.5.4, IX.7.2) of *thee* and *ye*, on the history of which forms much research is apparently still needed in dialect and Standard English.

1. The personal pronoun.
VIII.9.5 (a) We are; (b) We were. Under (a), *us* occurs as the subject at locality 1 only, and *we* at 2–7; under (b), *us* occurs at localities 1 and 2, *we* at 3–7 (cf. also VII.2.14 *we two*).
IX.7.9 We are. *Us* occurs as the subject at locality 1, *we* at 2–7. The use of the objective form *us* in unemphatic contexts for the subject *we* is found throughout the whole of Devon, in east Cornwall, and in single localities in Warwickshire, Oxfordshire and Berkshire.
VI.14.14 She wears the breeches. *Her* occurs as the subject at localities 1, 2, 5, *she* at 3, 4, 6, 7.
VIII.9.5 (a) She is; (b) She was. Under both (a) and (b) *her* occurs as the subject at localities 1–3, *she* at 4–7.
IX.7.7 She is. *Her* occurs as the subject at localities 1–3, *she* at 4–7.
IX.7.9 She is. *Her* occurs as the subject at localities 1–3, *she* at 4–7.

IX.7.2 Is she? *Her* occurs as the subject at localities 1–3, 6, *she* at 4, 5, 7.

IX.7.10 She isn't. *Her* occurs as the subject at localities 1–3, *she* at 4–7.

IX.7.3 Isn't she? *Her* occurs as the subject at localities 1–4, *she* at 5–7.

IX.7.6 Wasn't she? *Her* occurs as the subject at localities 1–3, 6, *she* at 4, 5, 7.

IX.7.8 (If) she were. *Her* occurs as the subject at localities 1–3, *she* at 4–7.
The subjective use of the form *her* is characteristic of the central and southern west Midlands and, except for west Cornwall, the south-western peninsula.

IX.7.2 Are they? *Mun*[1] ('them') occurs as the subject at localities 1, 3, *them* at 2, 6, *they* at 4, 5, 7.

IX.7.3 Aren't they? *Mun* occurs as the subject at localities 1, 3, *them* at 2, 6, *they* at 4, 5, 7.

IX.7.5 Aren't they? *Mun* occurs as the subject at localities 1, 3, *them* at 1, 2, 4–6, *they* at 7.

IX.7.6 Weren't they? *Mun* occurs as the subject at locality 3, *them* at 1, 2, 4–6, *they* at 7.
The objective form *them* is used in unemphatic contexts for *they* in the south-west and in much of the west-Midland region, as well as occasionally outside this area.

From the material tabulated above, it may be clearly seen that the forms *us, her, them* (*mun*), used as subjects, occur mainly in the eastern localities of Cornwall, while *we, she, they* are characteristic of the more westerly localities.

2. The verb To Be.

VIII.9.5 (a) I am. *I be* occurs at localities 1, 2, *I'm* at 3–7.

IX.7.7 I am. *I be* occurs at localities 1–4, 6, *I am* at 5, 7.

IX.7.9 I am. *I be* occurs at localities 1–4, 6, *I am* at 5, 7.

IX.7.1 Am I? *Be I* occurs at localities 1–4, *am I* at 5–7.

IX.7.10 I'm not. *I bain't* occurs at localities 1–4, 6, *I aren't* at 5, 7.

IX.7.4 Aren't I? *Bain't I* occurs at localities 1–4, 6, *aren't I* at 5, 7.

IX.7.5 Aren't I? *Bain't I* occurs at localities 1–4, *ain't I* at 6, *aren't I* at 5, 7.

VIII.9.5 (a) We are. *Us be* occurs at locality 1, *we'm* at 2–4, *we are* at 5–7.

IX.7.9 We are. *Us be* occurs at locality 1, *we be* at localities 2–4, 6, *we are* at 5, 7.

IX.7.2 Are you? *Art* occurs at locality 1, *be ye* at localities 2, 3, *art thee* at 4–7.

---

1. The origin of *mun* is obscure. It may derive from phrases such as [bɛɪn+ əm] *bain't 'em* > [bɛɪ+ nəm], with subsequent metathesis of [n] and [m], and then usage as an independent word 'them'. But *EDD*, recording *mun* (pronoun) from Somerset, Devon and Cornwall, suggests that the form arises from the dropping of *hy* from ME *hymen* 'them', a form derived from *hym*+ the inflexional suffix *-en*, added to differentiate *hym* 'them' from *hym* 'him', and found in south-western texts (cf. *MED Hemen*). *Mun* is also recorded from locality 5 at VII.2.11.

IX.7.3 Aren't you? *Bain't ye* occurs at localities 1–4 (also *artn't* at 1, *artn't thee* at 2), *aren't ye* at 5, *aren't thee* at 7, *ain't thee* at 6.

VIII.9.5 (a) They are. *They be* occurs at locality 1, *they'm* at localities 2–4, *they're* at 5–7.

IX.7.7 They are. *They be* occurs at localities 1–4, 6, *they are* at 5, 7.

IX.7.2 Are they? *Be mun* occurs at localities 1, 3, *be them* at 2, 6, *be they* at 4, *are they* at 5, 7.

IX.7.10 They aren't. *They bain't* occurs at localities 1–4, *they ain't* at 6, *they aren't* at 5, 7.

IX.7.3 Aren't they? *Bain't mun* occurs at localities 1, 3, *bain't them* at 2, *bain't they* at 4, *aren't they* at 5, 7, *isn't them* at 6.

IX.7.5 Aren't they? *Bain't mun* occurs at localities 1, 3, *bain't them* at 1, 2, 4, *aren't them* at 5, *aren't they* at 7, *ain't them* at 6.

The forms which occur in the above synopsis may be clearly seen to fall into two types which, for the sake of convenience, we may label '*be*' (which includes *bain't*)[2] and '*are*' (which includes *am*) types. It will be noted that, in general, the *be* type is to be found predominantly in east Cornwall, while *are* occurs in the west. From the accompanying map, map 23 (p. 178), drawn from the responses to IX.7.7 *I am*, it will be seen that *be* is now prevalent west of a line roughly approximating to Watling Street,[3] while *am* is restricted to the east of the country and is also the Standard English form. The map is, however, reasonably representative of the verb *to be* as a whole.

Historically, the present stem of the verb *to be* derives from two distinct roots, giving in OE (West Saxon) on the one hand sg. *eom*, *eart*, *is*, pl. *sint*, *sindon*, and on the other hand sg. *bēo*, *bist*, *biþ*, pl. *bēoþ*, infinitive *bēon*. It is not clear for how long there has been a territorial distribution of these two types, but it would appear that it is at any rate a post-ME phenomenon, since, on the basis of an examination of ME texts, it has been established that the normal forms in all ME dialects are: 1 sg. *am*, 2 sg. *art*, 3 sg. *is*, pl. southern and south-west Midland < OE *bēoþ*, east and west Midland *ben*, northern and north Midland < OE *(e)arun*, in the singular the *b*- forms being rarer and occurring mainly in early texts (they were common in OE). The only ME territorial distribution was thus between the various forms of the plural, and it therefore looks as if in the south-west these were later levelled out into the singular, giving the whole paradigm *b*- forms.[4]

2. *Bain't* looks like a blend of *be* and *ain't*, the latter regarded as a contracted form of *are not* by *OED* (s.v. *Ain't*), later extended to all persons of the verb, singular and plural. These problems cannot be solved, however, without full reference to the very wide variety of dialectal forms of the verb, positive and negative, obviously a problem requiring separate and detailed treatment.
3. On this isogloss, see M.F. Wakelin, *English Dialects* (1972), references in Index of Places.
4. See G. Forsström, *The Verb "To Be" in Middle English* (1948).

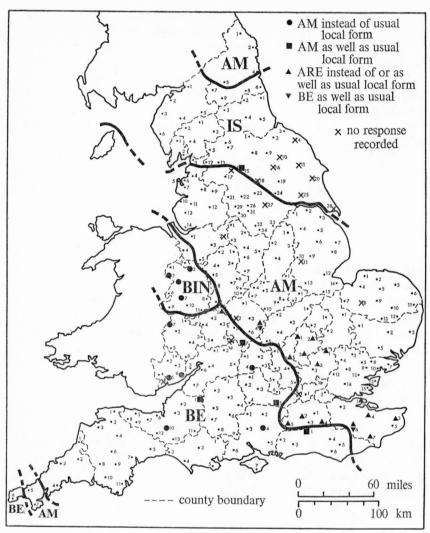

Map 23. I am (SED *IX.7.7*).

We'm, they'm, the contracted forms of *we am, they am*, occur at VIII.9.5 (a), localities 2–4, and are indeed common in the south-west. These simply represent the extension (presumably again of post-ME date, since there appears to be no trace of it in ME texts)[5] of the forms of the 1 sg. *am* to the plural.

5. See *MED*, s.v. *Bẹn* v.

Both in the personal pronouns and in the verb *to be*, it may be noted that locality 6 often has the dialectal form, which is surprising in view of the westerly situation of this locality. Frequently, moreover, as distinct from the other localities, it shows the form *ain't* or, on one occasion, *isn't*. In the case of the former, it appears that locality 6 is a 'boundary' locality, showing neither the dialectal nor the usual Standard English form, but perhaps an older form which at one time had a respectable place within Standard English (see *OED*, s.v. *Ain't*). *Isn't them* is an enigma, but has occasional parallels, e.g. at IX.7.5 Cheshire 4.

3. *A-* (< OE *ge-*) preceding the past participle.

IX.3.2 found, IX.3.5 broken, IX.5. 6 done, IX.6.4 got (illustrative material only) all show *a-* preceding them in localities 1, 2, but *a-* is absent in 3–7, this being a feature (in the country as a whole) of mainly south-western distribution.

4. The indefinite article *a* preceding a numeral.

VII.1.17 about ten (calves). *About a six, about a fourteen, a one* all occur as responses at locality 1, *a six, a one, about a four or five* at 2. *A* is absent from the responses at localities 3–7.

VII.2.8 about ten (o'clock). *A* occurs only at locality 1. This feature is widespread, occurring, for example, in Yorkshire as well as the south. It is, however, especially frequent in the south-west, occurring in the greater parts of Somerset, Wilts, Devon, Dorset and Hants.

It is hardly necessary to summarize the morphological material assembled above, or, indeed, to comment on it, since it speaks for itself, showing, on the whole, distributions which accord with those which emerge from the phonological material, namely on the one hand dialectal features penetrating the county from the east, extending down the peninsula even, in some cases, as far as locality 6, and on the other hand features which are plainly of a Standard English type. These facts will be taken into consideration in the general Conclusion.

7 Lexical features: the Cornish loan-words

During the *SED* investigation, some 20 to 30 words from the now extinct Cornish language emerged, either in the responses or in the incidental material. A detailed study of these words and of their distribution in the county both serves as a companion to the phonological and morphological material and supports the evidence available for drawing significant isoglosses.

The historical reasons for the presence of Cornish words in west Cornwall are set out in Chapters 3 and 4, and there is no need to cover this ground again, except to reiterate that as Cornish was last spoken in west Cornwall it is here that we should expect to find any surviving Cornish words, as indeed we do. Ellis, in *EEP*,[1] referring to his District 12, says, "many words of Cornish origin remain." This can hardly be said to have been substantiated by *SED*, but we must assume that many have disappeared since the time of Ellis's publication (1889).[2]

This is probably the main reason why so few Cornish words have been found by *SED*, but another reason is no doubt the universality of the *SED* questions. They were intended to elicit words for notions known over the length and breadth of the country, and could not be designed for special purposes at the same time: a questionnaire specially compiled to elicit mining or fishing terms or words for birds, flowers, and so on, would perhaps have produced a great many more Cornish words,[3] and it is to be hoped that this will soon be done.

1. p. 171.
2. Cf. H. Jenner, 'Cornwall a Celtic Nation', *The Celtic Review*, I (1905), 234–46. In this paper, read before the Pan-Celtic Congress at Carnarvon, Jenner states that a considerable number of words – perhaps a hundred or more, mostly names of things – were still in use among the Cornish working-classes (p. 241). In support of the *SED* findings, however, Mr I. Colquhoun, in 'Cornish Earth', *The Cornish Review*, XVIII (1971), 57–66, listing some 130 dialect words current in Penwith, cites only about ten of Corn. origin.
3. Cf. Jenner, *loc. cit.*, who states that a very large proportion of the mining and fishing terms are Cornish in origin. And it should be noted that there are a good many Corn. words in Nance's *Glossary*.

The absence of a substantial element of Cornish vocabulary, however, finds its parallel in medieval and early MnE documents from the same area. Such English manuscripts as are available for examination apparently show no trace of Cornish vocabulary,[4] any more than they show influence of Cornish phonology, morphology or syntax. It looks on the face of it, therefore, as if a large Cornish element has never been present in the English of the county, whether spoken or written. The most important element may have been confined to the specialized vocabularies of mining, fishing, and so on.[5]

One of the worst difficulties encountered in an investigation of Cornish vocabulary is the lack of early forms. What sources there are are mostly Cornish, and are pitifully few. A basic necessity is a Cornish dictionary on historical principles, but first the extant manuscripts need re-editing (for the most part). Meanwhile, it seems inadvisable to designate a word Cornish without evidence of either cognate (Welsh, Breton) or early forms. Many words may be simply of dialectal origins, taken into Cornish at the late stages of its history. It should be noted, incidentally, that the etymologies given in *EDD* are not always to be trusted. One reason for popular belief in the existence of a large number of Corn. loan-words in English dialect may, in fact, be attributable to erroneous ascription of some words to Celtic sources by early philologists. It seems very doubtful, for example, whether the words *clicky* 'left-handed', *click* 'left-hander', found by *SED* (VI.7.13) throughout Cornwall, as well as (N.B.) at Devon 8, 10, are genuinely from an Old Corn. *glikin* in *dorn glikin* 'left-handed', cited by *EDD* from Williams, and regularly accepted as Cornish even by present-day scholars, as much as merely imitative (cf. the other southern words for this notion – *coochy-*, *keck-*, *keggy-handed*, *squippy*, etc., etc.).

A second difficulty is the obscurity of Cornish phonology, which changed a good deal during the history of the language, especially in the last period of its existence, when the classical forms became broken down and mutilated.

4. J.H. Matthews, *A History of the Parishes of St Ives, Lelant, Towednack and Zennor* (1892), gives (p. 403) a short "list of the most curious Cornish words which occur in [fourteenth- to seventeenth-century] documents relating to the Saint Ives district", but these are merely surnames such as Moyl (< *moel* 'bald'), Engoff (? < *an gov* 'the smith'). Matthews reproduces a very considerable number of useful documents, and from an examination of these, I have found only one Corn. word, namely *porth* (< Latin *portus*) 'port', which occurs in the compound *porth-reeve* (spelled variously) from *c.* 1599 to 1639 and in the simplex *porth* in 1626. See my article 'Significant Spellings in the St Ives Borough Accounts', *Neophilologus* LVII (1973), 1–3.

5. Cf. Carew (*Richard Carew of Antony: The Survey of Cornwall*, ed. F.E. Halliday), 128, who admittedly was writing in east and not west Cornwall: "The other rude terms wherewith Devon and Cornishmen are often twitted may plead in their defence not only the prescription of antiquity but also the title of propriety and the benefit of significancy, for most of them take their source from the Saxon, our natural language, and continue in use amongst the Dutch [i.e. German] . . ."

Exactly how some sounds were pronounced is by no means certain – contemporary descriptions are not always very satisfactory – and this makes the question of dealing with the phonetic forms of the words very awkward. Orthography is chaotic in Middle and Late Cornish texts, and it is difficult to know how to interpret spellings. Added to this, some words have doubtless been subjected to the process of folk-etymologization, their forms being modified to conform to a mistaken notion of what they were thought to be.

Loan-words in Cornish

Some of the words discussed below are not Cornish in origin, but Latin, French or English. From an early period – even, for example, in the *Vocabularium Cornicum* of *c*. 1100 – Cornish was very susceptible to foreign influence, and the *Ordinalia* and later works abound not only in words and phrases in all three languages but also in chunks of verse in French and English, as we have already seen. This seems to reflect the actual situation in medieval Cornwall, in which Cornish, English, and, to a lesser extent, French, were all current. A substantial Latin element had been present in all the Brittonic languages from a very early period in the diffusion of that language. It is not surprising, therefore, that some of the words we are to consider here as Cornish have ultimately a different origin. These, however, have been allowed to stand, since – apart from other (e.g. phonological) indications – their presence in west Cornwall and nowhere else in the whole of England strongly suggests that they have come into English dialect through Cornish and not independently of it. The real interest of the English and French loans in Cornish is that they may preserve older, fossilized phonological or morphological forms, not available for scrutiny in 'normal' ME documents. From this point of view alone, the investigation of all extant Cornish documents is of the utmost importance.

Distribution

The Cornish words are distributed between *SED* localities 6, 7, 5, and 4, locality 6 having by far the greatest number. There are also one or two examples in localities 2 and 3. This means that they are mainly confined to the extreme west of the county, with an occasional example at locality 4 and further east. It was seen above (p. 93) that locality 6 (St Buryan), locality 7 (Mullion) and locality 5 (Gwinear) were three of the last places in which Cornish was recorded as having been spoken at the beginning of the eighteenth century, and that Cornish was apparently heard at locality 4 (St Ewe) as late as 1595. There thus seems to be a significant correlation. We can now establish an important isogloss between localities 4 and 5, an isogloss which very strikingly coincides with several others, namely:

1. Ellis's division between his Districts 11 and 12.

2. The place-name boundary between -*n*(*n*)- and -*dn*-, -*n* and -*dn*.

3. Some of the distributions of phonological features described in Chapter 5, e.g. the preponderance of some [æ] types from ME *a* in localities 5–7.

4. Some of the distributions of morphological features described in Chapter 6, e.g. the occurrence of *she* (as opposed to *her*), *we are* (cf. *we be*), and *am I* (cf. *be I*).

Sources of early forms

The following volumes, full references for which are given in the Bibliography, have been consulted.

1. English dictionaries and glossaries: *OED*; *MED*; *EDD* (which includes material from earlier glossaries, see p. 19, above).

2. Cornish dictionaries and glossaries (compiled from the extant Corn. texts, from earlier glossaries, and other sources; see p. vii of the Introduction to the *English-Cornish Dictionary*): R.M. Nance (ed.), *An English-Cornish Dictionary* (1952), and *A Cornish-English Dictionary* (1955) (treated as one work here, and abbreviated *Corn. Dict.*); R. Williams, *Lexicon Cornu-Brittanicum* (1865) (Williams used most of the early Corn. literature (see p. 24, above), and also E. Lhuyd, *Archaeologia Britannica* (1707) (see p. 24, above); W. Borlase's Vocabulary, chiefly derived from Lhuyd, printed in *Observations on the Antiquities . . . of the County of Cornwall* (1769); W. Pryce's Vocabulary, printed in his *Archaeologia Cornu-Britannica* (1709)—see p. 24, above; W. Stokes, 'A Cornish Glossary', *Trans. Phil. Soc.*, 1868–9 (a supplement to Williams' work, above, listing about 2,000 words from early sources); *ibid.*, 'A Glossary to the Cornish Drama *Beunans Meriasek*', *Archiv für Celtische Lexikographie*, I (1900), 101–42.

3. Place-names: J.E.B. Gover, 'The Place-Names of Cornwall' (1948); *PND*.

In the following discussion of the Cornish words, the item from *SED* is given, with its phonetic transcription, meaning, reference, and the locality where it was recorded. When the word has not been published (in *SED*), but has been extracted directly from the field-worker's recording-books, the spelling adopted is from *EDD*, and in these cases the reference given is to the entry in the recording-book.

When available, citations and comparable material are given from *EDD*, *OED* and *MED*, as well as comparable material from *SED* itself. The word's origin is given, with its Welsh and Breton cognates, if any, and its occurrence in early documents, including place-names. The remainder of the entry is self-explanatory, discussing phonological, morphological and semantic development.

The treatment of the semantic loans at the end is slightly different, but is self-explanatory.

bannel [banəɫ] a broom. V.3.2 (unpublished), locality 4

EDD Recorded from Cornwall only.

Origin and early forms Corn. *banallen* f., coll. *banal* 'broom flower or plant, besom', Old Corn. *banathel*. Bret. *balan*, Welsh *banadl, banal*.

Place-names ? Lamballa (*Lambadela c.* 1350, *Lambadala* 1380) in St Cleer; Benallack (*Benathelek* 1244, 1284, etc.; 'place of broom') in St Enoder; Benallack (*Benathelek* 1244, 1390) in Probus; Bonallack (*Benathelek* 1321) in Constantine; Benallick (*Benathlok* 1343) in Mabe; Carvannel (*Kaervanathel* 1302, *Carvanal* 1390; 'broom camp or fort') in Gwennap; perhaps Trevales (earlier *Trefathlas, Trevathelos,* etc.; ? for *Tre-vanathel-os* 'farm in the broomy place') in Stithians; Carvannel in Illogan; Rospannel (*Rospanal* 1329, *Rosbonal* and *Rosbanal* 1346; 'broom heath or hill') in St Buryan.

Commentary Cornish added a suffix *-en, -an* to create a singular form from a material noun, e.g. *būly, būlyen, scaw, scawen* (cf. below).[6] These nouns have come into English in their material forms, i.e. without suffix, but now have singular meanings, 'a broom, a pebble, an elder tree'.

bucca [bɒkə] scarecrow. II.3.7, localities 5–7

Words for scarecrow appear to be closely associated with those for hob-goblin, etc., both in Cornish and English (as well as other languages), and the following comparable material is therefore of obvious relevance, although not all the forms can carry the (? secondary) meaning of scarecrow as well as of hobgoblin, those that can being marked with an asterisk, except in the *SED* examples.

SED II.3.7 Scarecrow: *-boggart, -boggle, -bogle* from parts of the north of England (see vol. I); *bugalo, buglug* Dorset 5, *bogeyman* Bucks 4.

VIII.8.1 Bogey: *boggart, boggin* (Isle of Man), *bogle* from parts of the north of England (see vol. I). *Bogey(man)* is of general occurrence.

EDD Records the following forms with their variants and compounds: *bockie, bockle* (cf. *bock* v. 'to shy' (of a horse) – both from Cornwall only), *boggart** (note the form *bawker* from north-west Devon), *boggy-bo**, *boggin, bogie, bogle**, *bug, bugabo(o), bugan, bugger.* (Cf. also *bo* sb.1, *boll* sb. 3, *boodie, bull-beggar*.)

OED (with the earliest recorded instance of each) *Bog* sb. 2 1527, *boggard* 1570, *bogle** c. 1500, *bogy* 1836–40, *bug** sb.1 1388, *bugaboo* 1740, *bugbear* 1581, *buggard* 1575. (Cf. also *boll* sb.3, *bolly, boodie, bull-beggar, bull-bear*.)

To try to unravel the origin and relationships of the members of this

6. See H. Jenner, *A Handbook of the Cornish Language* (1904), 87–8.

large group (which seem to be in some way associated with exclamations such as *boo! bo!*) is beyond the present scope. A glance at the headings in *OED* will show the widespread, but uncertain, relationships.[7] Here we must restrict ourselves to a consideration of *bucca*.

Origin and early forms Corn. *bucca* m. 'hobgoblin, imp, bogy, scarecrow'. Cf. Bret. *bugelien-n, bugel-noz*, Welsh *bwgan*.

Place-names The following possibly contain the element *bucca*: Chybucca (*Chybucka* 1748; 'haunted house') in Kenwyn; Buckabarrow Downs (*Bukeborough* 1613; 'downs with haunted tumulus') in Lanreath; Bucklawren (*Bockelouwarn, Bockalowarn, Boklouwern* c. 1200, *Bokelewarn* 1263, and elements *Boke-, Boka-* 1284, 1302, 1311, 1339, *Buckelawre* 1535; the second element is 'fox', but the meaning of the whole is not clear) in Martin-by-Looe; Polbucky (*Polpoke* 1465, 1590, *Polpuckey* 1613; but the second element may be OE *pūca* 'mischievous demon', ME *puck*; 'haunted pool') in Talland, cf. Parkwalls (*Pokewallys* 1490, *Pokewalles* c. 1580, *Puckwalls* 1841; perhaps referring to haunted ruins or hut circles) in Advent; Buckabin (field-name, meaning obscure) in St Tudy; Bucky Tree (field-name; ? 'haunted tree') in St Cleer.

Commentary The basic meaning of *bucca*, as well as of the other forms listed above, is 'hobgoblin, ghost, object of dread', the meaning 'scarecrow' (which only some of them have) doubtless being a further semantic development. For further information on the *bucca* as hobgoblin, the reader is referred to *EDD* under the words listed above, and to Nance's *Glossary*, s.v.

bulhorns [bɒłaʳːŋʐ] snails. IV.9.3, locality 6

EDD Recorded from Cornwall only.

Origin and early forms Corn. *bulhorn* m. 'snail'.

Place-names There appears to be nothing relevant in Cornwall, but the name Bullhornstone (*Bolehorn(e)ston* 1287, *Bulhornston* al. *Bulston* 1574) in the parish of South Brent, Devon, should be noted. The Editors of *PND* suggest: "This would seem to mean 'bull horn stone', with reference to a stone of some particular shape, but no such stone is known here now."[8]

Commentary The usual Corn. word for snail was *melwhen*, which, in the form *melyen*, glosses Latin *limax* in *VC* (cf. *molhuiddzhan* in Lhuyd),[9] and is cognate with Bret. *melc'houed, -enn*, Welsh *malwen, melyen*, etc.

On the other hand, *bulhorn* is first recorded by Lhuyd.[10] It has no cognates, and is unknown in earlier Cornish literature. It is fairly clear that it is an English dialect nickname, although thought to be of Cornish origin by

7. J. Widdowson treats of the word *bogey* and its associates in 'The Bogeyman: Some Preliminary Observations on Frightening Figures', *Folklore*, LXXXII (1971), 99–115.
8. p. 290.
9. p. 79, s.v. *Limax*.
10. p. 48, s.v. *Cochlea*.

Lhuyd and later scholars. Stokes, in the 'Cornish Glossary' (p. 246), proposes an ingenious etymology *mulh-corn, *mulh- < *molc = Greek μαλακός 'soft' (cf. μαλακόσαρκος 'with soft flesh'), which seems unnecessarily complicated and hypothetical.

As an English dialect word, however, there are no references to *bulhorn* in *OED* or *MED*. It is presumably simply composed of *bull* + *horn*, the whole compound no doubt referring to the snail's horn-like tentacles. One might compare the large number of English words (mainly of doubtful origin) referring to trees and animals with the first element *bull*, e.g. *bullfinch*, *bulcard* (the smooth blenny).

Bulhorn may have been used in Cornish to indicate only the shelled garden snail. It would seem to be more specific than *melwhen*, which can also mean 'slug' (Lhuyd glosses *molhuidzhon*[11] as 'a naked snail'). The plural ending *-as*, given to *bulhorn* by the *Cornish Dictionary*, may be no more than the usual English plural suffix *-es*.

In a most interesting article on snail-charms,[12] R.M. Nance lists other, comparable, nicknames for the snail both from Cornwall and outside – from Cornwall *malorn*, *jinjorn*, *bull-jig* (cf. *bull-gog* from Lincs); *snarleyorn* from west Somerset, *snail-horn* from other counties. He notes that *bulhorn* has been generally accepted as part of the Cornish language since Lhuyd's citation of it in 1707, but that Cornish has "its own Celtic names" for the snail. He points out that, had he known it, Carew had great opportunities for using *bulhorn* as a name for his snail hero in *A Herring's Tail* instead of calling him 'Sir Lymazon' (French *limaçon*), and this suggests that *bulhorn* was not in familar use when Carew wrote. "On the whole it seems probable that *Bulhorn* was introduced to Cornwall in an English rhyme, its first syllable being 'bull' and its second a meaningless rhyme for 'horn', and that it had not long been known here when Lhuyd noted it."

(paving-)bullies [(peːvən)boɬtz] (paving-)cobbles. I.1.6 (unpublished), locality 7

EDD Recorded from Devon and Cornwall, as "a stone rounded by the action of water; a boy's large marble".

Origin and early forms Cf. Corn. *būljën* f., coll. *būly*, pl. *būlynow*, *būljow* 'rounded stone, pebble, boulder'.

Place-names Cabilla (*Cabulian* 1086, *Cabulion* 1211) in Cardinham. The early forms of this name look as if they are related to some of the examples given by Nance (below).

Commentary This word has no known cognates, and is probably, therefore, a loan-word in Cornish. The most likely source seems to be French

11. *Loc. cit.*
12. 'Bulorn and its Congeners', *OC*, v.7 (1956), 311–15.

boulet 'a small globe, sphere or ball' (*OED*), a diminutive of French *boule* 'ball', which gives MnE *bowl* (*OED Bowl* sb.2) 'a sphere, globe, ball'.

This word could apparently have entered English dialect from two sources. It may have been borrowed direct from French into English, making its first recorded appearance in English in 1605 (*OED*, s.v. *Boulet*), although doubtless existing in the spoken language before this (*MED* records (1419) the same word under *Bullet*, 'an official tag or badge of registration or identification'). But as we have it here, in locality 7, although the words show no phonetic or morphological evidence of Cornish mediation, it seems more likely that it was taken from Cornish into English dialect. We may therefore suggest the following sets of alternative series:

> *either* French *boulet* (< *boule*) > English *boulet* > *bully*
> *or* French *boulet* (< *boule*) > Corn. *būly* > English *bully*

Nance (*Glossary*) records *Bully(-stone)*, also *Caboolen(-stone)*, *Cabooly-stone*, *Camboolen*, *Cambooly-stone*, *Cambooly-shot*, all with the basic meaning 'stone'. Of *bully*, he suggests: "cf. F. *boulet*, diminutive of *boule*, a ball", and also notes that "a large rounded stone is a BOWLY." Under *Bowl(y)*, he suggests that this is an analogical imitation of *bully*, with augmentative sense. It seems more likely, however, that *bowl(y)* simply represents a form with retention of long *ū*, which is then assimilated to English *ū* and becomes [aɷ] (see p. 84, above), while *bully* shows a shortened form. For the other words, Nance suggests Corn. etymologies.

bussa [bɒsə] salting-trough. III.12.5, localities 6, 7;
  bread-bin. V.9.2, localities 5–7 (but at 7 "actually a salting-trough")

EDD Recorded from Devon and Cornwall as 'a coarse earthenware vessel'.

Origin and early forms See Commentary, below. *EDD* suggests cf. French (obsolete) *busse* 'espèce de tonneau'.

Place-names None.

Commentary The etymology of this word is uncertain. The *Cornish Dictionary* lists it, together with an older form *bōs-sēth* (i.e. *bōs* 'food' + *sēth* 'pot, jar, crock'), but continuity between these two forms has yet to be demonstrated. In fact, *bōs-sēth* seems an unlikely progenitor of *bussa* because this would mean that the final syllable had almost completely disappeared, a rather drastic reduction considering that the stress was probably almost equal in both elements of the compound.

I suggest, in agreement with *EDD*, that the word is first of all an English dialect word derived from ME *busse* < OF *buce*, *busse* 'barrel' and Medieval Latin *bussa*. *MED* (s.v. *Busse*) and *OED* (s.v. *Buss* sb.1) give numerous examples. French *u* ([y]) > English [ɒ] during the ME period as usual, as in, for example, *humble*, *judge* (but because of the preceding initial labial consonant, [ʊ] was retained in *buss*, as in *bush*, *push*, i.e. it did not go on to [ʌ]). The [ə] ending was retained, as is commonly the case with inflexional endings in south-western dialectal English, cf. the place-names in Cornwall Forda, Wooda, Beara (which retain the dative sg. ending in OE *ford*, *wudu*, *bearwu*, respectively), Prustacott (with genitive pl. ending in OE *prēost*), and for similar examples from Devon, see *PND*, p. xxxvi. Cf. also *dogga* (a dialectal name for the dog-fish, < ME *dogge*), cited in Nance's *Glossary*. The hypothesis of English dialectal origin (ultimately from French) explains the word's presence in Devon better than if it were Cornish in origin.

From English dialect, *bussa* seems to have got into Cornish, and, as noted above, it is listed in the *Cornish Dictionary* as a Cornish word with a Cornish origin. It does not appear, however, in any of the early literature, and has no Breton or Welsh cognates, and these facts alone suggest that it is more likely to be of extraneous origin.

As found in western Cornwall, *bussa* may be either merely the English dialect word, or it may, in fact, be part of the small residue of Corn. words. In either case there is a semantic development from the French meaning 'barrel' (? 'salting-barrel') to 'earthenware vessel, salting-trough'.

clunk [kɬʌŋk] to swallow. V.1.8 (unpublished), locality 5
clunker [kɬʌŋkəʳ:] windpipe. VI.6.5, locality 2

EDD Recorded from Devon and Cornwall s.v. *Clunk* v.2 'to swallow, esp. to swallow with an effort, to "bolt"'. Hence *Clunker* n. 'the uvula, "swallow"'.

Origin and early forms Corn. *lenky* 'to swallow', Bret. *lonkañ*, Welsh *llyngcu*, all from British **lunc-* 'to swallow'.

Place-names None (but Lank in St Breward may be from Corn. *lonk* 'gullet, throat' (hence ? 'whirlpool', etc.), related to *lenky*).

Commentary The origin of initial [kɬ] in these words is almost certainly not an imitation of a presumed Corn. unvoiced *l* (=Welsh *ll*) – for the existence of which there is little evidence[13] – as *EDD* implies, but is probably due to the compound *collenky* (< *cowal*, (when prefixed) *cowl-*, *col-* 'entire, whole, complete' + *lenky*) > *clenky > *clenk. (For the syncopation of unstressed *o*, cf. Corn. *clomyer*, etc., < Latin *columbarium*; and the place-name Treglum (in Tresmeer) ? < *tre* + *Columbanus* (personal name), *Tregloman* c. 1150.) For the development (to [ʌ]) of the stressed vowel, one must assume a series [ɛ] > [ə] > [ʌ], under the velarizing influence of the preceding [kɬ] and the following [ŋk], all velar sounds.

Clunker would then be derived from *clunk*, by means of the normal English *-er* suffix added to the base, cf. *SED* VI.6.3, Wilts 3, Berks 2, and

13. But cf. Norden (pp. 90–1, above), 26.

VI.6.5, Wilts 3, Devon 1 – *quilter* ('throat, windpipe') < *quilt* ('to swallow' – see *SED*, VI.5.13).

In dialect, the use of the words was possibly reinforced by their echoic effect, cf. *Clunk* v.1 in *EDD*, 'to emit a hollow, interrupted sound, as of a liquid issuing from a bottle or narrow opening'. (*EDD* records this word only from Scotland and Northumberland, and derives it from Norwegian *klunka* (dialectal) 'to emit a gurgling sound'. It is apparently unconnected with the words under consideration here.)

croust [kɹæv̆s(t)] snack. VII.5.11, localities 4–7

EDD The sense 'crust' is recorded from south-west England, but that of 'snack' from Cornwall only.

Origin and early forms Corn. *crowst* m. 'picnic lunch', etc. Recorded in *Origo Mundi*, 1901; Lhuyd, p. 89 (s.v. *Merenda*), *Krust*.

Place-names None.

Commentary Croust is not Cornish in origin. Ultimately, like English *crust*, it derives from OF *crouste*, Latin *crusta*. At least two paths of development suggest themselves:

1. OF *crouste*, Latin *crusta* > Corn. *croust* (then [u:] > [aɷ]; see p. 84, above).

2. OF *crouste*, Latin *crusta* > ME *crouste* ([kɹu:stə] > [kɹaɷst]), Corn. *croust*.

In other words, *croust* came into Cornish either direct from Old French and Latin, ultimately developing a diphthong by assimilation to ME *ou* ([u:]) words, or it came into Cornish via ME. Phonologically, either of these seems to be possible.

dram [dɹam], [dɹæm] swath. II.9.4, localities 5–7

EDD Recorded s.v. sb.3 from Cornwall only.

Origin and early forms Corn. *dram*. m., pl. *drammow*, Bret. *dramm*.

Place-names None.

Commentary Dram is cognate with Greek δράγμα 'a sheaf', literally 'as much as one can grasp', cf. δράξ 'handful' < δράσσομαι 'clutch, grasp'. The same root probably also appears in Irish *dreimm* 'to climb', and in Scottish Gaelic *dream* 'crowd, bundle'.

The notion of a handful is now remote from that of a swath 'a row of mown grass', but the word probably survives from the time when sickles were used to cut grass (i.e. before the advent of the scythe), a tuft of grass being grasped in one hand, while the sickle, held in the other, cut the handful of grass off at its roots.

flam-new [fɫamnʏ:], [fɫamnɪɷ], [fɫæmnɪɷ] brand-new. VI.14.24, localities 2/3, 5–7

EDD Flam sb.6 'flame' is recorded from Cornwall only; hence *flam-new*, from Cornwall only.

Origin and early forms The first element of the compound is Corn. *flam* m. 'flame', pl. *flammow*, < Latin *flamma*.

Place-names None.

fuggan [fʊgən] pastry dinner-cake. VII.5.12 (unpublished), locality 6

EDD Recorded from Cornwall only. (This entry should be consulted for the fuller meanings of the word.)

Origin and early forms Corn. *fūgen* f., pl. *-now*, *-gas*. Cf. *hoggan*, below.

Place-names None.

Commentary This word, *hoggan* (below), and probably also *hobban* (with similar meanings, but not recorded in *SED*) may all be further developments of Corn. *whyōgen* ('pastry dinner-cake'), *hoggan* by a simple shortening, and *fuggan* by a development of *wh* ([hw]) to *f* and obscure vowel change to *ū*, *ū* later being shortened to *u*. (*EDD* records alternative forms *fogan*, *-on*, which suggest a parallel Corn. base with *o* instead of *ū*.)[14] The sound-change [hw] > [f] is also attested in the south-west Cornouailles dialect of Breton: see K. Jackson, *A Historical Phonology of Breton* (1967), §§ 539–40.

gawky [gɔːki] stupid. VI.1.5, locality 6
gawk [gɔːk] a stupid person. VI.1.5, locality 4
Note. **gawky** also occurs at Devon 3 (and cf. [gʏːki] at locality 9), and **gawk** at Devon 3, 4. See also VIII.9.3, Devon 3 [gɔᵗːki].

EDD Both the adjective and the noun are stated to be of widespread distribution. Cf. also *Gowk* sb.1.

MED This work records ME *gōkī* n. and adj. < *gōk* 'cuckoo' < ON *gaukr*.[15] "Borrowed early in Cornish". *Gawky* occurs in Cornish as both noun and adjective, but as an adjective *MED* records this word in Cornish only; otherwise, it apparently occurs in ME only as a noun.

Origin and early forms Corn. *gōky* < ME *gōki*. Recorded (as noun and adjective) in *Origo Mundi*, 173; *Passio Domini*, 1149, 1662; *Resurrectio Domini*, 972, 983, 1136, 1273, 1454. The Corn. word is more easily explained as a loan-word from ME than as an adjectival formation from Corn. *cōk* 'empty, vain, worthless, one-eyed' < *cuic* 'luscus vel monoptalmus' (*VC*), as Williams would have it (see *Gocy*). The latter derivation requires explanation of the initial *g* (although this might be possible, cf. *gook*, below), and also of the suffixation of English adjectival *-y*, whereas derived adjectives in Cornish are mostly formed by adding *-ek* to a noun or verb.[16]

14. Were it not for the existence of Corn. *fūgen*, it would be tempting to explain *fuggan*, *fogan* as blends of *figgy* + *hoggan*: cf. *EDD*, s.v. *Hoggan* (sb. 1) – "sometimes called figgy hoggan or fuggan."
15. But see *OED*, s.v. *Gawk*, *Gawky*, where connexion with ON *gaukr*, etc., is denied.
16. Jenner, *op. cit.*, 91.

Place-names None.

Commentary The adjective *gawky* at locality 6 and the noun *gawk* (presumably a back-formation from *gawky*) at locality 4, may be from Cornish, as suggested above, but this origin need not be postulated for the same words in Devon, and obviously not for the rest of the country, where the forms with [ɔ:] go back directly to a ME *au* ([aɔ])[17] from ON *gaukr*. *Gooky* at Devon 9 must, however, go back directly to a ME *ọ̄* form (*ọ̄* > [u:] > [ʏ:]: see above, pp. 127ff.).

geeking [giː kən] gaping. VI.3.7, locality 6
                    peeping. VI.3.8, localities 5/6
Note. Cf. Devon 10 [iːz ɬʏkɪn geːki] he's looking geeky (i.e. 'looking steadily in astonishment').
EDD Recorded from Cornwall only.
Origin and early forms Corn. *gȳky* 'to peep', perhaps < English *keek*[18] (with lenition, perhaps arising from position in the sentence, and see further n.20, below), unrecorded in OE, but having Germanic cognate forms (see *OED*, s.v.).
Place-names None.

gook [guː k] bonnet. VI.14.1, localities 4/6
     (also **gook bonnet** at locality 4)
EDD Recorded from Cornwall only. Also in the form *gowk*.
Origin and early forms Presumably Corn. *cūgh*[19] m. 'head-covering, crown of hat, beehive cover', *pengūgh* m. 'hooded fur cloak, bonnet'. In *VC*, *pengūgh grec* glosses Latin *mastruga*. Cf. Welsh *cwch capan* 'crown of a hat', *penguwch* 'bonnet', Old Bret. *cuh* 'covering', Bret. *kouc'h*.
Place-names None.
Commentary Initial [k] of *cūgh* has become [g] although the word stands in isolation, probably surviving thus from the usage of the word in compounds, where the initial consonant was mutated as the result of the preceding part of the compound.[20]

Final [x] has become [k]. In English, after the stage had passed at which [x] became [f] or zero (as, for example, in *laugh*, *dough*), the natural simplification was to [k], a process shown in numerous place-names in Cornwall, and cf. *SED*, II, III.8.1 Cheshire 4 [mɒkɪnz] *mochyns* < Welsh *mochyn* 'pig'.

17. ON *au* was adopted in ME as *ọ̄, au, ou*, See K. Brunner, *An Outline of Middle English Grammar* (1963), §18.
18. A dialectal form now restricted chiefly to the north of England, according to *OED* and *EDD*. Cf. also *SED*, I, VI.3.8.
19. *Corn. Dict.* omits to mark the long vowel here, cf. cognate Irish *cúass* 'hole'.
20. See Jenner, *op. cit.*, 175, and cf. also 177: "In the latest Cornish there was a tendency to use the second state [i.e. *p>b, c/k>g, t>d, b>v, g>—, d>dh, m>v*] after nearly everything . . ."

In the *EDD* example, *gowk*, [u:] has been diphthongized to [aɔ], showing assimilation to ME *ū*, with usual further development (see p. 84, above).

griglans [gɾɪgɫənz] heather.
I.3.14 (unpublished), I.3.15, IV.10.11 (unpublished), locality 7
EDD Recorded from Cornwall only. But cf. *grig* sb.6 'heather', etc., recorded from Cheshire, Wales, Shropshire, ? Herefordshire, Norfolk and Cornwall.
OED Cf. *Grig* sb.2.
Origin and early forms Corn. *grüglon* m. 'heather-bush' (< *grük* coll. 'heath, heather, ling' + *lōn* m. 'grove, bush'). Cf. Welsh *gruglwyn*.
Place-names Perhaps found in Gregland in Withiel and Gregland in Roche (*Griglands* 1767), with lowering of [ɪ] to [ɛ] after unrounding of Corn. *ü* (see p. 145, above).
Commentary Williams records only *grig* 'heath' or 'ling', but notes that *griglan* "is used at the present day for 'heath' in Cornwall". He gives no early spellings. In late Cornish (from the sixteenth century), *ü* (perhaps [y]) was unrounded to [i] (see p. 84, above), and a lowered version of this appears in the dialectal form as recorded here. Final [z] presumably represents the English plural suffix -*s* (the Corn. plural was *grüglonow*), but the significance of a material noun (namely heather) is retained.

groushans [gɾæy̆dʒənz] dregs. V.8.15, locality 6
　　　　　[gɾæy̆ʒənz] dregs. V.8.15, locality 7
EDD See *Groushan* ([grū·ʃən]). The word also appears written *grooshan*, *grishen* (one of *EDD*'s quotations gives *grooshans*).
Origin and early forms Corn. *growjyon* pl. 'dregs, grouts' + the English -*s* plural suffix, forming a double plural. With regard to the further etymology of this word, Nance, *Glossary*, s.v. *Growjans*, states that it is a corrupt variant of *browjans* (q.v., 'small wreckage, timber fragments', etc.; < Corn. *browjyon*, *browsyon* 'crumbs, fragments', sg. *brows*), and adds: "Probably some confusion with 'growshans', the C. form of an E. dialect word meaning 'dregs', as of tea-leaves, coffee-grounds, etc."
An alternative derivation is from an Indo-European base **ghreu-* (Germanic **grū-*) appearing in *gruel*, *gruesome*, and, with an additional *d* (Germanic *t*) in *grit*, *grouts*. This base also appears in Corn. *grow* 'gravel, grit, sand', recorded in *VC* as *grou* 'harena'. With *d* suffix and plural ending -*yon* this gives *groud-yon*, with further development to [gɾæy̆dʒən], etc. (for [u:] > [æy̆], see pp. 147 ff, above).
Place-names None.

gurgoe [gəᵗ:go:] warren. VI.8.4 (unpublished), locality 6
EDD Recorded from Cornwall only. Also in the forms *gurgey*, *gurgy*.

Meanings: 1. A low hedge, a rough fence; the site of a former hedge; a gap in a broken-down hedge. 2. A deep rut; a ditch. 3. A long narrow lane.

Origin and early forms Corn. *gorgē* m., pl. *-ow* 'low or broken-down hedge' < *kē* 'hedge, fence, low wall', etc. (Bret. *kae* 'hedge, enclosure', Welsh *cae* 'hedge, enclosure, field'), with intensifying prefix *gor-*, causing 'soft' mutation of the following *k* in *kē*.[21]

Place-names The second part of Treworga in Ruan Lanihorne (*Treworge* 1314, 1334, 1342, *Treworga* 1483) is perhaps this word, and cf. Treworgey in St Cleer, Treworgie in St Gennys.

Commentary The *SED* form seems to have been adopted from the Corn. plural, with slight phonetic modification, while the *EDD* alternative forms seem to have been adopted from the singular.

Since its adoption into English, this Corn. word has come to embrace several new meanings. In Cornish, it seems to mean primarily a hedge or the like (cf., however, the Bret. and Welsh cognate forms), but since its adoption into English dialect it has come to mean various things associated with a hedge, the meaning 'deep rut, ditch' possibly developing as referring to that which is alongside a hedge, and – the rut notion being roughly comparable with the idea of a lane or narrow defile – easily spreading out to embrace the notion of warren.

Interesting comparisons may be made with the meanings of the Bret. and Welsh cognate forms, and also with such words as *haw* (OE *haga*), *OED*, sb.1 (corresponding to Swedish *hage* 'pasture-field', and Danish *have* 'garden'), and *hay* (OE *hege*), *OED*, sb.2, both of which originally meant 'hedge, fence', and which further developed the secondary meaning of 'enclosed space, enclosure'.

hoggan [ɒgən] pastry cake. VII.6.2 (unpublished), locality 5

EDD Recorded from Cornwall only.

Origin and early forms Corn. *hogen* f., pl. *-gas*. Cf. *fuggan*, above, and the remarks offered there, and *hobban* (not recorded by *SED*, but see *EDD*), with similar meanings.

Place-names None.

Commentary *EDD*, no doubt following Williams and Pryce, derives *hoggan* from Corn. *hogh* 'pig', and describes it primarily as a pork pasty. But, although the suffix *-en*, *-an* has a singulative or diminutive function, there is no evidence that it may have a derivative function, and so this explanation may be simply a folk-etymology. In any case, *hogh* + *-an* would give *hoghan* (i.e. [hɒxən]), and this would be more likely to end up as *hoffan* than *hoggan*. The word is, in fact, perhaps a shortened form of Corn. *whȳogen*,

21. Ordinarily, however, 'aspirate mutation' (i.e. *c/k* > *h*) would be expected, but cf. n. 20, above.

as may also be *hobban*, with change of [g] to [b]. Initial *h* may be due to popular association with *hogh*.

hoggans [ɒgənz] haws. IV.11.6, locality 6

EDD Recorded from Cornwall only.

Origin and early forms Corn. *hogan* m. 'haw' (pl. *hegyn*) + the English *-s* pl. suffix. Corn. *hogan* is probably borrowed from OE *haga* (modern *haw*), though a genuine connexion with Corn. *hogh* 'pig' is just possible (see below). The OE word was borrowed by Cornish (OE *a* (? [ɑ]) being heard as an [ɒ] type in this position),[22] and was regarded as a material noun, the singulative suffix *-an* therefore being added to give a singular or individual sense[23] (cf. *bannel*, above, and *scaw*, below). A new plural *hegyn*, with mutated vowel, was formed later.

The southern dialectal terms for 'haws' show a bewildering variety of forms: forms such as *aglons, eggle-berries, eagles, eggles, eglets, eglons, hags, hagags, haggles*, and so on, may all derive ultimately from OE *haga*, though the presence of *l* in some of them is enigmatic – as, indeed, are certain other characteristics.[24] The forms *hogasses* (more properly *hog-hawses*, a double pl.), *hoggans* (under consideration here) and *hog-hazels* also seem to belong to this category, although the occurrence (elsewhere in the south) of the expressions *pig-berries, -hales, -haws, -shells*, might suggest that the element *hog-* has in fact something to do with pigs, and is not from OE *haga*. It may be, however, that the *hog*-forms were in the first place derived from OE *haga*, but being subsequently folk-etymologized to an association with hogs, then gave rise to the idea that haws had some connexion with pigs. Clearly, an investigation into the folkloristic aspect of this group of words is demanded here.

Place-names None.

Commentary The most interesting aspect of this group of dialect words in Cornwall is the fact that while in localities 1–4 the words *eglets, eagles* and *aglets* are recorded, locality 5 has *eglons*, locality 6 *hoggans* and locality 7 *aglons*, i.e. here (and here alone in all the southern counties) we find forms ending in [ənz]. Whatever the ultimate derivation of Corn. *hogan*, it looks very much as if *eglons* in locality 5 and *aglons* in locality 7 have also adopted

22. See A. Campbell, *Old English Grammar* (1959), §32.
23. The possibility that *hoggan* derives from one of the oblique cases of OE *haga* (most likely *hagan*) must not be discounted – inflexional endings in nouns are often retained in south-western dialect (see p. 188, above).
24. It is not clear how OE *haga* can produce either the Corn. form or modern dialectal forms with [g], since OE *-ag-* regularly > *-aw-*, unless a base such as **hacga, *hagga* is postulated. *OED* records [g] forms first from the nineteenth century, but *hagges* is recorded as current in Lancs by Laurence Nowell, probably writing 1561–6. See A.H. Marckwardt (ed.), *Laurence Nowell's Vocabularium Saxonicum* (1952), s.v. *Haȝan*. Obviously, words such as *eagles* owe much to folk-etymological interpretation.

the *-an* ending by analogy with Corn. *hogan*, combined with an English first element (presumably < OE *haga*) and an English *-s* pl. suffix. It should be noted that *EDD*, s.v. *Haggle* sb.1, records *aglon, awglon, hagglan, orglon*, from Cornwall only.

kewny [kɪɒni] rancid. V.7.9, localities 6/7
(Also at locality 7 [ˈðat ˈbɛːkŋ‿z ˈkɪɒnɪḓ ˈɔːvəᵗ:] that bacon's kewnied over – i.e. has gone rancid)
EDD See *Cunie* n. 'scum', etc., recorded from Devon and Cornwall; hence *Cuny* adj. 'mildewed', recorded from Cornwall only.
Origin and early forms Corn. *kewnÿek* adj. 'mossy, mouldy, hoary', presumably from *kewny* coll. n. 'moss, mildew, mould, scum', etc.; *kewnÿa* v. 'to become moss-grown, mouldy', etc. Bret. *kivny, kinvy* n. 'lichen, moss'.
Place-names None.

muryans [mʌɾɪənz] ants. IV.8.12, locality 6
muryan-bank [mʌɾɪənbæŋk] ant-hill. IV.8.13, locality 6
EDD Recorded from Cornwall only.
Origin and early forms Corn. *muryon* f. coll. 'ants' (sg. *muryonen*) + the English *-s* pl. suffix, forming a double pl., the collective being used as a singular (cf. *bannel*, above). Bret. *merien*, Welsh *morion* 'ants', all from British **morịones*.
Place-names None.
Commentary The relationship of the Corn., Bret. and Welsh words with similar forms in other languages is obscure. Cf. *OED Mire* sb.2, also *Pismire*; *SED* IV.8.12 *Pissy-moors, -mowers*, etc., the second element no doubt < ON *maurr*, related by ablaut to the source (? OE **mīre*) of *mire*.

padgetty-pow [pædʒipɒl] newt. IV.9.8, locality 6
EDD Recorded from Cornwall only.
Origin and early forms Corn. *peswar-paw* (*peswar* 'four' + *paw* (presumably [paɒ] or ? [pɑɒ]) 'foot' < OF *powe*, or ME *pawe, powe* < OF *powe*).
Place-names None.
Commentary This compound, as it stands at present, is obviously the result of much phonetic corruption, some of it probably due to folk-etymologizing. The relevant phonetic changes are:[25]
1. *e > a*. This took place in Cornish. See Williams, s.v. *Padzhar, Paswera*, etc.; Lhuyd, pp. 15 (top of third column), 100 (s.v. *Nonaginta*).
2. *sw* ([dzw] or [ʒw]) > [dʒ].[26] Cf. Williams, s.v. *Padzhar*; Lhuyd, as above.

25. *-tty*, in examples in which it occurs (as in *EDD*), was probably added as an affectionate diminutive. It does not, in fact, appear in the *SED* form, whose spelling, however, is adopted from *EDD*.
26. See *LHEB*, 397.

3. *ar* (unaccented) > *er* and is reduced to *i*.

4. The substitution of *poll* for *paw* ([paω], etc., see above) was no doubt occasioned by phonetic confusion of final [ω] with final dark *l* ([ɫ]), *paw* being thereafter regarded as *pow*, *poll* 'head'. The forms cited in *EDD* are instructive in this respect, *padgetty-pow*, *padgey-pow*, *padzher-pou*, obviously representing a pronunciation with [aω], [oω] or the like. There would then be an obvious parallel with the word *tadpole* (ME *tadpolle*, etc., < *toad + poll* 'head'), and *padgy*, *padgetty*, etc., would function as an adjectival element of unknown but perhaps suggestive meaning in a pet or frivolous compound.

Finally, it should be noted that in Cornwall alone (localities 2 and 4) the newt is referred to as a *four-legged-evet* or *-emmet* (locality 4; the result of a confusion with *emmet* 'ant').[27] *Evet*, like *newt*, is < OE *efeta*, but the epithet *four-legged* looks like a calque on Corn. *peswar-paw*, which presumably meant 'the four-footed one', and could refer not only to the newt, but to the lizard and a water insect known as the ranatra (according to the *Cornish Dictionary*). Obviously, in English, a noun must be added to make *four-legged* more specific.[28]

peeth [piːθ] well n. IV.2.2 (unpublished), locality 6

EDD Recorded from Cornwall and the West Country.

Origin and early forms Corn. *pȳth* m., pl. *pȳthow*. The ordinary word for 'pit' in the extant Cornish literature is *pyt(t)*. This is so in Jordan's *Creation*, e.g. in lines 421, 922, 1722, except in line 329, where *pȳth* is used – *In pyth downe ythof towles* "In a deep pit I am cast", this seemingly being the first recorded instance of the word.

Place-names None.

Commentary The rise of this form and its further etymology are a puzzle. It looks as if it should bear some relationship to Latin *puteus*,[29] but there are the difficulties of the length of the vowel and of Corn. *th*. The regular representative of Latin *puteus* in Cornish is *pyt(t)*, borrowed through English, and, as noted above, the usual word in the extant literature and also in the place-names. The most likely suggestion, in spite of the formidable etymological difficulties, seems to be that *pȳth* is derived from an unrecorded Vulgar Latin form **putteus*[30] (the geminated *t* being necessary to give Corn.

27. Note that *EDD* (s.v. *Evet*) also records *emmet* ('newt' not 'ant') from Cornwall alone, suggesting a phonetic confusion of some standing between the two words. See M.F. Wakelin, *English Dialects* (1972), pp. 73–4.
28. Cf. in *EDD* (s.v. *Four*) *Four-legged cripple* for the newt or lizard.
29. Cf. H. Jenner's rather enigmatic statement: "This is a new word in Cornish, doubtless from the Latin *puteus*", on p. 538 of 'Traditional Relics of the Cornish Language in Mounts Bay in 1875', *Trans. Phil. Soc.* (1876), 533–42.
30. Cf. the geminated forms of various Vulgar Latin words, e.g. *tōttus*, cited by V. Väänänen, *Introduction au Latin Vulgaire* (2nd, rev. edn, 1967), §112.

[θ]). The stages of development here would be *putteus > *puth* (before the end of the sixth century) > *pūth* (c. 600) > *pŭth*[31] > *pȳth* (sixteenth century), modern dialectal *peeth*.

pig's-crow [pɪgzkɾæ̆ÿ] pigsty. I.1.5, localities 6/7
Comparable material

SED I.1.5 (*pig-*)*cree*, Northumberland and Durham.

pig-crew, Cumberland 1, Lancs 5–7, Derbyshire 4.

I.1.6 *hen-cree*, Northumberland and Durham.

hen-crew, Lancs 5–7.

I.1.9 *crew*, *crews*, *crew-yard*, Lincs, Notts, Leics, Rutland, Northants, west Norfolk.

EDD See *Cree, Crewe, Pig-cree, Pig's-crew.*

OED See *Crew 2, Croo.*

This whole family of words, as listed here, presents a fascinating complex which, however, it is not necessary to discuss, but merely to observe that the northern and Midland forms derive either from Brittonic sources via OE or ME, or from Gaelic sources mediated through ON. This group of words, including, of course, Corn. *crow*, is ultimately to be derived from a Common Celtic *krāu̯o*.[32]

Origin and early forms Corn. *crow*. Bret. *kraou*, Welsh *crau, craw*.

Place-names Crowdy Marsh (< *crow* + *dy* (< *ty* 'house') in Davidstow; Lancrow (probably originally *nant crow* 'valley with hovel') in Lanlivery; Carevick (*Crou* 1302, 1327, *Crowarthevick* 1529, *Carrevicke* 1602; the meaning of the whole is uncertain) in Cubert; Carines (*Crou* 1302, 1327, *Crouwoztheynys* 1349, *Crowarthenys* 1398, *Correynes* 1553, *Carrenys* 1620; perhaps 'hovel over against the well-watered land') in Cubert; Collgrease (*Crou* 1302, 1327, *Crowgres* 1497, *Crewgres* 1576, *Collgrease* 1667; the second element is perhaps *crēs* 'middle', but the meaning of the whole is uncertain) in Cubert; Crowgey (*Crougy* 1327; < *crow* + *dy*, as above) in Gwennap; Roscrow (*Roscro* 1208–13, *Roscrou* 1270, *Roscrow* 1284, *Roskrou* 1332; < *ros* 'hill, heath' + *crow*) in St Gluvias; Crowgey (*Crousi* 1338, *Creusy* 1372) in Wendron; Crowgey (*Croudy* 1284, *Creuthy* 1302, *Crugy* 1327, *Crowgy* 1522) in Constantine; Roscrowgey (*Roscreugi* 1285, *Roscrousi* 1358, *Roscrougy* 1359; < *ros* + *crow* + *dy*) in St Keverne; Crowgey in Ruan Minor; Crowlis (*Croures* 1327, *Creulys* 1345, 1360, *Melyncroulis c.* 1380 (*melyn* = 'mill'), *Crowlis* 1564; < *crow* + *lis* 'court, palace', but the first spelling suggests that the second element was originally *res* 'ford', and thus 'hovel at the ford') in Ludgvan. In Devon, *crow* possibly occurs in Crowdy Mill

31. On *pp, tt, cc* > *f, th, ch*, see *LHEB*, §147, and on lengthening, §§34, 35.
32. For fuller discussion, see M.F. Wakelin, '*Crew, Cree* and *Crow*: Celtic Words in English Dialect', *Anglia*, LXXXVII (1969), 273–81.

197

(*Croude* 1297, 1377, *Crowde* 1437, 1443; but the second element does not look like Corn. *dy*, above).[33]

rab [ɾab] gravel. VIII.5.9 (unpublished), locality 6

EDD Recorded from Northumberland and Cornwall.

Origin and early forms Cf. Corn. *rabmen* m. 'granite gravel'.

Place-names Rabman Zawn in Morvah (*zawn* < Corn. *saun* 'cleft', etc.).

Commentary The fact that *rab* is recorded from Northumberland makes it very unlikely that this is a Corn. word at all, although in the compound *rabmen* it is obviously affixed to Corn. *maen* 'stone'. There are no cognates in Breton or Welsh. The ultimate origin of the word is unknown. *EDD* derives it from Swedish dialectal *rabbe* 'remnants of a stone wall', but if this is correct it is not clear how it reached south-west England.

scaw(-tree) [skæv̆(tɾiː)] elder tree. IV.10.6, localities 5/7

EDD Recorded from Cornwall only.

Origin and early forms Corn. *scawen* f., coll. *scaw*. Bret. *skavenn* (earlier *scauenn, scawen*), *scav, skao* (earlier *scao, scaw, sco*), Welsh *ysgawen, ysgaw*.

Place-names Trescowe in St Mabyn; Scawn Hill (f.n.) in Pillaton; Scawn (*Schauan* 1290, *Skauen* 1296, etc.) in St Pinnock; *Scawen* 1338, a lost name in Perranzabuloe; Nanscow in St Breock; Penscawn (*Penscawen* 1306, 1327, etc.) in St Enoder; Enniscaven (*Enyscawen* 1472, etc.) in St Dennis; Nanscawn (*Nanscawen* 1338) in Luxulyan; Trescowe in Breage; Boscawen in Mawgan-in-Meneage; Liscawn in Sheviock, Boscawen-Noon and -Rose in St Buryan. Note Tresco (*Treskau* 1310, etc.) in Scilly.

Commentary The dialectal form is borrowed from the collective in Cornish, but is used as a singular.

stank [stæŋk] to walk, trample, step (on, in)

II.1.6 (='stepped' p.p.) (unpublished), locality 4; I.1.11, IV.1.3, IV.1.9 (='stepped' p.t.), IX.3.5 (='walked' p.t.) (all unpublished), locality 5; VI.6.1 (='stepped' p.t.) (unpublished), locality 6; IV.1.6 (='stepped' p.t.) (unpublished), locality 7

EDD See *Stank* v.5, recorded from Devon and Cornwall. Note sense 2, 'to walk quickly'.

Origin and early forms Corn. *stankya* 'to trample on or into'. Cf. *Bret. sankañ* 'to sink, thrust', etc., Welsh *sangu, sengi* 'to trample'.[34] The verb is cognate with a Primitive Germanic form *staŋkwjan*, OE *stencan* 'to scatter, disperse', 'to stench'; ON *stökkva* 'to leap, spring'; Gothic *stigqan* 'to thrust, strike', causative verb *gastagqjan* 'to collide with'.

---

33. *PND*, 325. The list of early spellings above is not exhaustive. See the article referred to in n. 32, above, for a fuller list.

34. On the development of Indo-European *st* in the Celtic languages, see *LHEB*, §122.

Place-names None.

Commentary The identical past tense and past participle are doubtless formed in English dialect by analogy with Class III strong verbs such as *stink*, *sink*, whose roots end in a nasal consonant and have *a* in the past tense.

tidden [tɪdn] tender. VI.7.14/15 (unpublished), locality 6 (at VI.7.14, *tidden* means 'nervous')

EDD Recorded from Cornwall only.

Origin and early forms Corn. *tyn*, later *tidn* (cf. *-whidden*, below) 'tight, firm, rigid', etc., 'cruel, painful, sharp, tender to touch, intense'. Recorded (as *tyn*) in *The Passion*, verses 171, 204; *Origo Mundi*, 402, 1351; *Passio Domini*, 1887; *Resurrectio Domini*, 1204.

Place-names None.

Commentary This word and *-whidden* below are the only examples of words elicited by *SED* to show the late Corn. sound-change *-n > -dn* (see pp. 76–7, above). 'Nervous' is an interesting extension of the word's semantic range.

(piggy-)whidden [(pɪgi-)wɪdn] weakling (of a litter of pigs) III.8.4, localities 5–7

EDD Recorded from Cornwall only.

Origin and early forms (*Piggy+*) Corn. *gwyn*, later *gwidden* (cf. *tidden*, above).

Place-names None.

Commentary Corn. [gw] > [w] in English.

In Cornish, the weakest pig of the litter could be termed the *pyg-bȳghan* ('small pig') or the *pyg-gwyn* ('white pig'), the first element being borrowed from English.

The point of greatest interest here, however, is why the epithet *gwyn* 'white' should be applied to the weakling. *Gwyn* in Cornish and Welsh, Bret. *gwenn*, in addition to the basic meaning of 'white', also means 'fair, pleasant, blessed, glorious, holy'. In *The Passion*, the adjective is applied, for example, to the soul (verse 204) and to the Blessed Virgin Mary (verse 171). *Bucca-gwidden* (q.v. in *EDD*) can mean 'good fairy'. *Gwyn* in Corn. place-names often conveys the notion of sacredness, e.g. Polwyn ('holy pool'), Ventonwin ('holy fountain'), and one may compare other British names, especially those containing elements referring to water, such as Wendover ('sacred water').[35]

Historical evidence clearly shows that the notion of sacredness can also be associated with the weakling. The smallest pig apparently belonged to the clergy during the Middle Ages; it was allowed to roam and did not have to be

35. See A.H. Smith, *English Place-Name Elements* (1956), II, s.v. **Winn* 3.

chained up to prevent it rooting.[36] Traditionally, it was often dedicated to St Anthony the Hermit,[37] and was (and is) for this reason known in some areas as an *anthony*[38] or (by metanalysis of *Saint* and *Anthony*) *tanthony*: *SED* records *anthony* only from Kent 3–5, but *EDD* (s.v. *Anthony-pig* and *Tantony*) records a much wider distribution (Cheshire, Derbyshire, Herts, Kent, Hants, Devon, Dorset). Cf. also *daniel* at *SED* Kent 4 and 7, which perhaps has some religious significance. All the words for this notion would certainly repay detailed study.

Semantic borrowings

There are one or two words recorded in the dialectal speech of Cornwall that have possibly undergone semantic influence from Cornish in different ways.

stiff[39] steep. IV.1.11, localities 4/7

> *EDD* Not recorded in this sense.[40]

The notions 'steep' and 'stiff' are (or may be) expressed by the single word *serth* in Cornish. It looks as if the functions of this word may have been separately translated into English, either of them being allowed to express the notion 'steep'. To complete the equation, the two words should be interchangeable (i.e. it ought to be possible to use *steep* for the notion 'stiff'), but there is no evidence of this. The modern sense of *stiff* 'steep so as to be difficult' (of an ascent or descent) is recorded by *OED* only from 1704 onwards, and is probably a new, figurative usage, which should be distinguished from the dialectal one under consideration.

white-neck weasel. IV.5.6, localities 5–7

> *EDD* See *White*, §3, p. 474 – 'white-throated weasel'. Recorded from Devon and Cornwall.

The *SED* and *EDD* citations appear to represent the only known occurrences of the word *white-neck*, and suggest comparison with *white-throat*, which occurs in Devon 9 and 11, and is also recorded by *EDD* (*loc. cit.*) for Suffolk, and Somerset (meaning 'stoat').

36. See G.C. Homans, *English Villagers of the Thirteenth Century* (1941), Chapter VII.
37. The pig is one of St Anthony's emblems, and is sometimes seen with him in medieval iconography. This is apparently because he was patron of an order of hospitallers founded in the south of France in 1095. These Antonines had the privilege of being exempt from an order which forbade men to allow their pigs to forage in the gutter. See R.L.P. Milburn, *Saints and their Emblems in English Churches* (2nd, rev. edn, 1957), 22–3.
38. See *MED*, s.v. *Antony*.
39. I have to thank Dr Peter Lucas for bringing this to my attention.
40. But cf. *stiff* (= 'hard' – of hearing), recorded by *EDD* from west Cornwall.

White-neck corresponds exactly to Corn. *conna-gwyn* 'weasel', *conna* meaning 'neck' and not 'throat' (which is *lonk*), and, because of its unique occurrence in these particular localities in west Cornwall, looks like a calque on the Corn. word.

four-legged-evet
   See p. 196, above.

8 Conclusion

It has been my aim in this book, by correlating linguistic features – phonological, morphological and lexical – of the present-day dialects of Cornwall with certain historical facts, to demonstrate that such features can be accounted for by reference to the county's linguistic past.

From the evidence presented in the chapters above it seems possible to draw two important isoglosses, defining three areas:

1. The area of early Anglo-Saxon settlement. As shown in Chapter 3, it is probable that the Anglo-Saxons had entered east Cornwall by the beginning of the eighth century. The main boundary between Saxons and Celts was pushed back to the Ottery–Lynher line where it remained for some time before the Saxons continued their advance down the county. The precise details of that advance remain unknown, but on general place-name evidence the north-east and the south-east were occupied – and probably had been for several hundred years – by the time of the Norman Conquest, while on the more precise evidence of the place-name elements *nant*, *bod*, and their further phonetic developments we can say that by *c.* 1100 the English language predominated in the county approximately as far west as Bodmin and the Camel–Fowey boundary, more or less coincidental with the easternmost lateral hundreds division.[1] This area, occupied in the first instance by men of Devon and the south-west, speaking a south-western dialectal form of English, is covered by *SED* localities 1 and 2 (or 1–3), which show predominantly south-western dialectal features, e.g. [ɣ(:)] < ME *ọ̄, u, iu*; [œɣ] < ME *ū*; [v, z, ð, ʒ] < ME *f-, s-, th-, sh-*; the use of grammatical forms such as *us, her* as subjects, *I be, bain't mun* and so on, and must therefore have formed something of a geographical linguistic unit for some hundreds of years, since the development of [ɣ(:)], for example, is not considered to have taken place before the early MnE period.

1. Obviously by this time the whole of Cornwall had been occupied, to a lesser or greater extent, but perhaps English settlements continued to be thicker in the east, and more scattered further west, so that the English language was predominant here and less so further west.

2. To the west of this area is a large central region stretching about as far as Truro, or perhaps approximately to the westernmost lateral hundreds division. In this area, between *c.* 1100 and *c.* 1500 (i.e. roughly the ME period) English spread slowly down the peninsula, leaving, according to the evidence of place-names and documents, pockets of Cornish-speaking peoples as it did so. At this stage, we are no longer concerned with English occupation and settlement, but with the dissemination of the English language which was going on bit by bit. This area is covered by *SED* localities (3,) 4 and 5 (except where 5 falls in with 6 and 7), and in this area dialectal types exist side by side with the types found in west Cornwall.

3. The westernmost area is that in which Cornish was spoken longest and was still current after *c.* 1500, gradually dying out over a subsequent period of about 200 years or so. Here, English penetrated last, and not until the early MnE period. This area is covered by *SED* localities (5,) 6 and 7. Many of the phonological types present here have been considered to be old Standard English ones, introduced in the early MnE period, and replacing other older (Cornish and English) forms of speech. This area is also the one in which morphological forms are more conformed to those of Standard English usage, and in which Cornish words are still found.

There have been earlier attempts to draw lateral isoglosses in Cornwall, for example that shown on the frontispiece map to Miss Courtney's and Mr Couch's *Glossary of Words in Use in Cornwall* (1880; see p. 26, above): "Sketch Map of Cornwall, showing approximately the point of dialectal division between East and West". According to this map, the line begins at Crantock Bay on the north coast and, passing just to the north-east of Truro, ends at Veryan Bay on the south coast. But the most celebrated attempt to distinguish between east and west Cornwall in respect of their dialects is that of A.J. Ellis. His deliberations in *EEP* about the division between his Districts 11 and 12 are quoted in Chapter 1 of the present book: Ellis finally followed the advice of the Rev. W.H. Hodge for the fixing of his boundary, but, as noted above (pp. 28–9), he also quotes the opinion of one Mr Sowell, whose proposed isogloss would be much further to the east. The Courtney-Couch isogloss falls between these two. The approximate positions are shown on map 24 (p. 204).

A significant point about these suggested dialect divisions is that they all fall within the central area described above. This, added to the lack of nineteenth-century agreement about the position of the line dividing east from west, reflects the fact that the investigators in question were reliant upon several (unspecified) dialectal features, perhaps, at least in some cases, merely upon 'general impression'. The evidence presented in this book shows that a single isogloss is insufficient, and that two major historical

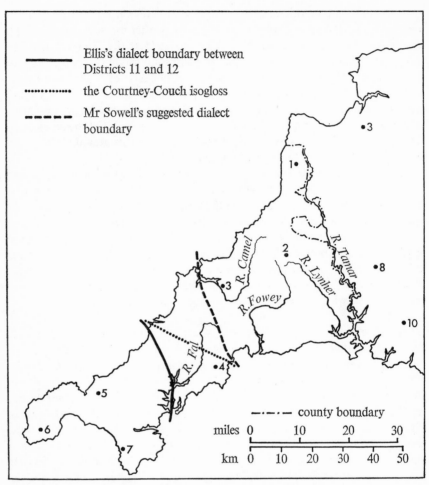

Map 24. Nineteenth-century dialect boundaries in Cornwall.

boundaries are needed, dividing the county into three regions, and accounting for some of the most important of the present-day dialectal isoglosses.

Present-day English in Cornwall bears the marks of a struggle[2] between languages in intimate contact. Here was a scattered race of people, the last speakers of a Celtic tongue which, already in the eighth century, had been pushed into the far west of England. English had been the 'upper' or 'dominant' language since the Anglo-Saxon invasions, and continued to be so in the early eighth century when the occupation of Cornwall began. The

2. Cf. L. Bloomfield, *Language* (1933), §§26.1ff.

result of the occupation was a territorial distribution of the two languages, Cornish in west Cornwall, English in east Cornwall, a long struggle along the border, and the ultimate defeat of the 'lower' language, Cornish. The struggle resulted in the lower language – in so far as it survived – bearing off large numbers of loan-words from the dominant language, as well as becoming phonologically assimilated to it in some details, and very early on adopting its orthographical features. On the other hand, the dominant language took in fewer loan-words and received no phonological influence from it, as far as can be ascertained. This is shown both by a study of the ME documents and from the present, more detailed, study of some aspects of the present-day dialects. This latter side of the struggle has been the subject of the present book, and the conclusions show an almost one-way influence, namely that of English on Cornish; in comparison, the influence of Cornish on English was negligible,[3] visible only in a quite small number of Cornish words found in the far west of the county.

3. This does not take into account the probable effect of Corn. intonation patterns on the English of west Cornwall, which need a full, separate, examination. See H. Jenner, *Handbook of the Cornish Language* (1904), 55 and n. 1.

Appendix

Andrew Borde's imitation of dialectal speech from Cornwall, 1547 (see p. 25, above).

The following 26 lines are reproduced from F.J. Furnivall's edition of *The Fyrst Boke of the Introduction of Knowledge*, EETS, ES 10 (1870), 122–3, and are followed by a commentary.

Iche cham a Cornyshe man, al[e] che can brew;	1
It wyll make one to kacke, also to spew;	
It is dycke and smoky, and also it is dyn;	
It is lyke wash, as pygges had wrestled dryn.	
Iche cannot brew, nor dresse Fleshe, nor vyshe;	5
Many volke do segge, I mar many a good dyshe.	
Dup the dore, gos! iche hab some dyng to seg,	
"Whan olde knaues be dead, yonge knaues be fleg."	
Iche chaym yll afyngred, iche swere by my fay	
Iche nys not eate no soole sens yester daye;	10
Iche wolde fayne taale ons myd the cup;	
Nym me a quart of ale, that iche may it of sup.	
A, good gosse, iche hab a toome, vyshe, and also tyn;	
Drynke, gosse, to me, or els iche chyl begyn.	
God! watysh great colde, and fynger iche do abyd!	15
Wyl your bedauer, gosse, come home at the next tyde.	
Iche pray God to coun him wel to vare,	
That, whan he comit home, myd me he do not starre	
For putting a straw dorow his great net.	
Another pot of ale, good gosse, now me fet;	20
For my bedauer wyl to London, to try the law,	
To sew Tre poll pen, for waggyng of a straw.	
Now, gosse, farewell! yche can no lenger abyde;	

Iche must ouer to the ale howse at the yender syde;
And now come myd me, gosse, I thee pray,   25
And let vs make merry, as longe as we may.

Commentary

Line 1. *Iche cham, che;* cf. 1.5, etc., *iche,* 1.9 *Iche chaym,* 1.14 *iche chyl.* The
retention of [ʧ] in ME *ich* (< OE *ic*) 'I' was a southern feature in late ME
and early MnE, and is used as such for effect on the Elizabethan stage. At
a later period, however, it became confined to a much smaller area: Ellis's
'Land of Utch',[1] Variant v of his District 4, "occupied the angular space
between the two railways which have their vertex at Yeovil, Sm., on the
b[order] of Do.", and Ellis names about a dozen villages in this area which
"were named as using *utch*". Together with *us*, perhaps a further development of *utch*,[2] *utch* is recorded (but unfortunately unpublished) by *SED*
in Somerset alone, and it is clear that this once-common southern feature
has now receded to a small and remote area. In examples such as *chill,
chud* ('I will', 'I would'), final [ʧ] becomes attached to the following verb:
Borde's *Iche cham, iche chyl,* etc., with apparent gemination of [ʧ], either
represent a long medial consonant, i.e. [ʊʧ:ˡam, ʊʧ:ˡʊl], or are simply con-
ventional dialect spellings of each separate word, the *ch* element thus being
unnecessarily duplicated.

3. *dycke, dyn;* cf. 1.7 *some dyng.* In these words ME *th-* ([θ]) has become [d],
presumably via the intermediate stage [ð] which is fairly commonplace in
the dialects of the south and south-west today, initial [d] being currently
attested, however, in only two words, namely *thatch*(-) and *thistle* (see p. 161,
above). In Cornwall, the feature is limited to the east and centre of the county.

4. *dryn* 'therein'; cf. 1.19 *dorow* 'through'. These may simply be examples
of the change [θ] > [ð] > [d], as in 1.3, above (*dorow* representing 'thorough'),
but, perhaps more likely, they may represent the combinative south-western
sound-change [θɾ] > [ðɾ] > [dɾ], attested in words such as *three*: see p. 162,
above. This presupposes syncopation of the vowel in *there-*. Again, the
results of this sound-change are recorded by *SED* only in east and central
Cornwall.

5. *vyshe;* cf. 1.6 *volke,* 1.13 *vyshe,* 1.17 *vare;* and also (with initial *f*) 1.5 *Fleshe,*
1.8 *fleg,* 1.9 *fay,* 1.11 *fayne,* 1.15 *fynger,* 1.20 *fet,* 1.23 *farewell.* No examples
of the voicing of initial *s* are shown. Of the words above which show initial
voicing, only *folk* (actually *folks*) occurs in *SED* (s.v. VIII.2.12 *people*). It

---

1. *EEP*, 84–5. But *ich*, etc., also occurs, according to Ellis (see p. 30), in his District 1,
"western Celtic Southern", where he records it in his Forth and Bargy (Wexford) classified
word list.
2. Cf. *EEP*, 84 (bottom).

has initial [v] in localities 1–3, but localities 4–7 have only *people*, so that no proper comparison, as to initial voicing, can be made. But, as shown in Chapter 5, above, initial voicing is a feature characteristic chiefly of localities 1–3, and falls off considerably in the west of Cornwall.

6. *segge;* cf. ll.7, 13 *hab*, l.7 *seg*. These forms represent the southern retention of OE *secg-, habb-* (*secgan, habban*) in Class III weak verbs, whereas in the north and usually in the Midlands they are replaced in ME by forms derived from the 2 and 3 present indicative, (modern) *say, have*.[3] No modern dialectal parallels to Borde's forms are recorded in *SED* or in *EDD*.

do segge; cf. l.15 *iche do abyd*. These are examples of the south-western periphrastic *do*, as found, for example, at *SED* VIII.7.5 *burglars steal them*. Periphrastic *do* now seems to occur in Cornwall only from locality 4 westward, and is not usual in Devon and most of Somerset, though it is in some other parts of the west and south-west.

7. *Dup* 'shut'. Not recorded in *SED*. See *EDD*, s.v. (v.1).

gos (for *gossip*) 'friend', etc. Cf. l.13, etc., *gosse*. Not recorded in *SED*. See *EDD*, s.v. *Gossie* (apart from this reference, *gos* is given only for Scotland. Cf. *OED*, s.v. *Goss* sb.1, *Gosse* 2, *Gossy*).

8. *fleg*. This word presumably=*fledge*<OE **flycge* (*OED*), adj. 'fit to fly'. Final *g* must (?) here represent [dʒ] (cf. line 7 *seg*), [g] being characteristic of northern forms. Cf. *EDD Flig* adj., recorded from Northumberland, Yorks, Cheshire, Leics, Northants, Warwicks and Shropshire.[4] This proverbial saying is untraced.

9. *afyngred* 'a-hungered'<OE *of-hyngred, -od*<*of-hyngran, -ian*. See *OED*, s.v. *Afingered, Ofhungered* (recorded in ME southern and western texts). Cf. l.15 *fynger* n., no doubt representing a back-formation with initial *f* from the verb-form prefixed by [əf], OE *of-*. Neither *afingered* nor *finger* are recorded by *SED* or *EDD*, and *finger* seems not to be recorded anywhere.

10. *nys. Ne+is* does not seem to make very good sense here, and *ne+has* seems to be the only possible derivation for the word. See *EDG*, §435, which states that some of the southern and south-eastern dialects have a 1 sg. verbal ending in *s, z* or *əz*. No trace of this for *have* has, however, been found in *SED*.

soole 'soul', i.e. flavouring, meat, <OE *sufel, -ol*. Not recorded in *SED*. See *OED*, s.v. *Sowl*; *EDD*, s.v. *Sowl(e)*. The word seems to be chiefly found in northern and Midland dialects (but also in Pembroke and Glamorgan,

3. See Brunner, *An Outline of Middle English Grammar* (1963), 81, who states that forms such as are given by Borde persist in the south into the fifteenth century, although the forms from the 2 and 3 present indicative also appear in this area (e.g. in Chaucer) in the fourteenth century. Obviously the old forms lingered on for a longer period in Cornwall.
4. For the possibility that *segge, seg, fleg* actually represent forms with final [g], cf. *lig, liggan* 'deposit, manure', etc., recorded by Nance, *Glossary*, and by *EDD* (sb. 1) from Cornwall only, and perhaps connected with OE *licgan*.

according to *EDD*), and it is significant in this respect that Borde uses it (spelled *sole*) again in his representation of Scottish speech.

sens. This form, although common, perhaps shows characteristic south-western lowering of [ɪ] to [ɛ]. See p. 145, above, where examples from *SED* are given.

11. *taale.* The meaning of this whole sentence is completely obscure. *Taale* seems to be *tale* v. (< OE *talian*) 'say, speak, tell (of), talk, gossip, account, reckon, consider, count up'.

ons. Perhaps 'once', but 'on (= of) us' is a possibility, though with what possible significance is not clear.

myd (also ll.18 and 25) < OE *mid* 'with'. See *OED*, s.v. (prep. 1), which states that this form became obsolete before the end of the fourteenth century. No doubt it was retained longer in Cornwall, but no modern descendant is recorded in *SED* or *EDD*.

12. *Nym* < OE *niman.* This appears to mean here 'give' (? 'get for me'). From *c.* 1600, the word usually meant 'steal' in general dialect and slang (see *OED*, *EDD*, s.v. *Nim*), but is not recorded even with this meaning for Cornwall (*EDD* records it from Devon, however).

13. *a toome* 'at home'. This is an example of common dialectal metanalysis. Cf. the local pronunciation of the place-name St Ewe, namely [sənˈtˈu:]. (The reference to fish and tin is an obvious one, these being industries for which Cornwall has always been specially noted.)

15. *watysh.* Untraced – ? *what* + an obscure element.

16. *bedauer* (also l.21) < *bed-ifere* 'bed-fellow'. See *OED*, s.v. *Bedauer* and *Bed-fere.* The longer form was apparently retained in south-western dialect until the sixteenth century; *bed-fere* was a literary form until the seventeenth century. Not recorded in *SED* or *EDD*.

17. *coun* perhaps = *OED Cond, Cund* 'to conduct, direct', etc., recorded in Carew. See also *OED Con* v.2, of which *Coun* (q.v.) is a form.

vare < OE *faran* 'go, travel', etc. Recorded in *EDD* (v.2), but not from Cornwall.

18. *comit* 'cometh'. The use of final unstressed *t* for *th* has not been paralleled from Cornwall.

starre. This word is completely untraced.

20. *fet* 'fetch' < OE *fetian*, as distinct from *fecc(e)an* (? altered from *fetian*). Not recorded by *SED*, but, according to *EDD*, formerly in general dialectal use, including Cornwall.

22. *sew* ? = 'sue' in its modern sense of 'institute legal proceedings against' (*OED*, s.v., §13).

Tre poll pen. "By Tre Pol Pen you shall know the Cornishmen" is the well-known jingle alluding to the large number of Cornish surnames beginning with these elements.

23. *lenger* < OE *lengra*, ME *lenger*, which was later replaced in Standard English by a new comparative formation from the positive *long*. The last examples in *OED* are dated 1561 and 1590, but the latter is from Spenser's *Faerie Queene*, and perhaps a conscious archaism. It is not recorded in *SED* and *EDD*.

24. *yender* < OE *geond* + *-er*, but with shift of accent, *géon* (as distinct from *geón*). See *EDD*, s.v. *Yonder* (in general dialectal use). Not recorded in *SED*.

It must be admitted that there are many unresolved obscurities in this passage. Some words are completely without explanation; a few others, namely *gos(se)*, *?fleg*, *soole*, seem to be more characteristic of northern dialect. Others still are merely generally dialectal. It is not, of course, impossible that Borde occasionally confused his dialects. He had spent a year in Glasgow (?1536–7), studying and practising medicine, and it is conceivable that he had heard words there which he later ascribed to the south-west.

On the whole, however, although some of the features of the passage are characteristic of general south-western or 'Mummerset' (stage) dialect as it was conceived of in the sixteenth century (e.g. the use of *ich* and the voicing of initial fricative consonants), other phonological, morphological, syntactical and lexical features of the passage suggest that Borde had in fact genuinely recorded this material – or the greater part of it – in Cornwall. If this is so, then it can hardly be doubted from characteristics such as voiced initial fricative consonants (as in *vyshe*, *volke*), together with [d] in *dycke*, *dyn*, etc. – features recorded by *SED* in east and central Cornwall but not in western Cornwall – that it was from the eastern part of the county that Borde made this specimen.

The extract, if it has any degree of real accuracy, is of further interest in that it shows the retention of archaic features in Cornwall, e.g. the *seg*, *hab* forms and the use of *myd*.

Bibliography

W.G.V. Balchin, *Cornwall* (London, 1954).

A. Ballard, *British Borough Charters 1042–1216* (Cambridge, 1913).

A. Ballard, *The Domesday Inquest* (London, 1906).

A. Ballard and J. Tait, *British Borough Charters 1216–1307* (Cambridge, 1923).

M.W. Barley and R.P.C. Hanson (eds), *Christianity in Britain 300–700* (Leicester, 1968).

D. Barrington, 'On the Expiration of the Cornish Language', *Archaeologia*, III (1786), 279–84.

M.V. Barry, 'Traditional Enumeration in the North Country', *Folk Life*, VII (1969), 75–91.

J. Bartholomew, *The Survey Gazetteer of the British Isles* (9th edn, reprinted Edinburgh, 1963).

R.M. Barton, *An Introduction to the Geology of Cornwall* (Truro, 1964).

Bede, *Historia Ecclesiastica*, in *Venerabilis Baedae Opera Historica*, ed. C. Plummer, 2 vols (Oxford, 1896).

H.S. Bennett, *Life on the English Manor* (Cambridge, 1937).

W.H. Bennett, 'The Southern English Development of Germanic Initial [f s þ]', *Language*, XXXI (1955), 367–71.

M.W. Beresford, *New Towns of the Middle Ages* (London, 1967).

C. Berry, *Portrait of Cornwall* (2nd edn, London, 1971).

J. Betjeman, *Cornwall: A Shell Guide* (London, 1964).

P.H. Blair, *An Introduction to Anglo-Saxon England* (Cambridge, 1956).

B. Blomé, *The Place-Names of North Devonshire* (Uppsala, 1929).

L. Bloomfield, *Language* (New York, 1933).

H. Bohman, *Studies in the ME. Dialects of Devon and London* (Goteborg, 1944).

W. Bonser, *An Anglo-Saxon and Celtic Bibliography (450–1087)*, 2 vols (Oxford, 1957).

W. Bonser, *A Romano-British Bibliography (55 B.C.–A.D. 449)*, 2 vols (Oxford, 1964).

A. Borde. See F.J. Furnivall (ed.).

W. Borlase, *Natural History of Cornwall* (Oxford, 1758).

W. Borlase, *Observations on the Antiquities, Monumental and Historical, of the County of Cornwall* (Oxford, 1754; 2nd, rev. edn, London, 1769).

W.C. Borlase, 'A Collection of hitherto unpublished Proverbs and Rhymes, in the Ancient Cornish Language; from the Manuscript of Dr. Borlase', *JRIC* (April 1866), 7–17.

W.C. Borlase (ed.), 'Copy of a MS. in Cornish and English from the MSS. of Dr. Borlase', *JRIC*, xxi (1879), 182–9.

N. Boson. See preceding item, and R.M. Nance (ed.).

J. Bosworth, *An Anglo-Saxon Dictionary* . . . edited and enlarged by T.N. Toller (Oxford, 1882–98; reprinted 1929, 1954). *Supplement*, by T.N. Toller (Oxford, 1908–21; reprinted 1955).

E.G. Bowen (ed.), *Wales, A Physical, Historical and Regional Geography* (London, 1957).

J. Bowring, 'Language, with Special Reference to the Devonian Dialects', *TDA*, I.5 (1866), 13–38.

J. Braidwood, 'Ulster and Elizabethan English', in *Ulster Dialects: An Introductory Symposium* (Ulster Folk Museum, 1964), 5–109.

G.L. Brook, *English Dialects* (London, 1963).

R.L.S. Bruce Mitford, 'A Dark-Age Settlement at Mawgan Porth, Cornwall', in *Recent Archaeological Excavations in Britain*, ed. R.L.S. Bruce Mitford (London, 1956), 167–96.

K. Brunner, *An Outline of Middle English Grammar*, trans. G. Johnston (Oxford, 1963).

E. Campanile (ed.), 'Un Frammento scenico medio-cornico', *Studi e Saggi Linguistici* (Supplement to *L'Italia Dialettale*, xxvi), III (1963), 60–80.

A. Campbell, *Old English Grammar* (Oxford, 1959).

R. Carew. See F.E. Halliday (ed.).

Census 1951 England and Wales, County Report: Cornwall (H.M.S.O., 1955).

Census 1951 England and Wales: Populations of Ecclesiastical Areas (England) (H.M.S.O., 1955).

H.M. Chadwick, 'The End of Roman Britain', in *Studies in Early British History*, ed. N.K. Chadwick (Cambridge, 1959), 9–20.

H.M. Chadwick, 'The Foundation of the Early British Kingdoms', in *Studies in Early British History*, 47–60.

N.K. Chadwick (ed.), *Celt and Saxon: Studies in the Early British Border* (Cambridge, 1962).

N.K. Chadwick, *Celtic Britain* (London, 1963).

N.K. Chadwick (ed.), *Studies in Early British History* (Cambridge, 1959).

N.K. Chadwick (ed.), *Studies in the Early British Church* (Cambridge, 1958).

R.P. Chope (ed.), *Early Tours in Devon and Cornwall* (Exeter, 1918); reprinted, with a new Introduction by A. Gibson (Newton Abbot, 1967).

E. Classen and F.E. Harmer (eds), *The Anglo-Saxon Chronicle* (Manchester, 1926).

R. Cleasby and G. Vigfússon, *An Icelandic-English Dictionary* (2nd edn, with a Supplement by W.A. Craigie, Oxford, 1957).

R.G. Collingwood and J.N.L. Myres, *Roman Britain and the English Settlements* (2nd edn, Oxford, 1937).

R.G. Collingwood and R.P. Wright, *The Roman Inscriptions of Britain, I: Inscriptions on Stone* (Oxford, 1965).

I. Colquhoun, 'Cornish Earth', *The Cornish Review*, xviii (1971), 57–66.

T.Q. Couch, 'A List of Obsolete Words, still in use among the folk of East Cornwall', *JRIC* (March 1864), 6–26.

T.Q. Couch, 'Appendix to a List of Obsolescent Words and Local Phrases in use among the folk of East Cornwall', *JRIC* (April 1870), 173–9.

M.A. Courtney and T.Q. Couch, *Glossary of Words in Use in Cornwall:* West Cornwall by Miss M.A. Courtney; East Cornwall by T.Q. Couch. EDS, XXVII (1880).

W. Cunningham, *Alien Immigrants to England* (London, 1897; 2nd edn, with a new Introduction by Charles Wilson, London, 1969).

B. Danielsson, *John Hart's Works on English Orthography and Pronunciation 1551 . 1569 . 1570. Part II: Phonology* (Stockholm, 1963).

H.C. Darby and R.W. Finn, *The Domesday Geography of South-West England* (Cambridge, 1967).

W.Ll. Davies, *Cornish Manuscripts in the National Library of Wales* (Aberystwyth [private press of the National Library of Wales], 1939).

Devon and Cornwall: A Preliminary Survey. Report issued by the Survey Committee of the University College of the South-West, Exeter (Exeter, 1947).

T.F.C. Dexter, *Cornish Names: An Attempt to explain over 1600 Cornish Names* (London, 1926; reprinted, Truro, 1968).

M. Dillon and N.K. Chadwick, *The Celtic Realms* (London, 1967).

E.J. Dobson, 'Early Modern Standard English', *Trans. Phil. Soc.* (1955), 25–54.

E.J. Dobson, *English Pronunciation 1500–1700* (2nd edn, 2 vols, Oxford, 1968).

R.H.M. Dolley, 'The Tywardreath (Fowey) Treasure Trove', *Numismatic Chronicle*, 6th Series, xv (1955), 5–9.

W. Dugdale, *Monasticon Anglicanum*, ed. J. Caley, H. Ellis and B. Bandinel. 6 vols (London, 1846).

Earle-Plummer. See C. Plummer (ed.).

E. Ekwall, *English River-Names* (Oxford, 1928).

E. Ekwall, *The Concise Oxford Dictionary of English Place-Names* (4th edn, Oxford, 1960).

E. Ekwall, *Studies on the Population of Medieval London* (Stockholm, 1956).

W.D. Elcock, *The Romance Languages* (London, 1960).

L.E. Elliott-Binns, *Medieval Cornwall* (London, 1955).

A.J. Ellis, *On Early English Pronunciation: Part I* (London, 1869); *Part III* (London, 1871).

A.J. Ellis, *On Early English Pronunciation, Part V: The Existing Phonology of English Dialects* (London, 1889).

F.T. Elworthy, *Specimens of English Dialects, I: Devonshire*. EDS, XXV (1879).

F.T. Elworthy, *The Dialect of West Somerset*. EDS, VII (1875).

Encyclopedia Britannica, 24 vols (London, 1966).

A. Ewart, *The French Language* (London, 1933).

S. Feist, *Etymologisches Wörterbuch der Gotischen Sprache* (Halle, 1909).

H.P.R. Finberg, *Lucerna: Studies of some Problems in the Early History of England* (London, 1964).

H.P.R. Finberg, *Roman and Saxon Withington: A Study in Continuity* (Occasional Paper No. 8 of the Department of English Local History of the University of Leicester, Leicester, 1955; reprinted in *Lucerna* [preceding item], 21–65).

H.P.R. Finberg, 'Sherborne, Glastonbury, and the Expansion of Wessex', *Transactions of the Royal Historical Society*, 5th Series, III (1933), 101–24. Reprinted in revised form in *Lucerna* (see above), 95–115.

H.P.R. Finberg. *The Early Charters of Devon and Cornwall* (Occasional Paper No. 2 of the Department of English Local History of the University of Leicester, Leicester, 1963).

R.W. Finn, *Domesday Studies: The Liber Exoniensis* (London, 1964).

R.W. Finn, *The Domesday Inquest and the Making of Domesday Book* (London, 1961).

G. Forsström, *The Verb 'To Be' in Middle English: A Survey of the Forms* (Lund, 1948).

M. Förster, 'Die Freilassungsurkunden des Bodmin-Evangeliars', in *A Grammatical Miscellany offered to Otto Jespersen* (Copenhagen, 1930), 77–99.

D.C. Fowler, 'The Date of the Cornish "Ordinalia"', *Medieval Studies* (Toronto), XXIII (1961), 91–125.

A. Fox, *Roman Exeter* (Manchester, 1952).

A. Fox, 'Roman Exeter', in *The Civitas Capitals of Roman Britain*, ed. J.S. Wacher (Leicester, 1966), 46–51.

A. Fox, *South West England* (London, 1964).

C. Fox, *The Personality of Britain* (Cardiff, 1932; 4th, rev. edn, 1943).

F.J. Furnivall (ed.), *The Fyrst Boke of the Introduction of Knowledge made by Andrew Boorde, of Physycke Doctor*. EETS, ES 10 (1870).

T. Garland, 'A List of Words in common use in West Cornwall', *JRIC* (April 1865), 45–54.

G.N. Garmonsway (trans.), *The Anglo-Saxon Chronicle* (London, 1953: Everyman's Library, No. 624).

E. Gibson, *Camden's Britannia, Newly Translated into English, with Large Additions and Improvements* (London, 1695).

A. Gil, *Logonomia Anglica* (1621), ed. O.L. Jiriczek (Strasbourg, 1903).

D. Gilbert (ed.), *Mount Calvary; or, the History of the Passion, Death and Resurrection of Jesus Christ* (London, 1826).

D. Gilbert (ed.), *The Creation of the World, with Noah's Flood* (London, 1827).

D. Gilbert, *The Parochial History of Cornwall*, 4 vols (London, 1838).

A.C. Gimson, *An Introduction to the Pronunciation of English* (2nd, rev. edn, London, 1970).

J.E.B. Gover, 'Cornish Place-Names', *Antiquity*, II (1928), 319–27.

J.E.B. Gover, 'The Place-Names of Cornwall', 1948. In manuscript.

J.E.B. Gover, A. Mawer and F.M. Stenton, *The Place-Names of Devon*. EPNS, VIII, IX (Cambridge, 1931–2).

E. Van T. Graves (ed.), *The Old Cornish Vocabulary* (University Microfilms Incorporated, Ann Arbor, Michigan, 1962).

A Hackman, *Catalogi Codicum Manuscriptorum Bibliothecæ Bodleianæ, Pars Quarta, Codices Viri Admodum Reverendi Thomæ Tanneri, S.T.P., Episcopi Asaphensis, Complectens* (Oxford, 1860; reprinted 1966).

A.W. Haddan and W. Stubbs, *Councils and Ecclesiastical Documents relating to Great Britain and Ireland*, 3 vols (Oxford, 1869–78; reprinted 1964).

F.E. Halliday, *A History of Cornwall* (London, 1959).

F.E. Halliday (ed.), *Richard Carew of Antony: The Survey of Cornwall* (London, 1953).

F.E. Halliday, *The Legend of the Rood* (London, 1955).

W. Hals, *The Compleat History of Cornwal*, vol. I (Truro, 1750).

M. Harris (trans.), *The Cornish Ordinalia: A Medieval Dramatic Trilogy* (Washington, D.C., 1969).

J. Hatcher, *Rural Economy and Society in the Duchy of Cornwall 1300–1500* (Cambridge, 1970).

R. Hemon, *Dictionnaire Breton Français* (3rd, rev. edn, Brest, 1964).

H. O'N. Hencken, *The Archaeology of Cornwall and Scilly* (London, 1932).

C. Henderson, *Essays in Cornish History*, ed. A.L. Rowse and M.I. Henderson (Oxford, 1935).

215

C. Henderson, 'Nicholas Boson and Richard Angwyn', *OC*, II.2 (1931), 29–32.

C. Henderson, *et al.*, *The Cornish Church Guide and Parochial History of Cornwall* (Truro, 1925; reprinted 1964).

F.C. Hingeston-Randolph (ed.), *The Register of John de Grandisson, Bishop of Exeter* (*A.D. 1327–1369*), 3 vols (London, 1894–9).

W.T. Hoblyn, 'In English and Not in Cornowok', *OC*, II.11 (1936), 11.

J.B. Hofmann, *Etymologisches Wörterbuch des Griechischen* (Munich, 1949).

G.C. Homans, *English Villagers of the Thirteenth Century* (Harvard, 1941).

E.G.R. Hooper, 'Dialect as a Gateway to Cornish', *OC*, II.2 (1931), 34–5.

W.G. Hoskins, *The Human Geography of the South West* (George Johnstone Lecture, 1968), (South Western Electricity Board, 1968).

W.G. Hoskins, *The Westward Expansion of Wessex*, with a Supplement to *The Early Charters of Devon and Cornwall* by H.P.R. Finberg (Occasional Paper No. 13 of the Department of English Local History of the University of Leicester, Leicester, 1960).

W.G. Hoskins, *Two Thousand Years in Exeter* (Exeter, 1960).

K. Hughes, 'British Museum MS. Cotton Vespasian A. XIV ('Vitae Sanctorum Wallensium'): Its Purpose and Provenance', in *Studies in the Early British Church*, ed. N.K. Chadwick (Cambridge, 1958), 183–200.

K.H. Jackson, *A Historical Phonology of Breton* (Dublin, 1967).

K.H. Jackson, *Language and History in Early Britain* (Edinburgh, 1953).

K.H. Jackson, 'The British Language during the Period of the English Settlements', in *Studies in Early British History*, ed. N.K. Chadwick (Cambridge, 1959), 61–82.

U. Jacobson, *Phonological Dialect Constituents in the Vocabulary of Standard English* (Lund, 1962).

F.W.P. Jago, *An English–Cornish Dictionary* (London, 1887).

F.W.P. Jago, *The Ancient Language, and the Dialect of Cornwall, with an enlarged Glossary of Cornish provincial words* (Truro, 1882).

A.K.H. Jenkin, *The Story of Cornwall* (London, 1934; reprinted, Truro, 1962).

H. Jenner, *A Handbook of the Cornish Language* (London, 1904).

H. Jenner, 'An Early Cornish Fragment', *Athenæum*, 2614 (1 Dec. 1877), 698–9.

H. Jenner, 'Cornwall a Celtic Nation', *Celtic Review*, I (1905), 234–46.

H. Jenner, 'Descriptions of Cornish Manuscripts – II', *JRIC*, xx (1915), 41–8.

H. Jenner, 'The Cornish Drama'. Four unpublished lectures given at Exeter University, *c.* 1928, now in the Morton Nance Bequest at the County Museum, Truro.

H. Jenner, 'The History and Literature of the Ancient Cornish Language', *JBAA*, xxxiii (1877), 137–57.

H. Jenner, 'Traditional Relics of the Cornish Language in Mounts Bay in 1875', *Trans. Phil. Soc.* (1876), 533–42.

O. Jespersen, *Mankind, Nation and Individual* (London, 1946).

D. Jones, *An Outline of English Phonetics* (9th edn, Cambridge, 1962).

E. Jones, *Towns and Cities* (Oxford Paperbacks University Series, Opus 13, 1966).

R. Jordan, *Handbuch der Mittelenglischen Grammatik, Erster Teil, Lautlehre* (2nd edn, rev. H.C. Matthes, Heidelberg, 1934).

T. Kerslake, 'The Celt and the Teuton in Exeter', *Archaeological Journal*, xxx (1873), 211–25.

A. Kihlbom, *A Contribution to the Study of Fifteenth Century English* (Uppsala, 1926).

J. Kjederqvist, *The Dialect of Pewsey* (London, 1903).

E. Klein, *A Comprehensive Etymological Dictionary of the English Language*, 2 vols (Amsterdam, 1966–7).

H. Kurath, *A Phonology and Prosody of Modern English* (Heidelberg, 1964).

H. Kurath and S.M. Kuhn (eds), *Middle English Dictionary* (Ann Arbor, Michigan, 1952–).

W.S. Lach-Szyrma, 'Manx and Cornish: The Dying and the Dead', *JBAA*, xliv (1888), 273–8.

A.G. Langdon, 'Early Christian Monuments', in *The Victoria History of the County of Cornwall*, ed. W. Page (London, 1906), 407–49.

A.G. Langdon, *Old Cornish Crosses* (London, 1896).

A.F. Leach, *Educational Charters and Documents 598–1909* (Cambridge, 1911).

A.F. Leach, *English Schools at the Reformation 1546–8* (London, 1896).

A. Lewis and H. Pederson, *A Concise, Comparative Celtic Grammar* (Göttingen, 1937).

G.R. Lewis, *The Stannaries: A Study of the English Tin Miner* (Boston and New York, 1908; reissued Truro, 1965).

E. Lhuyd, *Archaeologia Britannica* (Oxford, 1707; facsimile by Scolar Press, No. 136, 1969).

W.B. Lockwood, *Indo-European Philology, Historical and Comparative* (London, 1969).

C.E. Long (ed.), *Diary of the Marches of the Royal Army during the Great Civil War; kept by Richard Symonds*, Camden Society, lxxiv (1859).

R. Longsworth, *The Cornish Ordinalia: Religion and Dramaturgy* (Cambridge, Mass., 1967).

K. Luick, *Historische Grammatik der englischen Sprache*, 2 vols (Leipzig, 1914–40).

D. and S. Lysons, *Magna Britannia, Vol. III: Cornwall* (London, 1814).

R.A.S. Macalister, *Corpus Inscriptionum Insularum Celticarum*, 2 vols (Dublin, 1945–9).

A. McIntosh, 'A New Approach to Middle English Dialectology', *English Studies*, XLIV (1963), 1–11.

A.H. Marckwardt, *American English* (Cambridge, 1958).

A.H. Marckwardt, 'An Unnoted Source of English Dialect Vocabulary', *JEGP*, XLVI (1947), 177–82.

A.H. Marckwardt (ed.), *Laurence Nowell's Vocabularium Saxonicum* (Ann Arbor, Michigan, 1952).

I.D. Margary, *Roman Roads in Britain* (3rd, rev. edn, London, 1973).

J.H. Matthews, *A History of the Parishes of Saint Ives, Lelant, Towednack and Zennor* (London, 1892).

W. Matthews, 'South Western Dialect in the Early Modern Period', *Neophilologus*, XXIV (1939), 193–209.

A.L. Mayhew (ed.), *The Promptorium Parvulorum*. EETS, ES 102 (1908).

A. Mee, *The King's England: Cornwall* (2nd, rev. edn, London, 1967).

R.L.P. Milburn, *Saints and their Emblems in English Churches* (2nd, rev edn, Oxford, 1957).

Monumenta Germaniae Historica, Scriptores II, ed. G.H. Pertz (Hanover, 1829; reprinted, Stuttgart, 1963).

S.A. Moore (ed.), *Letters and Papers of J. Shillingford, Mayor of Exeter, 1447–50*. Camden Society, New Series, II (1871).

S. Moore, S.R. Meech and H. Whitehall, *Middle English Dialect Characteristics and Dialect Boundaries* (Ann Arbor, Michigan, 1935).

J.A.H. Murray, H. Bradley, W.A. Craigie and C.T. Onions (eds), *The Oxford English Dictionary*, 13 vols (Oxford, 1933, 1961).

R.M. Nance, *A Cornish–English Dictionary* (Marazion, 1955).

R.M. Nance, *A Glossary of Cornish Sea-Words*, ed. P.A.S. Pool (Marazion, 1963).

R.M. Nance, *A Guide to Cornish Place-Names with a List of Words contained in them* (Marazion, n.d. [1951]).

R.M. Nance, *An English–Cornish Dictionary* (Marazion, 1952).

R.M. Nance, 'Bulorn and its Congeners', *OC*, v.7 (1956), 311–15.

R.M. Nance, 'Cornish in 1756', *OC*, II.5 (1933), 44.

R.M. Nance, 'Glossary of Cornish Dialect'. In manuscript.

R.M. Nance (ed.), *John of Chyannor or The Three Points of Wisdom*, by Nicholas Boson (Cornish Language Board, 1969).

R.M. Nance, 'More about the Tregear Manuscript', *OC*, v.1 (1951), 21–7.

R.M. Nance, 'New Light on Cornish', *OC*, iv.6 (1947), 214–16.

R.M. Nance (ed.), 'Nicholas Boson's "Nebbaz Gerriau dro tho Carnoack"', *JRIC*, xxiii (1930), 327–54.

R.M. Nance (ed.), 'The Charter Endorsement in Cornish', *OC*, ii.4 (1932), 34–6.

R.M. Nance, 'The Plen An Guary or Cornish Playing-Place', *JRIC*, xxiv (1935), 190–211.

R.M. Nance, 'The Tregear Manuscript', *OC*, iv.11 (1950), 429–34.

J. Norden, *Speculi Britanniae Pars: A Topographical and Historical Description of Cornwall* (1610; ed. London, 1728).

E. Norris (ed.), *The Ancient Cornish Drama*. 2 vols (London, 1859; reprinted, New York and London [Benjamin Blom], 1968).

J. Ogilby, *Britannia*, vol. I (London, 1675).

L.C.J. Orchard, 'Some Notes on the Cornish Language in the Fourteenth Century', *OC*, iii.2 (1937), 79–80.

H. Orton, 'An English Dialect Survey: Linguistic Atlas of England', *Orbis*, ix (1960), 331–48.

H. Orton and E. Dieth, *Survey of English Dialects* (Leeds, 1962–71). *Introduction*, by H. Orton (1962); vol. I (Northern), ed. H. Orton and W.J. Halliday (1962–3); vol. IV (Southern), ed. H. Orton and M.F. Wakelin (1967–8); vol. II (West Midland), ed. H. Orton and M.V. Barry (1969–71); vol. III (East Midland), ed. H. Orton and P.M. Tilling (1969–71).

H. Orton and E. Dieth, 'The New Survey of Dialectal English', in *English Studies Today*, ed. C.L. Wrenn and G. Bullough (Oxford, 1951), 63–73.

W. Page (ed.), *A History of the County of Cornwall, Part 5: Romano–British Remains* (London, 1924).

W. Page (ed.), *The Victoria History of the County of Cornwall* (London, 1906).

R.E. Palmer, *Thomas Whythorne's Speech* (Copenhagen, 1969).

J.J. Parry, 'The Revival of Cornish: An Dasserghyans Kernewek', *PMLA*, lxi (1946), 258–68.

E.H. Pedler, 'Notes on the Names of Places, etc., mentioned in the preceding Dramas', in Norris, *The Ancient Cornish Drama* (see above), 473–514.

R. and O.B. Peter, *The Histories of Launceston and Dunheved in the County of Cornwall* (Plymouth, 1885).

E. Phillimore, 'The *Annales Cambriæ* and Old-Welsh Genealogies from *Harleian MS*. 3859', *Y Cymmrodor*, ix (1888), 141–83.

C. Plummer (ed.), *Two of the Saxon Chronicles Parallel . . .* on the basis of an edition by John Earle, M.A., 2 vols (Oxford, 1892–9).

R. Polwhele, *A Cornish–English Vocabulary; a Vocabulary of Local Names, chiefly Saxon, and a Provincial Glossary* (Truro, 1808, 1816, 1836).

R. Polwhele, *The History of Cornwall*, 3 vols (London and Falmouth, 1803).

M.K. Pope, *From Latin to Modern French with Especial Consideration of Anglo-Norman* (Manchester, 1934).

T.G.E. Powell, *The Celts* (2nd, rev. edn, London, 1959).

W. Pryce, *Archaeologia Cornu-Britannica* (Sherborne, 1790).

W.O. Pughe, *A Dictionary of the Welsh Language*, 2 vols (London, 1803).

A Questionnaire for a Linguistic Atlas of England, by E. Dieth and H. Orton (Leeds Philosophical and Literary Society, 1952; reprinted in revised form in the *Introduction* to *SED* by H. Orton [Leeds, 1962]).

C.A.R. Radford, 'The Cultural Relations of the Early Celtic World', in *Proceedings of the Second International Congress of Celtic Studies* (Cardiff, 1966), 1–27.

W.L.D. Ravenhill, 'Cornwall', Chapter V of H.C. Darby and R.W. Finn, *The Domesday Geography of South-West England* (Cambridge, 1967).

W.L.D. Ravenhill, 'Cornwall and Devon', in 'Rural Settlement in Ireland and Western Britain' (Report of a symposium), *The Advancement of Science*, xv.60 (1959), 342–5.

W.L.D. Ravenhill, 'The Settlement of Cornwall during the Celtic Period', *Geography*, xl (1955), 237–48.

P.H. Reaney, *A Dictionary of British Surnames* (London, 1958).

P.H. Reaney, *The Origin of English Place-Names* (London, 1960).

M. Richards (trans.), *The Laws of Hywel Dda* (Liverpool, 1954).

B.S. Roberson, *The Land of Britain: The Report of the Land Utilisation Survey of Britain, Part 91: Cornwall* (London, 1941).

Rotuli Parliamentorum; ut et Petitiones, et Placita in Parliamento, 6 vols [n.1., n.d.].

J. Rowe, 'Cornish Emigrants in America', *Folk Life*, iii (1965), 25–38.

J. Rowe, *Cornwall in the Age of the Industrial Revolution* (Liverpool, 1953).

A.L. Rowse, *Tudor Cornwall* (2nd, rev. edn, London, 1969).

J.C. Russell, *British Medieval Population* (Albuquerque, New Mexico, 1948).

M.L. Samuels, 'Some Applications of Middle English Dialectology', *English Studies*, xliv (1963), 81–94.

W. Sandys, *Specimens of Cornish Provincial Dialect* (London, 1846).

P.H. Sawyer, *Anglo-Saxon Charters: An Annotated List and Bibliography* (London: Royal Historical Society, 1968).

W. Scawen, *Antiquities Cornu-Britannick* (*c.* 1680), in 'Observations on an Ancient Manuscript entitled Passio Christi . . .', Appendix V of D. Gilbert, *Parochial History of Cornwall* (see above).

J. Shillingford. See S.A. Moore (ed.).

A.H. Shorter, W.L.D. Ravenhill and K.J. Gregory, *South West England* (London, 1969).

W.W. Skeat, *A Concise Etymological Dictionary of the English Language* (Oxford, 1882; revised 1901, 1911).

W.W. Skeat, *Nine Specimens of English Dialects*. EDS, LXXVI (1896).

A.H. Smith, *English Place-Name Elements*, 2 vols (Cambridge, 1956).

A.S.D. Smith, *The Story of the Cornish Language: Its Extinction and Revival* (2nd edn, rev. E.G. Retallack Hooper, Camborne, 1969).

L.T. Smith (ed.), *The Itinerary of John Leland in or about the Years 1535–1543* (London, 1906–10; reprinted in Centaur Classics, 5 vols, London, 1964).

T. Smith (ed.), *English Gilds*. EETS, 40 (1870).

R. Southern, *The Medieval Theatre in the Round* (London, 1957).

J.L. Stackhouse, 'Obsolete Words still in use among the folk of East Cornwall', *JRIC* (October 1864), 75–6.

F.M. Stenton, *Anglo-Saxon England* (3rd, rev. edn, Oxford, 1971).

L. Stephen and S. Lee, *Dictionary of National Biography* (London, 1885–).

H.S. Stokes, 'County and Parochial Histories and Books Relating to Cornwall', *JBAA*, xxxiii (1877), 35–45.

W. Stokes, 'A Cornish Glossary', *Trans. Phil. Soc.* (1868–9), 137–256.

W. Stokes, 'A Glossary to the Cornish Drama *Beunans Meriasek*', *Archiv für Celtische Lexikographie*, i (1900), 101–42.

W. Stokes, 'Cornica', *Revue Celtique*, iii (1876–8), 85–6.

W. Stokes, 'Cornica', *Revue Celtique*, iv (1879–80), 258–64.

W. Stokes (ed.), *Gwreans an Bys, the Creation of the World: A Cornish Mystery, Trans. Phil. Soc.* (1864), pt IV.

W. Stokes (ed.), *The Life of Saint Meriasek, Bishop and Confessor: A Cornish Drama* (London, 1872).

W. Stokes (ed.), *The Passion, A Middle-Cornish Poem*. Appendix to *Trans. Phil. Soc.* (1860–1), 1–100.

J.F.S. Stone, *Wessex before the Celts* (London, 1958).

B.M.H. Strang, *A History of English* (London, 1970).

B.M.H. Strang, 'The Tyneside Linguistic Survey', *Zeitschrift für Mundartforschung*, Beihefte, Neue Folge, Heft IV (1968), 788–94.

Subsidy Rolls, Muster and Hearth Tax Rolls and Probate Calendars of the Parish of St Constantine (Kerrier), Cornwall (Exeter: Devon and Cornwall Record Society, 1910).

H. Sweet, *A History of English Sounds* (Oxford, 1888).

R. Symonds. See C.E. Long (ed.).

The Cornish Language: A Selected Hand-list of Works published since 1900. (Redruth, Institute of Cornish Studies, 1972).

A.C. Thomas, *Britain and Ireland in Early Christian Times* (London, 1971).

A.C. Thomas 'Cornwall in the Dark Ages', *Proceedings of the West Cornwall Field Club*, II (1957–8), 59–72.

A.C. Thomas, *Gwithian: Ten Years' Work 1949–1958* (Camborne, 1958).

A.C. Thomas, 'Settlement-History in early Cornwall, I: The Antiquity of the Hundreds', *Cornish Archaeology*, III (1964), 70–9.

J. Thomas, *Randigal Rhymes and a Glossary of Cornish Words* (Penzance, 1895).

H.S. Toy, *The History of Helston* (Oxford, 1936).

J.T. Tregellas, *Peeps into the Haunts and Homes of the Rural Population of Cornwall* (Truro, 1868).

W.H. Tregellas, *Cornish Worthies*, 2 vols (London, 1884).

J. Trevisa, *Polychronicon Ranulphi Higden Monachi Cestrensis*, ed. C. Babington and J.R. Lumby. Rolls Series, 9 vols (1865–86).

J. Tuckett, 'A Devonshire Song', *Notes and Queries*, 2nd Series, X (1860), 462.

V. Väänänen, *Introduction au Latin Vulgaire* (2nd, rev. edn, Paris, 1967).

G.J. Visser, 'Celtic Influence in English', *Neophilologus*, XXXIX (1955), 276–93.

M.F. Wakelin, 'A Dialect Note: South-Western *Breakfast* in the *Survey of English Dialects*', *Orbis*, XIX (1970), 47–8.

M.F. Wakelin, '*Crew, Cree* and *Crow*: Celtic Words in English Dialect', *Anglia*, LXXXVII (1969), 273–81.

M.F. Wakelin, *English Dialects: An Introduction* (London, 1972).

M.F. Wakelin, 'Names for the Cow-house in Devon and Cornwall', *Devon and Cornwall Notes and Queries* (April/July 1968), 52–6; reprinted in *Studia Neophilologica*, XL (1970), 348–52.

M.F. Wakelin, 'Significant Spellings in the St Ives Borough Accounts', *Neophilologus*, LVII (1973), 1–3.

M.F. Wakelin, '*Skippet, Skibbet* and *Skivet*: Consonant Mutations in Cornwall', *Devon and Cornwall Notes and Queries* (Summer 1972), 152–3.

M.F. Wakelin, 'Welsh Influence in the West of England: Dialectal *Tallet*', *Folk Life*, VIII (1970), 72–80.

M.F. Wakelin and M.V. Barry, 'The Voicing of Initial Fricative Consonants in Present-Day Dialectal English', *Leeds Studies in English*, N.S. II (1968), 47–64.

M. Weinbaum, *British Borough Charters 1307–1660* (Cambridge, 1943).

R. Weiss, 'The Greek Culture of South Italy in the Later Middle Ages', *Proceedings of the British Academy*, XXXVII (1951), 23–50.

J. West, *Village Records* (London, 1962).

J. Widdowson, 'The Bogeyman: Some Preliminary Observations on Frightening Figures', *Folklore*, LXXXII (1971), 99–115.

B. Widén, *Studies on the Dorset Dialect* (Lund, 1949).

H. Wiegert, '*Jim an' Nell' von W.F. Rock: Eine Studie zum Dialekt von Devonshire*. Palaestra, 137 (Berlin, 1921).

J.J. Wilkinson (ed.), *Receipts and Expenses in the Building of Bodmin Church A.D. 1469 to 1472*. Camden Miscellany, VII (1875).

Willelmi Malmesbiriensis Monachi, De Gestis Regum Anglorum, ed. W. Stubbs. Vol. I, Rolls Series, 90 (London, 1887).

R. Williams, *Lexicon Cornu-Britannicum* (Llandovery and London, 1865).

D.M. Wilson and C.E. Blunt, 'The Trewhiddle Hoard', *Archaeologia*, XCVIII (1961), 75–122.

M. Wollaston, 'Coast, Clay, Cream and Foreigners', *Sunday Times Magazine* (25 Sept. 1966), 26–39.

E.S. Wood, *Collins Field Guide to Archaeology* (London, 1963).

C. Woolf, *An Introduction to the Archaeology of Cornwall* (Truro, 1970).

R.N. Worth, 'Some Inquiry into the Association of the Dialects of Devon and Cornwall', *JRIC* (April 1870), 180–3.

C.L. Wrenn, 'Saxons and Celts in South-West Britain', *Transactions of the Honourable Society of Cymmrodorion*, Session 1959, 38–75; reprinted in the author's *Word and Symbol: Studies in English Language* (London, 1967).

J. Wright, *The English Dialect Dictionary*, 6 vols (Oxford, 1898–1905).

J. Wright, *The English Dialect Grammar* (Oxford, 1905).

J. and E.M. Wright, *An Elementary Historical New English Grammar* (Oxford, 1924).

J. and E.M. Wright, *An Elementary Middle English Grammar* (2nd, rev. edn, Oxford, 1928).

J.T. Wright, 'Urban Dialect: A Consideration of Method', *Zeitschrift für Mundartforschung*, XXXIII (1966), 232–46.

H.C. Wyld, *A History of Modern Colloquial English* (2nd edn, London, 1921).

H.C. Wyld, *A Short History of English* (3rd, rev. edn, London, 1927).

H.C. Wyld (ed.), *The Universal Dictionary of the English Language* (London, 1934).

J.C. Zeuss, *Grammatica Celtica* (2nd edn, by H. Ebel; 2 vols. Berlin, 1871).

General index

General index

Callington, 57, 70, 169, 170
Camborne, 21, 33, 41, 43, 47, 49, 70, 75, 76 n.15, 79
Camden, William, 18 n.4, 92
Camel, River, 37, 38, 47, 57, 75, 95, 140, 146, 154, 202
Camelford, 29, 41, 45, 68, 111, 139–40, 147, 152, 167
Cardinham, 29, 66, 111, 139, 147, 152, 167, 168, 186
Carew, Richard, 18 n.4, 25, 42, 43, 83, 89–90, 93, 94, 96, 97, 98, 99, 100, 181 n.5, 186
Carn Brea, 47
Carnmenellis, 36
Castle Dore, 50 n.6, 51
Celts, 48ff.
Centwine, King, 55, 57
Cenwealh, King, 53
Ceolnoth, Archbishop, 52
Charles I, King, 45
'Charter Fragment', 78, 80, 81
Charters, early, 59, 67
Chaucer, Geoffrey, 208 n.3
Cheshire, 179, 191, 192, 200, 208
Chiverton, 44
Christianity, early, 49, 51–3
Chun, 51
Church, 57–8, 59, 79 n.26, 83, 91, 97, 98–9
Chysauster, 48
Civil War, 91, 99
Clicker Tor, 44
Cnut, King, 67
Cockney, 141, 142
Conan, Bishop, 60
Connerton, 62
Constantine, 47, 184, 197
Cooper, Christopher, 115 n.9
Cornish, 22–5, Chap. 4 passim, 144, 146, 154, 172–4, Chaps. 7, 8 passim; documents in, 22, 23–4, 67, 74, 78–86, 182; influence of on English, 22, 87 (see also Substratum); loan-words in English dialect, 21, 30, 46, Chap. 7 passim, 205; sounds: a, 125, eu, ew, yu, yw, 145, i, 83–4, ? unvoiced l, 188, oi, 85, ou, 84, ü, 84–5, 145, 192, ǖ, 84, 145, u, eu, ue, 84, wa, 84
Cornwall: archaeology, 47ff.; communications, 45–6; documents relating to, 7, 21, 74, 86–8, 181; early settlement, 38 n.7, 47ff.; geology, 36; holiday industry, 41, 44, 45, 46; hundreds and other units, 37, 38–40, 60 (see also Boundaries); occupations, 42–4; parishes, 40, 51; population trends and settlement

patterns, 40–1, 61–7, 68–9; rivers, 37–8 47, 62; towns, 69–71, 97–8; woodland, 37. For historical periods see separate headings
Courtney, M. A., and Couch, T. Q., *Glossary of Words in Use in Cornwall*, 26, 29, 30, 203–4
Crantock, 167
Crantock Bay, 26, 203
Creation, W. Jordan's, 24, 79, 80, 81, 96, 196
Crediton, 53, 60
Crowan, 79, 80
Cubert, 28, 68 n.64, 76 n.15, 168, 197
Cubertus, St, 68 n.64
Cumberland, 197
Cuðred, King, 56
Cynewulf, King, 56

Danes, 56, 57
Dart, River, 48
Dartmoor, 36, 47–8, 49, 55
Davidstow, 197
Dedications, church, 51, 52, 61, 68 n.64
Déisi, 52
Delabole quarries, 44
Derbyshire, 197, 200
Devon, 22, 43, 47, 50 n.6, 52, 53ff., 58, 60, 61, 62 n.52, 63, 64–5, 84, 96–7, 98, 99, 102, 120, 168 n.91, 202; dialect of, 28, 29, 30, 73, 84 n.51, 91, 92, 94, 100, 120, 127, 128, 131, 133, 138, 141 n.51, 142, 146–7, 150–4, 161, 171, 175, 176 n.1, 179, Chap. 7 passim, 202, 208
Devonport, 146
Dialect: regional, Chap. 1 passim, 46, 73–74, 97, 99, 100; urban, 18 n.3, 21, 99. *See also under* Fishing, Middle English, Old English
Domesday Book, 37 n.5, 38, 39, 61–7, 69, 75, 174
Dorset, 57, 60, 61 n.51, 84, 120, 122, 127, 153, 179, 184, 200, 207
Down Derry, 29
Dumnonia, 48–9, 50, 53, 55, 57, 58, 60–1
Dumnonii, 48, 50
Durham, Co., 35, 197
Durotriges, 48
Dutch population in Cornwall, 97 n.83
Dyfed, 59 n.38

Ealdred, Bishop, 60
East, hundred of, 38
East Wheal Rose, 44
Education, influence of on speech, 74, 100
Edward I, King, 96

226

Index of words

This index is in two parts, the first of which lists all the words discussed, the second all the place-names cited as linguistic evidence. Other place-names are listed in the General index, above.

A, indef. art., 179
About, 148, 149, 153 n.80, 179
Abuse, 136
Adder, 103
Afingred 'a-hungered', 208
After, 105–6, 111, 118, 172
Afternoon, 105–6, 118, 172
Aglets, Aglons 'haws', 194–5
All, 106, 111–12, 118, 119
Alter(ed), 107, 119
Always, 106, 111, 119
Angle-touches 'earth-worms', 25
Ankle, 104
Another('s), 125
Anthony 'weakling', 200
Anvil, 104
Apple-, 103; Apples, 103, 112–14
Arm, Armful, Armpit, 109
Around, 149
Arse, 109, 124
As, 111
Ash(-), Ashes, 103, 115
Ask, 105, 116, 117; Asked, 111
Ass, 124
A-took 'taken', 147
Aunt, 104, 115
Axle, 103

Backwards, 103
Bad, 103, 111
Badger, 103
Bag, 103–4, 115
Bald(-), 106, 119, 120

Ball(s), 106, 119
Bannel 'a broom', 184, 194
Bar, 109
Bare-footed, 125
Barn, 109
Barrel, 103
Bat, 103
Bawker 'bogey', 184
Be, dialectal forms of, 176–9, 183, 202; OE and ME forms, 177
Beauty, 136
Bedauer 'bed-fellow', 209
Bird, 84
Bite, 153 n.80
Blood, 127, 131
Blue, 135, 136, 137, 144, 145 nn.63, 68
Bo(o), exclam., 185
Bo 'bogey', 184–5
Bock 'shy' (of a horse), v., 184
Bockie, Bockle 'bogey', 184
Corn. bod (bos, boj) 'dwelling', 75–7, 202
Bog, Bogey(man), Boggard, -art, Boggin, Boggy-bo, Bogle, 'bogey', 184–5
Bogeyman, (-)boggart, -boggle, Boggy-bo, (-)bogle, 'scarecrow', 184–5
Boll(y) 'bogey', 184–5
Boodie, 'bogey', 184–5
Boot(s), 125, 127, 131, 139, 141
Boughs, 148

Bowl(y) 'globe, sphere, ball, stone', 187
Branch, 104, 115
Broth, 130
Brother, 126, 127, 128, 131, 133, 141–2
Browjans 'fragments', etc., 192
Bruised, 136
(-)brush, 131, 133, 173
Bucca 'scarecrow', 184–5; Bucca-gwidden 'good fairy', 199
Bug 'bogey, scarecrow', 184–5
Bugabo(o) 'bogey', 184–5
Bugalo, Buglug 'scarecrow', 184–5
Bugan, Bugbear, Buggard, Bugger 'bogey', 184–5
Bulcard 'smooth blenny', 186
Bulhorns 'snails', 185–6
Bull, 131, 132, 133, 144
Bull-bear, -beggar 'bogey', 184–5
Bullet 'tag, badge', 187
Bullfinch, 186
Bull-gog, -jig (snail-names), 186
(-)bullies 'cobbles', 84, 186–7
Bulling, Bullward 'on heat', 131
Bush(es), 131, 133, 188
Bussa 'salting-trough, bread-bin', 187–8
But, 135
Butcher, 131, 134, 135
Butter, 131, 135, 141

Index of words